DIGITAL
GUERRILLA
VIDEO

DIGITAL
GUERRILLA
VIDEO

A Grass Roots Guide
to the Revolution

Avi Hoffer

Miller Freeman Books

San Francisco

Published by Miller Freeman Books
55 Hawthorne, Suite 600, San Francisco, CA 94105

 Miller Freeman
A United News & Media company

Distributed to the book trade in the U.S. and Canada by
Publishers Group West, 1700 Fourth Street, Berkeley, CA 94710

Cover Art: Cody Harrington, Black Coyote Productions, Inc.
Interior Design and Composition: Brad Greene

Library of Congress Cataloging-in-Publication Data

Hoffer, Avi
    Digital guerrilla video: a grassroots guide to the revolution/by Avi Hoffer
       p. cm
    ISBN 0-87930-575-4 (alk. paper)
    1. Video recordings—Production and direction. 2 Cinematography.
    3. Low budget motion pictures. I. Title.
PN1992.94.H64 1999
791.43.023—dc21   99-43361
                                   CIP

Printed in the United States of America

99 00 01 02 03 04   5 4 3 2 1

Dedication:

This book is dedicated to my father
Emanuel Hoffer
who thought I might like this program called MacPaint
that came with his Mac 512k
and to
Augusto Daniel Lewkowicz
who showed me what a real jungle looks like and
provided the conditions to write a good portion of this book.

Thanks to:

Cody Harrington
Doug Barnard
Flavio Kampah
Yvette Hoffer
Kristi Foster
John Agnew
Dorothy Cox

Special Thanks to:

Radius/Digital Origin, Artville, Planet Art, Digital Vision, Electric Image,
Corel, Rubberball Productions, Stockbyte, Classic Pio Partners,
walnut creek CDROM, CMCD Library, Adobe, Avid,
Artbeats, MetaCreations and Equilibrium Software

Preface

The idea for this book comes from my career experiences during the 1990s. Many books and journals have used the word "Pioneer" to describe the early adoptors of digital video technology. I seldom felt like a pioneer; mostly I felt like a poorly trained soldier trying to fight in thick mud with defective weapons. Many nights, when buggy software failed at the crucial moment, I seriously reconsidered the vision, enthusiasm, and incredible naiveté that had sent me into this foxhole.

It was during this period, the early '90s, that in many basements, spare bedrooms, cramped offices, and university labs around the world, an anonymous army of fools had started using personal computers to make moving images. Under technologically primitive conditions, this scattered underground of digital guerrillas armed and trained themselves. These artists, tinkerers and geeks never actually identified themselves as members of any "revolutionary movement" but there were certain tell-tale signs of a bold shift towards a different way of doing things: They were people who would say yes to almost any video project even if they had almost no clue as to how to accomplish it; they could be found using pre-release beta software without a user's manual to finish a deadline critical project; never completely trusting a product manufacturers' claims, they relentlessly traded anecdotal information at sparsely attended conferences, user group meetings and via (pre-World Wide Web) BBS's and online services.

It was also during those years of desperate tech support calls with confused technicians with no production experience, that I often fantasized about a book, a kind of manifesto, that would help me cut some corners and make the binary life a bit less painful; a book that would tell the truth about this new technology—the good, the bad, and the downright nasty. There was no such book then…but now perhaps, for some other intrepid mediamaker reading this page, here is that book. During the period this book was written (so gracefully endured by the publisher), so many tools and technologies have moved forward that there was no point in trying to be current or advocate a particular kind of gear. I'll let magazines and the web and your friends keep you abreast of that stuff. Instead, I have tried to concentrate more on creative approaches and production problem-solving which don't get dated nearly as quickly. I hope this information is useful and valuable and well-worth the money. Even if it isn't, the cover will intrigue your colleagues when they see it on your bookshelf.

Table of Contents

Introduction

"He did not plan the course of events that followed. He merely slipped his ready fingers into History's waiting glove."
—Arundhati Roy, *The God of Small Things*

It was sometime during the winter months of 1989 when I saw an early version of Adobe Photoshop and Macromind Director. I was living in New York, trying to do something useful with my film production degree and had stumbled onto a freelance gig doing desktop publishing layout in the graphics department at American Express World Headquarters. I worked evenings so when the workload was light and the supervisor stepped away from his desk, I played around with these applications on a speedy 25-mhz Apple Macintosh "packed" with 24MB of RAM.

I had been trained in school as a traditional cel-animator and quickly grasped the power of Director's approach to digital animation. The animation "score" looked similar to a traditional animation exposure sheet except that the computer ran the animation in real-time without shooting the art on an animation stand; modifications in any of the layers could be made instantly. Despite some obvious crudeness, I knew that I had glimpsed something wonderful, something that I had been imagining in my mind since my father had showed me his first computer, a black-and-white Macintosh 512K back in 1984. Someday, I thought, postproduction for a feature film or commercials will be accomplished entirely in two rooms, one for video and one for audio, connected by a network of some kind. Stop dreaming, kid.

I was fired from American Express because I was told I wasn't a team player. I wasn't sure what that meant when you were given all your work in a solitary cubicle without even a local area network connecting you to other computers. "What about wearing a tie to work knotted with a tight power-cone double windsor? Wasn't that ample evidence of team player?" I wondered. Nevertheless, my desktop publishing career in jeopardy, I went back to catering parties to pay the mortgage and bided my time.

It was not until 1990 that I saw my first Avid Media Composer. It was very close to how I'd imagined such a system. It used the metaphors of organizing from traditional film, the "clip" and the "trim bin" but added the timeline metaphor. It could access shots instantly from the hard drive without tape winding. It was very buggy but very cool. I nodded my head and thought, "finally, it's happening". Then I saw the $70,000 price tag. The revolution had begun all right but it was still too expensive for the revolutionary.

The next year I bought a used Macintosh IIfx with 16MB of RAM and a giant 330MB hard drive for $5,000. When the software developer who sold it to me heard that I was into animation, he mentioned this new thing from Apple called Quicktime. He showed me some of the first sputtering grainy samples of "movies" playing on a computer screen and explained that it was a resolution independent, scaleable architecture. Moving images now had a standard file format on a personal computer. This was very good news.

A short time later I saw an ad in MacWorld magazine for a device called Video F/X from a company in Mountain View called Digital F/X. It was a VTR controller, Digital Frame Buffer and editing software package for a Macintosh computer for under $13,000. It even had primitive non-linear editing capabilities built in. Despite its limitations, it was something potentially affordable for an independent upstart, and after a few demos, I called a friend from film school and began to convince him that we could run a business based on "desktop" video equipment. He didn't understand a word of what I was saying.

I came out to LA and we began to look at hardware and software. The Lightworks editing system was beta testing and looked exciting but it was expensive and only did one thing: edit. The more affordable Video Toaster from NewTek had started making waves but it had no non-linear editing capability. I was used to using a computer for multiple uses and wanted that swiss army knife flexibility that the Video F/X system represented. At the time, it also looked like the manufacturer was much more serious about professional video than NewTek. By November of '91, we were looking for office space in Santa Monica with a 33mhz MacIIfx as our "video workstation" and a Mac SE/30 as our "audio workstation."

So there we were, my partner and I, open for business as a digital post production studio with no track record and no business experience. We had an extremely vague business plan ("if we build it, they will come") and no real identified market niche other than, "we'll do it for less." This kind of approach might seem ludicrous in hindsight (as I recall, there was also a sinking feeling that it was ludicrous at the time) but it did create the opportunity for an incredibly diverse array of projects with new challenges and problems to solve.

Digital video technology was developing at an unprecedented pace so that it was difficult to tell clients what was and wasn't possible. Today we're much more acclimated to that constant rate of change but then it seemed like one long rollercoaster ride. For our clients, it was often a game of Release Date Russian Roulette, anxiously waiting for new versions of software to hit the streets. One week, a product wouldn't support drop frame time code; the next week, there would be a patch available that corrected that function. A 1.0 version release of VideoBlahBlahPro wouldn't support alpha channel masking and a month later, version 1.01 was alpha channel enabled. There was a somewhat dysfunctional family relationship between these start-up companies and their loyal smattering of enthusiastic users. A constant back and forth of cajoling requests and aggressive demands for new features. Like self-indulgent drug addicts, each software upgrade made us want a stronger fix.

Then there was the schizophrenia of evangelizing the desktop video technology (the "desktop" phrase stuck first because it wasn't quite all digital yet) to clients ("yes, it will work perfectly") and cursing it to companies developing it ("bastards, you said it would work!"). I found that the manufacturers of products like Video F/X, Adobe Photoshop,

Macromind Director and Specular Infini-D didn't really have the answers to a lot of questions I had about field dominance, vertical blanking, C-Mode EDL assembly, square pixels vs. round pixels, D-1 aspect ratios, RGB, YUV and NTSC color palettes—the kinds of questions I was being asked by the engineers at the bigger post houses when I brought in material for transfer. They usually smiled or laughed when I said that I was creating video on a Macintosh. In their eyes, I was playing with toys. Slowly, sometimes painfully and sometimes at high financial cost, I learned what it took to bridge the vast gap between computers and broadcast video.

Towards the end of that first year in business, I got a call from an editor for a new IDG magazine then called *Desktop Video World* (later to be called *Digital Video* and still later *DV Magazine,* eventually purchased by the publisher of this book). She asked me to write an article about the Video FX system for the premiere issue. I had always thought those people who wrote in magazines knew an incredible amount of technical stuff, way more than any mere mortal. It then dawned on me that, as one of the early end-users, I now knew things about this system that even the people who designed it weren't even aware of. I had accidently become a technogeek without even noticing.

After a year and a half in business, my partner decided that he was sick of computers and the stress of trying to master all these tools; this is not what he moved his soul for, so he left the company to pursue directing. (Things change and evolve. At last report, he had trained to become an Avid editor.) It was about this time, in the spring of 1993, that non-linear editing was really starting to become a major buzz word around Los Angeles. While Avid and to a lesser extent Lightworks were getting all the big-budget Hollywood attention, the first generation of useful inexpensive QuickTime compression boards were rolling onto the market. You could finally, almost reliably, edit and deliver full screen video on a personal computer...if you kept it short.

An inexpensive program like Adobe Premiere, originally conceived as a homespun editing package for multimedia producers, was now blurring the lines between editing, animation, and special effects for broadcast. For the first time, despite important limitations, a $3,000 Radius VideoVision sytem with Adobe Premiere could accomplish certain editing and imaging operations that even a fully loaded $200K Quantel Henry couldn't perform. A new market was born.

There were now enough cool toys around for other kids to want in on the game. In fact, there were so many games to play—CD-ROM production, broadcast graphics, editorial, audio mixing and of course, special effects—and all benefitted from these digital tools. Getting outfitted was cheap and easy enough; however, making all the components of a system work smoothly together was another matter. In the previous paradigm, one purchased a turnkey system from a vendor who guaranteed reliability. In an open-platform world, compatibility was only a theoretical concept. This was understandable from a computer geek's point of view but quite foreign to a traditional video editor or animator unaccustomed to setting up their own system with pieces from multiple manufacturers.

Now that the cost of entry into this industry was manageable and a critical mass of true believers had been reached, independent digital video artists began to ooze from every dark corner overlooked by larger post houses. For instance, in 1991 there were relatively few independent players in the obscure world of televison promotional "bumpers" (10-30 second ads to identify the network or a particular program) but by mid-'94, an entire cottage industry had formed around the "bumper" transforming them into glitzy, hypergraphic eye-candy designed by one or two artists on a personal computer for a very competitive price.

It was around this time that one of my clients (and later, friend), John Agnew, started me thinking of what I was doing as a kind of guerrilla warfare. He was working at an advertising agency doing a lot of new business strategy and it was becoming fashionable to present clients with a video pitch in addition to the traditional presentation boards like Darrin Stevens used to show his clients on "Bewitched."

John would typically walk in with some rough-hewn, poorly lit, Hi-8 footage and start complaining about how little time they had to get this together. So we would load his footage into the computer, either a

SuperMac Digital Film set-up or an early Media 100 system, and start to play around with ideas. We would filter the video, add graphics, animation, sound effects and music, and shape the piece to powerfully communicate the ad pitch. It was actually fun to work side-by-side with the client because we could try things out so fast and get a creative rhythm going.

At the end of the day, John was no longer sulking about his impossible task. Instead, he was struting around the studio, arms raised like Muhammed Ali, shouting, "I am the king of guerrilla video." And so he was (with a little help from his friends).

Thus, this kind of scene defined for me the philosophy of the Diguerrilla (read dij-ur-ila, as in digital+guerilla): no time, no budget, elements of varying quality, limited equipment, and quick wits. Though I've worked on many projects since then with significantly larger budgets, the guerrilla ethic has remained.

The diguerrilla is distinct from the concept "Digerati," another label that has floated around the digital media industry. For me, the word digerati has conjured up images of people with research grants and prestigious speaking engagements and business cards that say "evangelist" on them as opposed to someone who has five days and two computers to deliver a 30-second commercial. It's a completely different state of mind. This is where, to paraphrase a committed analog guerrilla, Ernesto "Che" Guevara, the render meets the road.

Questionnaire

Q: Are You Reading the Right Book?

Review Questionnaire Alpha if you already work with digital video on some level. Review Questionnaire Beta if you aren't working with digital video at the moment but would like to.

Questionnaire Alpha: Determine Whether You Are a Digital Guerrilla.

1. Do you have more than two SCSI/IDE chains full of peripheral devices?
2. Do have at least 18GB of storage crammed at max capacity?
3. Do occasionally pirate copyrighted images assuming that you can manipulate them beyond recognition?
4. Can you tell the difference between a rasterized vector and an antialiased bitmap?
5. If you were shipwrecked with a camera, a scanner, and a robust PC, would you be able to complete a video project without any assistance?
6. Are you a software fanatic, hoarding software (acquired both legally and illegally) most of which you rarely even use?
7. Does a 12-hour workday sound reasonable to you?
8. Have you ever gone over 48-hours at your workstation without more than meal and bathroom breaks?
9. Do you have an astonishing collection of different types of spare cables and adaptors?
10. Do you often synchronize your personal sleep cycle with your computer's rendering cycle?
11. Do you find yourself agreeing to take on projects and then figuring out how to execute them on the fly?

12. Have you ever used beta software with known bugs to complete a client's project?

13. Do you usually find that technical support people don't understand what you're trying to do with their software or have never conceived of the specific operation you are attempting?

14. Will you risk personal injury to capture a really killer live-action shot?

15. Do you gain a perverse pleasure from seeing what kinds of strange images you can generate from peripheral hardware by pushing it close to the point of malfunction or mechanical failure?

16. Do you have skewed fiscal distribution in your worklife (in other words, do you have a $15,000 computer workstation on top of a $29 used folding table)?

17. Have you ever had a dream about a piece of software (erotic or otherwise)?

18. Can you look at a moving image and guess it's frame rate ±1 frame?

19. Can you calculate SMPTE timecode durations in your head?

20. Do you look at art history books and wonder what took them so long?

Questionnaire Beta: Determine Whether You Might Have Guerrilla Tendencies.

1. Do you tend to stockpile digital images and sounds for no reason other than that you may need them someday?

2. Do you obsessively collect graphics and video software plug-ins just because they're cool?

3. Do you fool around a lot with camcorders with the intention of somehow editing something interesting later?

4. Are you in a related graphics field (desktop publishing, web design, etc.) and find yourself constantly thinking about making your designs move?

5. Do you watch commercials and programming on television and envision how you might accomplish something similar with your own PC?

6. A week after working with the fastest personal computer on the market, do you find yourself thinking it's too slow?

7. Do you watch video and unconsciously edit it in your head?

8. Do you find yourself hooked for hours playing around with the simplest animation tools (e.g. GIFbuilder)?

GIFbuilder

9. Do you find yourself thinking that the Powerpoint presentation you are preparing could be better demonstrated with motion video?

10. Do you dabble, asking theoretical questions in video-related SIGs and moderated discussions on the Net?

11. Do you catch yourself window-shopping or comparing prices for video compression boards and other digital video devices when you have no immediate need?

12. Do you already own a monster personal computer even though you're currently only running video games, internet browsers and a word processor?

13. Are you a traditional animator or videographer who thinks this digital revolution thing might be okay if it were cheaper?

14. Have you seen a demo or taken a seminar on digital video and caught the production bug?

15. Have any of your friends or family ever identified you as a control freak?

16. Do you posess this unique combination of characteristics: an manic urge to do things fast and efficiently, and an extraordinarily long attention span?

17. Do you have a short learning curve for technical data and an aptitude for learning software with a poorly written user manual?

18. Can you, just using your mind, intuitively switch between thinking in 2-D and 3-D space?

19. Have you answered "yes" to many of these questions not because they apply 100% but more because you're naturally cocky and just know you're a digital guerrilla at heart?

20. Instead of purchasing this book outright, did you borrow it from someone?

Scoring

15–20

If you answered yes to at least 15 questions, you're definitely reading the right book; in fact, you should've bought it last year before it was written; in fact, you should probably buy two—one to put by your workstation to read while you're rendering and the other to keep in your bathroom which is probably the only other place to find you when you're not at your computer.

10–15

This is the right book for you and you're buying it at the right time, just as you're starting to mature as a diguerrilla, appreciate some of the finer points of this so-called revolution and look for ways to avoid learning everything the hard way.

5–10

There's a lot here in the book for you if you want to find it. It may kick-start you to the next level of boldness and guile. Then again, you may get depressed because you're the type that always picks up these books and then puts them down, preferring the pipedream of making your own digital video rather than demonstrating enough grit to boot up your workstation and do something about it.

0–5

This might be a nice gift for a friend who really likes this stuff.

Essence of Diguerrilla Warfare

> 66 *The Revolutionary idea should be diffused by means of appropriate media to the greatest depth possible* 99
>
> —*Che Guevara,* Guerrilla Warfare *(1960)*

If we, the grandchildren of Marx and Coca-Cola, indeed now live in the media-spun "Global Village" that Marshall McLuhan once envisioned, then the digital guerrilla is the village blacksmith. He does not claim to spin straw into gold; however, with a bit of sweat and basic tools, he can craft keen weapons of communication.

A lone blacksmith, working in the age of mass production, appears as an underdog. At a glance, he seems no match for the machinery and consolidated capital of the mass-media age. Nevertheless, the digital guerrilla, catalyzed by technology, sees this struggle as not only survivable but winnable.

In this chapter you will be introduced to the following guerrilla production principles, as quoted from the diguerrilla manifesto:

1. It is possible to win against a larger army.

2. It is not necessary to wait until all conditions for victory exist before taking action; action itself can create the conditions for victory.

3. Strategy and tactics exist for fighting on both favorable and unfavorable ground.

> ➤ **Demographic Shifts:** A buddy of mine who lives in Arizona was here in LA trying to get work in the video business. He's a total guerilla video guy. And he could not find work in LA because he was too much of a generalist. In LA the market is very specialized, same with New York. You're here to do one thing. There are unions. They make sure you only do that one thing. And your bosses make sure you only do that one thing, 'cause there's enough people who specialize in other areas. You're supposed to be really good at one thing. And my friend, he's a generalist, he is the kind of guy that you say, "You know, I want some skiing footage of blah, blah, blah, blah, people flying through the air and all that." And he just takes care of it. He goes, gets the camera, grabs some people, goes and gets it done, edits it, brings it back, and there it is. He couldn't find work here. He's very happy in Arizona, he's got all the work he needs. (Barry Silver, CEO-Trakker Technologies, video editor)

Whether your current base camp is a university, a home studio, a small production company, or the media department of a corporation, you have probably been hit by a malaise of cynicism and resignation at one time or another. No matter how creatively brilliant you are, there exists an occasional nagging voice in the back of your mind. It echoes the prevailing wisdom that when push comes to shove, you are no match against a highly trained army of big-league production professionals equipped with the latest arsenal of supercomputers so powerful that they can compress video, brew cappuccinos, and disinfect your bathroom tile faster than you could shade a simple polygon.

➤ **In Demand:** I started in video in the early '80s and people would say, "Oh, there's so many people in the video world." You couldn't even get a job at an entry level. Now with the computer stuff it's a whole new situation. There's a whole lot of new jobs available. People are getting jobs. People are working. People are advancing fairly quickly. (Barry Silver)

This defeatist attitude can take you out of action in several ways. Perhaps you might not even attempt a project because you don't think it's possible without "turboradiosity, vector-based, subraster fuzzylogic kernels" or some other such whiz-bang feature available only in the silicon towers of the largest digital production palaces. Or else you might play it safe and succumb to the conspiracy of mediocrity. You will complete the project at hand but you will lower your sights and do no more than what you know you can accomplish easily while thinking to yourself, "If only I had more _____ (time, resources, money...you fill in the blank), I would produce something really great." Or finally, you may take an ill-fated kamikaze approach, fighting a losing battle trying to create your visionary digital epic on equipment that barely handles a decent screensaver.

> ➤ **The Space Race:** *Every SIGGRAPH or NAB [trade show] the new stuff comes out and I immediately say, "Hey that is just the greatest thing ever. But I didn't know it existed ten minutes ago." And now I'm walking around saying, "Hey, you mean software B doesn't do this. Well how could they even bear to keep their doors open being such slackers?" (Doug Barnard, Virtual Acreage, 3D animator)*

Given these pitfalls, new methods and techniques are necessary in order to prevail. The digital guerrilla fights against this conspiracy of mediocrity. The diguerrilla will not accept the prevailing wisdom that more money and more tools are the only ways to ensure success. Why does the diguerrilla bother to fight, one might ask? Why does any revolutionary pick up a gun or a pen or

⇨ ⇨ ⇨ **BIRTH OF A DIGUERRILLA**

I was doing a lot of freelance [desktop publishing] work and still getting minor things happening but not really feeling I was doing what I needed to do with a lot of the 2D stuff. And, you know, typography is typography, you know, it gets old after about the tenth page. So I wanted to kind of, get back to my sculptural roots. I'd always been drawing and sculpting, building weird things ever since I was but a wee lad and my father trusted me enough to use power tools. Which was a very big mistake. The thing about tools, I've decided is, success depends on when you make the transition from coffee to beer. If you make that transition just a day too early, you're a wreck; if you make it too late, you're jittery. It's very important to time that correctly; if you can get that down, the rest comes easy. (Doug Barnard) a mouse and fight? They fight in order to change the system, to change the way things have been done in the past, to make themselves heard. In the digital age, it is not enough to merely redistribute the means of production; the very concept of "production" itself must be reinvented.

Tabla Raster: The Blank Screen

Before we get into the keystrokes and shortcuts that are most effective, we should address the ideology of imagemaking. Ultimately, clever use of technology amounts to very little without a unique point of view. Let us begin with the question behind all questions: Why bother? In other words, what is the point of this dubious digital journey?

Start with our own personal CPU, the mind and the imagination. To reinvent the game, you need to be willing to think outside the box—free from the constraints of what's currently in fashion, what you have accomplished in the past, what you think is reasonable to achieve. You must establish what unique approach you are bringing to the design and architecture of your images; you must figure out the best way to inject into your work a distinct expression of self (whether we're talking about a soft drink commercial or training film for a hotel chain or a video kiosk for a trade show).

This need not be an overly profound inquiry. It may be as basic and crude as asking yourself, like my philosophical Texan friend Jeff once said, "Who's f—ing this dog, anyway?" A digital

> ➤ **Mind Over Megahertz:** Seems like I've been configuring for about two years now and refining and upgrading. It took me away for a few years trying to learn the tools and ask for the right tools. You ask the different companies you're working with to make tools that allow us to express ourselves really. And I really feel that now I'm there. I've got tools that I can express myself, they're working, they're really solid. And now it's just up to me to become the guerrilla filmmaker again with it. Otherwise it's all this horsepower and incredible code waiting for something to do. So nothing can really replace your intent to create a film or tell the story and I'm finding when all the configuration's said and done, I'm sitting there with a blank piece of paper still, and now what can I do with it? (Cody Harrington)

guerrilla usually doesn't have time for a long artistic discussion. Just ask yourself three questions while you're waiting for your computer to reboot:

- How will I hold the viewer's interest from beginning to end without losing the message?

- How will I get a client/viewer to notice me among all the competing companies using similar or superior technology?

- How will I be able to use the project at hand (no matter how modest) to further my ultimate goal of global industry domination?

⇨ ⇨ ⇨ **THE ZEN OF LOGOS**

For me it was really a journey of discovery. I was just having fun learning the new tools and was amazed that you could have a [digital] tool set that you could express yourself in a filmic way. You know, like editing on a little personal computer. You could actually start to do these little tiny movies. Of course they were very little and very tiny. But you didn't have to have a big Quantel box, or you know, spend hundreds of thousands of dollars. And of course it was low res but it still told a story. It was a way of expressing myself and I really was attracted to that. I was still able to find plenty of corporate clients that were wowed by this. You know like, "Oh, flying logo." And I started doing flying logos in 3D and that's what really lit. And they paid good money for that. Flying logos are really how I started in the business. (Cody Harrington)

Finding the Strike Zone

Creating and aligning on a thoughtful design approach and well-conceived preproduction strategy is essential to achieving your objectives, smashing the chains of mediocrity, and outmaneuvering larger opponents who want to snag your client. If you are fortunate to have the opportunity to conceive a project from scratch, attack this opening and go for broke (creatively, that is, not financially). This is what I call, "setting up a creative strike zone." When you set up a creative strike zone for the project, the appropriate guerrilla tactics will begin to naturally reveal themselves. You will also be much better equipped to deal with the inevitable adjustments necessary in the heat of battle.

This insight may seem obvious, and yet, I have dealt with

many producers and clients that had only the vaguest clue of why they were doing the project and what they wanted to communicate. I remember dealing with an ad agency that wanted a series of drugstore commercials emphasizing different special sale offers for various holidays. They wanted to go beyond a drab static design and have something that would really catch the viewer's attention. It became very clear during the production that they had no idea of what that really meant: we would go back and forth getting them to sign off on various elements, only to have them reverse their decision a few days later.

While I freely admit that we could've managed the client's expectations differently from the outset, I can also assert that this kind of aesthetic Alzheimer's is rampant in broadcast and interactive media; if left unchecked, it will infect your entire project, leaving you cranky, nauseous, and possibly catatonic. If you have any kind of guerrilla spunk and grit, you will survive, but not without scars to show for it.

Setting up the strike zone, like any good Marxist dialectic between pitcher and batter, is constituted by juxtaposing opposites whose proportions give definition to your artistic target. In baseball, the armpits and knees of the batter define the vertical range while the inside and outside of home plate define the horizontal range of the strike zone. Any pitch outside those boundaries is not optimally effective. You are not in control.

Below is a sample table to help you set up a creative strike zone. I call it a perception matrix. Some descriptors are common concepts in the art world; others are more philosophical or emotional. You need not use all of them, but if you pinpoint where your ideas might fall inside a few domains of perception, you will become much clearer about where you will need to aim the ball in designing the project.

To illustrate how these descriptors operate, I have chosen an existing project as a demonstration. The project, All Surface Running, is a broadcast *documercial* for the Athletic Footware Association who wanted to show that running with your friends—anywhere, anytime—was a fun thing to do.

By diagramming the All Surface Running Project using the matrix below, I could begin to assess what the specific needs of the project are. Identifying areas of contrast and harmony are powerful ways to get to the heart of what works and what does not. From this grid, there is enough creative information to design the production and create a script and/or storyboard.

Spectrum	Pertinent elements	Possible ideas/expressions
dream/reality	documentary footage	create an urban "movement"
dominant/recessive	environment vs. shoes	bring kids' personalities to fore-ground; not a shoe commercial
tension/release	running vs. talking	manic running footage combined with short interviews
contrast/blend	individual personalities vs. group activity	show kids' quirks but use long-shot to show group interacting with urban landscape
thought/action	viewer participation, static bystanders vs. running	bystander interviews, website promo...get involved
sweet/sour	kids vs. anchor	adult anchor made to look sillier and dumber than the kids
hidden/revealed	youth speaking out	provocative interview bites, expressing point of view
rough/soft	music and editing	vary the pace so that the viewer is taken on a long journey in only a few minutes
serious/funny	exercise vs. gags	personal feelings vs. sight gags, running in funny situations
brain/heart	health vs. spirit	express feelings through words and music
big/small	society vs. individual	make All Surface Running a revolutionary act
slap/kiss	physical vs. emotional	the aggressiveness of running contrasted with the kids' personal feelings

⇒ **Possible Pitfall:** Using this creative framework as a substitute for tight scripting and storyboarding. It is not a substitute.

Zoning, Scripting & Boarding

There are many books that go over the principles of scripting and storyboarding technique—I won't delve into them here; diguerrillas can figure out what scripting and storyboarding methods work best for themselves. The essential point, I feel, is to clearly delineate the creative framework for the project so that every subsequent step in the process targets the creative strike zone. This will not only save time and money over the long term, there will also be far less chance of winding up with something that barely resembles your initial concept.

After you have established this strike zone for the project, you can turn from overall strategy to tactics. Some basic production questions to tackle are

- Are we acquiring images or generating everything purely digitally? Does this piece contain video or film images?

- Would it benefit from a special "look" (digital manipulation, compositing, motion effects)?

- To what degree should type or still graphics play a role in this project?

➤ **Storyboards—Second Opinion:** I hate storyboards. To me, and I've never been one of those guys who sat around sketching, which is probably why I didn't work out in any design studios. Those guys, boy, they sketch like crazy and they, I'm more one of these guys to sit down and stare out the window and form an idea and then just get to work. Trying to form an idea and then just record it by putting it down on paper or in a computer. Obviously it's gotta be somewhat of a hazy concept, because even though we like to think of ourselves of being able to come up with a perfect mental picture, rarely does it work like that. (Doug Barnard)

➤ **Rebuttal:** The preproduction process is real important. You have to have a clear understanding, especially with the budget, of what's expected, and storyboards are the only way, and they always have been the only way. So much production is done so fast that people gloss over the storyboards and what I don't like to do is to try to teach the client to know their mind instead of changing it in the beginning. If you get that done in the beginning, really, the rest is going to fall in line. (Cody Harrington)

- To what extent should animation play a role in this project? What kind (2D, 3D, hybrid techniques)?

- What is required of the audio? Narration? Music? Sound effects?

- What is the best way to composite/edit all of the disparate elements?

These kinds of questions should be fairly easy to address if you relate them back to your strike zone. If you are creating from a blank slate, this is the time when your imagination can run wild, and the strike zone will assist you in measuring your ideas against the overall objectives and will be instrumental in keeping you focused when presenting in front of your client.

In the case of the All Surface Running project, a strike zone of youth, spontaneity, self-expression, and fun emerged. With that framework in place, it became apparent early on that the kids themselves would carry the piece. No narration was really necessary; the adult anchor of the show seemed very flat and one-dimensional when compared with the spirit of the kids, and so his role was minimized in the editing process. No matter how uninspired or inarticulate the kids might have been during the shoot, in postproduction we made them look like they were philosopher-rebels out having a blast.

Strong music segues and wild jump cuts punctuated the reactions of the kids running around their city. The kind of *Hard Day's Night* atmosphere created by odd camera angles, motion effects, and music made this roving band of All Surface Runners pop out of their environment like a jolt of electricity instead of just a bunch of young joggers huffing and puffing along some city streets. Lastly, because this formula would be repeated with different kids in different cities, we would be communicating, without saying it directly, that this was some sort of national movement that you, the viewer, might want to get involved in personally.

Avoiding the Mistakes of Others

Another important aspect in designing your project with a guerrilla budget is to become a student of what doesn't work.

While you learn the most from your own mistakes, they are often costly. You can learn almost as much from the mistakes of others, and the price is a lot more reasonable.

Unlike the military, who guard their techniques and approaches, designers and media producers are show-offs by nature. They want people to see and examine their work. They are usually willing to talk about it and share some of the speed bumps they hit along the way.

Successful diguerrillas keep a close watch on who and what is current in whatever market niche they are carving out. If you are going after commercial, corporate, or entertainment work, begin to collect demo reels from various companies and artists. You will watch them, and one of two things will happen. Either you will be inspired by the images, the design, and the execution, or you will marvel at what schlock gets created and somehow sold. Both responses can be insightful.

Most often, it is the well-intentioned effort that misses the mark that provides the most useful instruction. Just as you might redirect a movie scene in your mind that you think could've been better, you can observe the flaws in commercials, music videos, instructional tapes, or documentaries and find the source of their creative defects.

Ask yourself these questions:

1. If you could define the strike zone for this project, what would it be?

2. Has the filmmaker stayed within this zone or added elements that don't support the message or vision?

3. Does the pace and flow enhance the subject matter and make the piece more "readable"?

4. Is there a cohesive visual design (image, graphics, type)?

5. Is there any audio design, or is audio an afterthought?

6. What kind of feeling and message do you walk away with as a viewer?

By doing these virtual filmmaking excercises, you will train yourself to be very conscious of details and you will find that your instincts for experimentation are greatly sharpened.

> ⇒ **Possible Pitfall:** Honing your critical skills to the point where you stifle your own creative energy through self-censorship. Get someone else to be your personal critic; you've got work to do.

The Rules of Engagement

Before heading into the fray, it is useful to assess your own personal strengths and weaknesses in relationship to the project. One of the drawbacks with using powerful digital tools is thinking that you have the time and expertise to pull off every aspect of your production. Sometimes, a diguerrilla will have much more time than budget and might be able to do a diligent job in a production area they don't normally handle. In the majority of cases, however, it is better not to overextend. It is more effective to have a firm grip on the capacity of your studio and plan accordingly.

Where are you rock solid and where are you vulnerable? Are you basically an outstanding editor with a little bit of graphics capability? Are you a good shooter with a little editing experience? Whatever your balance sheet reveals, you can begin to explore what kinds of digital alliances you might need to create with others and how you can design a project to embrace your assets and minimize the aspects that aren't as well developed.

Carpe Data

Once you have laid the creative groundwork for a successful project, you must be prepared to fight it out on the ground, in the real world. This is a test not only of your ideas and talent but of your improvisational skills during production. The diguerrilla is extremely mobile and flexible, rapidly adapting to all circumstances. He or she anticipates the corrupted sound file, the missing reverse angle shot, the wrong resolution graphic, the overnight render crash, the file conversion problem, the disk space squeeze, the mismatched lighting, the temperamental network server, the PAL to NTSC conversion, the mixed-format source tapes, the broken address track, and the occasional power outage. The diguerrilla is a master at managing uncertainty.

Handling these production hiccups creatively is the reason your clients will love you and why you will continue to grow professionally. It is never a case of how much equipment you own but how fast you can solve a problem that is ultimately decisive. You don't need to own every piece of hardware and software, but you do need access to the people and equipment that can save your life without costing you the job.

Designing for Change

A guerrilla force which has just begun its development must follow three conditions in order to survive: constant mobility, constant vigilance, constant distrust.

—Che Guevara

As any well-travelled diguerrilla will tell you, clients, producers, and sometimes even you, gentle reader, are wont to change their minds…sometimes many times a day. Fighting this process will take a toll on your sanity and respiratory system. Instead, do what guerrillas do best: stay light on your feet. Prepare from the start with change in mind. This includes everything from file management methods to shot selection.

⇨ ⇨ ⇨ **LAW AND ORDER**

I think that if you have an orderly way of going about things, if you have processes that you've mastered, individual processes, it's more like you're plugging things into a system and this is also making sure to leave a lot of fallback positions. Sort of like, "We won't [destructively] change this file until we know that this is what everyone wants." If anything, I have a tendency to pound on clients to say, "Look at this. Is this what you're thinking of? Are we marching to the same beat here? Do we know what we want?" So, I think a lot of it has to do with refining the ideas in the beginning. (Doug Barnard)

If you know exactly how your project is constructed, and you carry along some spare parts, the odds of you going into toxic shock when a change comes up is greatly diminished. Many of the production details will be covered in subsequent chapters. In the conceptual stage it is useful to keep certain production principles in the back of your mind so that you avoid backtracking and scrambling at later stages of the campaign.

Excerpts from the Diguerrilla Field Manual

When gagged and bound, work around. —*Anonymous*

We made 24 of those [features] a year. We had the following schedule: Monday and Tuesday, you wrote your script and prepared the production; Wednesday and Thursday, you shot; Friday, you cut; and Saturday, you went to gamble in Tijuana. —*Edgar G. Ulmer, Director*

Basic Principles:

- *The fundamentals:* Yes, you can make video without knowing what timecode is or create animation without knowing what a Bezier curve is. However, your progress will be slowed by the holes in your training. Go to boot camp. Learn the basics. It will help you understand *why* your tools do what they do and what options you have when something goes wrong.

- *Push your limits:* This is probably self-evident but deserves emphasis. Discover what you can do. Know your bread-and-butter tools well and find ways to squeeze more out of

them. There are always undocumented maneuvers that manufacturers have never tested or understood the application for. Find them. Exploit them. If you know your fundamentals, you will know where to look.

○ *Creative coverage*: When gathering footage (either stock or production footage), make your camera work as hard as you do. A successful shoot is not just getting a dozen takes of a line reading. It doesn't take much time to gather unscripted loose "B-roll" shots, close-ups, and cutaways that might not seem immediately useful given the shooting script. However, in the editing room, they may save your tender bottom.

Make a list at the location of at least 10 extra 5-second shots to grab "just in case." Sometimes you just need to let your subconscious select additional shots that just occur to you in the moment (e.g., a hand gesture, a car passing, a wall clock, a longshot in a hallway). When the client starts asking you to recut interview footage or create a new segue, you'll have someplace to start.

○ *Stay modular*: Does every shot depend on the preceding shot? If the piece is *too* linear, it will require more effort than if the piece is constructed in such a way that shots can be reshuffled or eliminated without impacting the overall integrity and message. Think of symbiosis rather than interdependence between media elements and you will create more flexible structures. For example, if you zoom in at the head of the shot, zoom out at the end. You may end up liking the back end better than the front; extra gestures—head turns, pauses, pointing, leaving frame, entering frame—all leave more options in the editing room. In interviewing, after you let the subject ramble, ask them the question again along the lines of: "if you had to answer in one sentence…" That way, you get the in-depth and the sound bites.

o   *Loose timings*: Often animation, music, and audio cues get left until the end of postproduction and need to be crammed into existing space based on the length of a shot or transition. This can lead to all sorts of unforeseen problems. For instance, that animated transition that you crammed into six seconds just doesn't flow like you thought it would. Now you have two choices: live with something you don't like, or spend time/money recutting and reanimating. By incorporating temp music or a few sequential key frames representing the animation (often called an "animatic"), you can make much better timing choices and create the final elements parallel to the editing process.

o   *Precomps in compositing*: Just as it is more efficient to bring ready-made dips, spreads, and dressings on a picnic rather than the base ingredients, begin to envision labor-saving recipes that taste just as good as complicated ones with dozens of ingredients. Do you have to composite the sky, the buildings, and the water in the final composition, or can you bring a precomposited section called "cityscape" into the final composite and save placement, effects, and render time in the process.

o   *Nothing wasted*: In a digital world, everything is always raw material for something else. How can you optimize your media assets? Yesterday's news doesn't have to be tomorrow's fish-and-chips paper; it might be the back-

ground for your next composite. Become a master of repurposing media in creative ways.

o *File health and hygiene*: How much time can you afford to waste looking for files and identifying the latest versions? From your mother telling you to clean up your room to your accountant telling you to systematize your expenses, the world keeps telling you to get organized.

Now you might say that a run-and-gun revolutionary thrives on chaos, serendipity, and the occasional act of God. It might be true, but God gets busy with her own productions sometimes. The rude awakening is that Mom and the IRS are on the right track even if their ideas of organization are a bit one-dimensional. The bottom line is that if you misplace critical files, you either have to waste time recreating them, or in some cases, you are dead meat. The good news is that the diguerrilla is free to invent an administrative structure that works best for the project and the team. It need not be some Dewey decimal-inspired nightmare; simplicity is more durable. Several examples will be discussed in subsequent chapters; in the meantime, look at your project right from the start as a mosaic of digital tiles that you will need to prevent from falling into the shag carpeting.

Infrastructure Checklist

(Specifics will be covered in subsequent chapters.)

1. *Equipment redundancy:* Are you prepared for your best machine to go down? Many independent artists make the mistake of having just one or two souped-up hot rod computers. A vanilla-model PC used for light duty like a scanning station may be called into service for other tasks in an emergency.

2. *Removeable media/high-speed network:* Do you have adequate storage and archiving for big jobs? Do you have a fast internet connection? (If you're still using a dial-up

connection then you're either living in a remote "unwired" area or you're a traitor to the revolution.) Is your studio a data island, or can you move your data around quickly? Around your studio? Around town? Around the world?

3. *Open-system savvy:* Do you know how to take full advantage of a digital media universe? Are your workstations extensible with plug-ins or other "add-ons"? Can you extract useful datasets like motion and color information and map them into other applications for other uses? Do you have production tools that can talk to other applications and exchange media in an intelligent fashion? Do you have conversion tools that allow you to shoehorn almost any media file into a relevant format?

4. *Proper display:* Can you view your work adequately? Are your RGB and NTSC monitors of adequate size and quality for you and your clients?

Survival Kit

○ *CPU and RGB monitor:* Big screen (or dual-monitor setup), lots of RAM, lots of fast storage.

○ *NTSC or PAL monitor:* At least 13", high resolution, with as many input flavors as possible (RGB/YUV/YC/composite or more) and 16:9 image support.

○ *Speakers:* Two pairs recommended—one inexpensive pair for listening to lowest-common-denominator output (multimedia quality) and a set of studio speakers for hearing the full dynamic range of your mix.

○ *Audio mixer:* Minimum 8-channel, preferably 12 or 16. Should have some phantom power for microphone inputs.

○ *Video compression board:* Part of a turnkey system or separate component (e.g., Targa Series, Miro, DPS, Media 100, Matrox, etc.) with a 5:1 compression threshold or better. The board should handle at least two channels of 16-bit audio input. Better boards will have a breakout box with various input/output configurations (including a FreWire option). A desirable bonus feature is convolution option to output your computer monitor's contents as an NTSC/PAL (you will invariably want to capture moving images off a CD-ROM or DVD and transfer them to tape quickly and easily).

○ *Video camera:* Something (analog or digital) to capture pictures to tape. FireWire connection and manual audio/video settings options a plus.

○ *VHS VCR:* This format is the paper napkin of video recording: not the most efficient but certainly cheap and functional for a lot of different uses, from logging shots to watching movies when you're waiting for something to render.

○ *Microphone:* A good studio mike for scratch tracks and the occasional voiceover is indispensible.

○ *Digital still camera:* Something to capture still images and transfer them to disk without the time and expense of analog photographic processing (some DV cameras capture stills as well as motion video).

○ *Digital scanner:* Preferably two—one larger format cheap 11 x 17 and another cheaper 8.5 x 11 scanner.

○ *CD-R/CD-RW drive (DVD-RW drive):* Something to store large amounts of data cheaply. Good for archiving and distribution of elements such as digital graphics, video, and audio.

○ *Laptop computer:* A beefy color laptop with a big hard drive; good for a number of functions in the field such as presentations, video logging, and project administration.

○ *Media libraries (font, audio, graphics, 3D):* Royalty-free elements purchased or collected for various postproduction uses.

○ *Nonlinear video editing application:* Either part of a turnkey system or an application that will run on third-party hardware to edit clips into a program.

○ *Compositing application:* May be part of the editing application or a separate application that allows stacking and keying of video and graphics with animatable settings.

○ *Paint/image editing application:* A bitmap-oriented program that allows custom brushes, masking, and detail procedural work on the pixel level of the image.

○ *2D drawing application:* A vector-based drawing program for tweaking font outlines and drawing scalable PostScript objects such as logos, masks, and other shape-based art.

○ *3D application:* Though you may not be an expert modeler, you will inevitably need to create some simple 3D object or animation even if it is just a spinning globe.

○ *File conversion utility:* Something that reads files across platforms and applications and performs the necessary number crunching to make the round peg fit in the square hole.

o *Digital compression utility:* The corollary to the file conversion utility. Since compression is a fact of digital video life, you'll need an application that takes your flavor of digital video and helps you squeeze it into whatever delivery format is requested. (MPEG encoding is highly desirable.)

o *Software codec collection:* Many manufacturers now offer a software codec (compressor/decompressor) to view their media files on workstations that aren't equipped with the necessary hardware for realtime playback. The best part is that most of these codecs are free, so you don't need to be caught shrugging your shoulders when you encounter files digitized with "foreign" gear.

Useful Extras

o *VTR w/TC:* Though you can survive without a professional VTR (rent when you need it), you will probably want to own one because a high-quality timecode accurate deck is constantly in demand.

o *Laserdisc/CD combo player or DVD:* DVD is taking root, but there is also a ton of laser disc software out there already on the cheap. Besides, though analog, Laserdisc has no digital compression artifacts like DVD.

o *DAT player:* Though we are rapidly approaching the point of purely disk-based audio with MP3 and other high-fidelity audio formats, a lot of audio studios routinely use digital audio tape and expect that anyone using audio professionally will be able to play their tape.

○ *UPS:* Uninteruptible power supply and voltage conditioner. Depending on the size and your power draw, these battery/current stabilizers will give you 30 minutes to an hour of additional juice when there is an interruption of service. Cheaper than having a generator around, and those extra few minutes could make all the difference.

○ *Cable adaptors:* A diguerrilla's life is often filled with tape and bandages. A large collection of computer/video (even video game) cables and adaptors will save the day on a regular basis. You can never predict what extra piece of gear you will want to patch into your system or what strange dub routing you'll think up.

Digital Dogma

Thus far, I've tried to give you an overall sense of what kinds of things the digital guerrilla needs to consider before battle to increase the chances for success. The quickest, cheapest changes are possible when you are previsualizing and discussing details in preproduction, never when you are behind the camera or in an editing bay.

Unfortunately, this is the kind of precautionary wisdom that only becomes clear after you've made a costly error that could've been avoided with some better preparation. Everyone will, no doubt, get burned at the stove at some point. The question is

> **Passing the Mouse On:** What I eventually see in my future is teaching, because to me, every senior citizen should be teaching. Because theoretically if they're not teaching, they should sit down and shut up. Because the one thing that you've got after your youth and beauty is fading is experience, and the only way to get experience is to live through it. So the fact that we live in a society in which we don't necessarily pay for everything that we get, that I think the way that we return it to society is to try to take our experience load, pass it on to the next generation of people so that they can either use it or listen to us and laugh at us and go off their own way, but at least they have the benefit of that experience. (Doug Barnard)

whether it will be a surface wound or a hideous deformation requiring reconstructive surgery.

This chapter has been about fusing creative intention with pragmatic financial and logistical assessments. You would do well to read it twice—once to skim for tips and suggestions and a deeper reading for developing your own sense of mission. For that has been the other purpose of this chapter, preparing yourself mentally for the challenge in front of you. David did not slay Goliath with a fluke toss. He knew who he was up against; he chose the best stone and knew exactly where to place it. He also had his harp along in case he needed a soundtrack. A true diguerrilla, one who survives professionally, clocks his target dead on time and on budget no matter what. The following chapters will provide insight on how to accomplish that and still make it home for dinner occasionally.

Gathering Images

> **"** *I would also like to compose shots that are magnificent in themselves like Fritz Lang, but I can't. So I do other things.* **"**
> —*Jean-Luc Godard*, Cahiers du Cinema *interview*, December 1962

This chapter is about some of those "other things." It's about getting the right images for the job using whatever means of acquisition you deem appropriate. Not that there's anything wrong with beautifully photographed footage. You may be a brilliant cinematographer or photographer; if so, you have a skill that will serve you well in this endeavor, but don't let the cult of the camera become your only means of imagemaking. Besides, not every image is a point-and-shoot affair, some images don't readily exist in the everyday world. These images must somehow be teased out from your mind and into your computer. The digital guerrilla must never rely on only one method for acquiring material. The eggs-in-one-basket pitfall can produce bottlenecks in the production schedule if the acquisition method, for logistical or budgetary reasons, becomes untenable. As guerrilla adman John Agnew reminds me, "Never forget, the true guerrilla uses whatever's at hand to put the enemy on the back foot!" There are many ways to bag an image, and this chapter explores what options are available and what challenges they entail.

Original Sin

Now that you have previsualized your project and laid the foundation for its realization, you will need to begin to accumulate the raw materials, namely, pictures and sound. A diguerrilla must be willing to invent, capture, find, buy, borrow, and even steal images on occasion (though this last category does have certain legal ramifications). In some instances, this may require the sublimation of a certain amount of ego because some of the approaches outlined in this chapter are not as glamorous (nor tedious) as standing on the set of an expensive film shoot. In other cases, this may require creative ephiphany to capture material that is difficult to obtain, under any budget. Regardless of the media required, this book takes a by-any-means-necessary approach to getting you what you need under almost any budget.

The guerrilla instinct is a by-product of the 20th century. It is defined by the collision of industry and art, the interplay of economics and inspiration. In 1935, Walter Benjamin wrote about the role of art in a technologically changing world:

For the first time in world history, mechanical reproduction emancipates the work of art from its parasitical dependence on ritual. To an even greater degree the work of art reproduced becomes the work of art designed for reproducibility. From a photographic negative, for example, one can make any number of photographic prints; to ask for the "authentic" print makes no sense. But the instant the criterion of authenticity ceases to be applicable to artistic production, the total function of art is reversed. (*Illuminations*, 1935).

He was concentrating on the impact of photography on a world where the entire notion of art had been previously based on one-of-a-kind uniqueness. The thought was that art, no longer primarily measured or valued by its rarity, was now primarily a vehicle for ideas. His writing foreshadowed artists like Andy Warhol for whom factory-like reproducability became the entire foundation of the art. The mindshift from one-of-a-kind to dime-a-dozen has become even more acute in the digital age, where images can be copied, distributed and ingested like a virus.

Cody Harrington: On the Diva project, we started with designs and storyboards of what the product [an interactive television interface] would look like. And I was really brought on to work with the backgrounds digitally. You know, we were supposed to decide, "Ok, what's the look and feel of the backgrounds and the foregrounds?" So we were trying to design the storyboards around it, the designs around this concept, but we didn't have enough time really to create 15 hours of continuous digital backgrounds.

loops

> ➤ **Loop-de-Loop:** Loops, or cycles, are named for strips of film that are spliced head-to-tail for continuous projection. It's well worth the effort to find or create short pieces that loop—that is, the last frame seamlessly loops back to the first frame without looking "jumpy." When well executed, they are efficient to use and conserve disk space. A good loop is long enough to have a little variation in it (perhaps 5–25 seconds) and is subtle enough so that the repetition of images isn't obvious (e.g., reflections moving on the water's surface, a bird flapping its wings a few times). Loops are important building blocks in animation and make excellent moving backgrounds for graphics and other superimposed layers. Like symphonic music, entire compositions can be constructed using only looping bits of images. Thus, a long sequence can be generated from less than a minute's worth of material.

Avi Hoffer: That's interesting, to me that represents the whole paradigm shift where a client can ask for 15 hours of digitally manipulated footage. Even a few years ago that would be inconceivable. How could you generate that kind of quantity? You don't buy stuff by the pound do you?

CH: Well, it was a task and we didn't have very much time to do it. I just ended up making short loops that you could tell were looping but it wasn't in your face. So even in the edit session I was coming up with short little linear loops that we just had to tack together since it was a linear-based system. I just threw together 20 different loops. It was the only way we could make it work.

AH: Does that come out of your exposure to cell animation? Understanding how loops could work together?

CH: Yeah, it came from trying to minimize the cost of in-betweening. That's where you learn the tricks. So, a lot of my cel-based training taught me how to work efficiently. I guess I'm lazy. I want to get the job done as fast as possible, but make it look good.

So what to do in a digital world where art has become cheap (original analog masterworks notwithstanding) and the process for creating it even cheaper? Although the human creative instinct yearns to do something new and different, it becomes more obvious than ever that creativity does not operate in a vacuum, and as Ecclesiastes put it, "There is nothing new under the sun." Creativity exists in dialogue with the real world, and that world is referenced whenever an image is created.

In the latter part of this century, we have become so referential that now our images reference other images instead of something out in the physical world. There is a spectrum between "direct quote" and "inspired by" that defines the huge bulk of visual communication. For a digital guerrilla, this referencing, this *homage*-nization, is not something to fear; it is something to embrace whole heartedly. Practically speaking, digital guerrillas are less concerned about the *authorship* or uniqueness of their images and more with their unique application.

There are three ways to acquire images for digital media use:

o Photographically (including high-tech methods such as laser photography, thermophotography)

○ Computer generated (including other computerized devices that deliver realtime computer-generated images such as game consoles, special effects boxes, etc.)

○ Reproducing existing images (scanning or importing existing stock images)

Within those categories, there are a number of strategies and techniques worth mentioning. Many, I'm sure, you are already familiar with to some degree. For the diguerrilla, however, familiarity can also breed contentment. I would like to challenge you to become unfamiliar with your equipment again; it is essential that you recapture that new-toy twinkle in your eye, find that urge to see just how far you can push yourself and your gear. Every weird experiment will have within it the seed of something wonderful.

DIGUERRILLA WANTED: I am looking for an Art Director with complete production skills to work on a pitch tape for a new TV show. Naturally, because it is a pitch tape, there is no footage of the show, and no talent. The tape will be very compositing intensive, with some 3D as well. Anyone interested MUST have an amazing reel, with plenty of high-end experience. Additionally, they MUST be able to take this project from concept to final online by themselves. The chosen person will need to work at the client's facility on a brand spankin' new MACINTOSH setup that will be purchased by the client. Software required for the gig will include After Effects, Premiere, Photoshop, Illustrator, Commotion, and one of the high-end 3D packages (either C4D, El Broadcast, or Lightwave). Here's the rub... Because of the massive amount of research and design time involved, the project will require AT LEAST a six-week commitment. The amount of money involved should make it worth the while of most people. The client needs help, and they are willing to put some money up front. This project could end up being an amazing addition to someone's reel.

Found Footage

In the '50s and '60s, some would-be filmmakers who couldn't even afford the basic materials—a camera and film—began to scrounge through dumpsters outside of film laboratories and salvage celluloid. People like Bruce Conner and Stan Brakhage began to understand that you could communicate a unique visual message with recycled images. And it was a cheap way to work.

Pictures, whoever happens to shoot them, are ultimately just pictures, raw materials in a larger process. They can be like bits of information, like words or hieroglyphics that can be reshuffled and recycled to mean many things. It's not the individual words that are so important, but rather their collective meaning. Though not all images are interchangeable, in this context, the underlying idea becomes more important than the individual image.

For the guerrilla, this is an important tenet of the unofficial manifesto. Not that you need to give up the idea of shooting your own images or using original material, but there is a lot of stuff out there that is either licensable stock footage, royalty-free buy-out footage, or public domain.

There's also what I call "white pirates"—those who cruise the low-fly zone under the radar of copyright law by altering existing copyrighted images beyond recognition and thus transforming the images from one thing into another. It's like a form of biodegradability—if you can't identify what it originally was or where it came from, then you've somehow made it your own. This statement may inspire the Feds to read my email and look through my garbage,

> ⇨ ⇨ ⇨ **YOUR TAX DOLLARS AT WORK**
>
> Sometimes, it is okay to ask, not what you can do for your country, but what can your country do for you. One of the perks of paying taxes in the United States (besides watching the money be misspent) is that you automatically become a "part owner" of the National Archives, or at least, under the Freedom of Information Act, a potential user. The National Archives and Records Administration has a vast library (http://www.nara.gov/nara/searchnail.html) of text, images, moving images, and sound recordings. There is an ordering procedure (http://www.nara.gov/research/ordering/broad.html), and if you want broadcast quality transfers, you will have to pay transfer costs...but other than that, the footage is royalty-free.
>
> This is not a resource for yesterday's news footage. It usually takes 20–30 years for records from federal agencies to reach NARA—this is government we're talking about after all—and 4–6 weeks to reach you once the order is received. So this isn't a last minute resource, but you can use NARA to build a library of elements for future projects.

but it's accurate: diguerrillas around the world transform copyrighted material into unrecognizable "original" images every day.

Steal This Image

Sometimes, when pitching a new job, your showreel may not be enough; the client wants to see something specifically related to their job before they buy. Sometimes, the job is awarded, and there is still a need to see some sort of mock-up quickly so they can sell it to *their* client. Whatever the case, it usually doesn't make tremendous sense to shoot a lot of new footage that may never be used in the final project. Short on cash and high on creativity, the Rip-O-matic was born.

The name affectionately stems from the concept of an animatic, a moving storyboard (usually with a scratch soundtrack) that provides the basic timings of the scenes to be either animated or filmed. It allows the production team and the client to get a sense of the commercial spot or program before the real expenses begin. A Rip-O-matic is the same idea except that the images used are ripped off; in other words, instead of having an artist draw storyboard panels, the producers pirate existing (usually copyrighted) footage and lay out the structure of the piece.

The advantage of a Rip-O is that you can experiment without a lot of risk. Your head is a vast storehouse for images that you saw somewhere once; now you can recall them, hunt them down at the video store or on the Net, and see how they all fit together. Once you are happy with the images that you've ripped off from magazines, TV, and movies, you can begin to lay the final images on top of the Rip-O's and match the timings. Some Rip-O-matics, however, have been so creatively put together that the producers eventually decided to license some of the *ripped* material and use it in the final cut.

Your local video store is one huge source for Rip-O-matic material. I prefer DVD or laser disc sources to VHS because of the superior picture and sound. However, in a Rip-O, image quality isn't always the highest priority.

Parental Warning: As a concession to government overlords and to the last vestiges of artistic integrity, please let me make one thing perfectly clear: I am not condoning the pirating of copyrighted images for commercial use (unless I receive a clandestine percentage of the proceeds in small unmarked bills). Use of copyrighted material is suggested as a visualization tool only. Subsequent commercial use must be done with proper licensing agreements. ■

Scavenging the Digital Dumpster

With a century of motion picture technology and half a century of videotape under our collective belts, our planet is awash in footage. The following section deals with using other people's pictures—specifically, locating what you want, negotiating the rights and/or fees to use it, and receiving the footage in a format that you can use. One of the more invaluable analog tools I've found is a resource book published by Second Line Search called, rather appropriately, *Footage* (http://www.footagesources.com). This book is updated annually and contains descriptions of over 3,000 moving image sources and all the steps necessary to research, screen, and license the footage.

> ➤ **Seen and Not Heard:** While this chapter is devoted primarily to images, it should be noted that the "acquisition mode" applies to sound also. There is also a large market for stock sound effects and music as well as a number of creative ways of aquiring them yourself. They will be covered in a subsequent audio chapter.

Taking Stock

The artistic ego in you may want to resist using someone else's images in your project, but there are just too many compelling reasons not to consider your "stock options." In this end of the millennium craze, so many business and advertising concepts are focused on globalization and a fast-moving century of progress. Unless you illustrate it symbolically, globalization usually implies showing images from around the world. How often does your budget include 21 days of shooting in 12 different countries? And there are so many things that you could afford to shoot, but it may not be the best use of your time and resources just to get that time-lapse shot of fruit rotting in a bowl when it has been done many times before you. Also, there's always the client wondering if you could just put a bigger mountain in the background. Another reason might be efficiency: do you really want to create every single graphic background from scratch when they'll only be on screen for a second? Whatever the motivation, when strategically deployed, stock savviness is an extremely potent guerrilla weapon.

Rules of the Game

Within the stock image category, there are two basic models for licensing images for production. Rights-protected images are licensed for specific use, for a negotiated fee based on a number of factors like geographic distribution, type of commercial use, and level of exclusivity. There can also be research and duplication fees involved. The rights-protected model has been the backbone of the stock footage industry for several decades. It has the advantage of providing the customer some information on how the image has been used in the past and usually insures that competitors may not use the same image within a certain time frame.

The second model is royalty-free licensing: for a one-time standard fee, the user licenses the images for nearly unrestricted use. The advantage to royalty-free image licensing is that the image can be reused without incurring additional fees and traditionally is less expensive since the collection is designed with volume sales in mind. Royalty-free libraries have traditionally been the domain of still photography and graphics, but now several companies have begun to develop digital video products on CD-ROM that are of tremendous use to professionals in all areas of media production.

Stock vs. Schlock

Because of the ease of producing a CD full of images, there is an abundance of royalty-free product out on the market that looks and sounds quite similar in the mail-order catalogs. In fact, the quality and content varies a great deal, so some diligent shopping will make the difference between purchasing material that fills a real production need rather than sitting on the shelf next to your 12 America Online Trial CDs. In the still-image class, PhotoDisc is one of the pioneers of CD-ROM and Web-based digital image distribution. Their library now tops 60,000 images, of which 25,000 are available on over 130 CD-ROMs. The variety, depth, and quality of their library make them a reliable brand to turn to as a primary resource. The premium brand carries a higher price tag ($139–$299 per CD), but the photography quality in both concept, composition, and execution is uniformly excellent.

The industry standard is normally 100 images per disk, usually in at least two usable resolutions, accompanied by some kind of browsing software. While most images are drum scanned and color corrected, be prepared to do some image editing even if it's just cropping and resizing. The largest market segment for still images is print, so most products are separated with CMYK color and need RGB conversion. Corel uses the PhotoCD format for its images, which I find a useful format for video work since all the images will have a 35mm film aspect ratio. The middle resolution (768 x 512 pixels) is close enough to a D-1 video frame size to require minimal cropping or resizing. Clipping paths and masks are a nice bonus, but only a minority of manufacturers take the trouble.

Window Shopping on the Web

Most of the general market companies have similar sounding libraries with categories themed around business, sports, travel, health, objects, backgrounds, and so on. Without browsing the distributor's website, it's difficult to really know if the CD is worth purchasing. The Web has added a powerful dimension to this market by offering online search and purchase capability on a per-image basis. Not only does this make it easier to locate that Bolivian Lawn Bowling Association photo, you can "try before you buy" (often a low-resolution image is downloadable free for comp-ing purposes), and thus limit your expense to the single image (usually between $20 and $40) you need instead of a disk full of images that you may never use.

The pay-per-pic model is much like the rights-protected model for still images except that it's much cheaper. For video professionals, unless you have an incredibly specific need or an insanely picky client, royalty-free is a great way to go for still images. There's a lot of selection available, and for most still images, they're either used as part of a layered composition or they tend to appear briefly on screen. However, if you need something that is highly unconventional in style or content, the royalty-free market may not have what you're looking for.

Buying images individually is especially practical in categories where you know that the visuals date themselves quickly. For example, buying a disk full of technology images, unless they'll all be used right away, might seem a poor investment when you know that technology,

> **Tech Pics:** The downloadable product-info sheets from manufacturers' websites are an excellent source for up-to-date technology images. Commercial use is usually easy to clear with their PR people. If you're nice, they may even provide you with a whole CD full of press images.

particularly computer technology, starts to look dated every six months or so (that's why a lot of metaphorical business collections tend to show only mice, keyboards, and the edges of monitors since they stay in fashion longer).

Evergreen Bargains

On the other hand, there are a number of "classic," niche, or obscure categories that won't get dated easily, if at all. Strictly speaking, classic evergreen examples would be wildlife and nature (earth and beyond), weather (everyone needs a shot of lightning once in their life), babies (naked preferably, even diaper styles get dated), body parts (not dismembered, mind you, just no hair or clothes), native "primitive" cultures, food (raw ingredients), and classic landmarks and architecture (I don't think they'll be tearing down the Vatican anytime soon). Niche categories might be vintage/retro images (they're supposed to look dated), textures (abstract and organic), maps, and everyday objects (like an 8-ball or a traffic light). Obscure evergreens are unique collections that won't get everyday use but may fill a particular production need, like X rays, cemeteries, and acoustic musical instruments.

What I might call blue-chip categories—not 100% evergreen but close enough—include money, sports, elderly people, costume events (e.g., Carnival in Rio), and aerial photography. Another category worth investing in is stock illustration, which needs to be in its own category. Though obviously subjective, many drawing and painting styles have a timeless quality and are impervious to the changes in lighting trends, film stocks, and lens optics that impact photography.

Financially, these types of collections make purchasing an entire CD a good investment because the per-image cost is so much less. Even if you buy at the high end, using only 6 or 7 images will amortize your cost. For the bargain bin CDs ($39 and under), even if you use a single image, you've gotten your money's worth. Be aware that the cheaper disks aren't as thoughtfully conceived and occasionally have imperfections in the photography and sometimes less-than-inspired composition.

Bodies in Motion

Okay, still images are cool, but you make your living getting pictures to move. What's out there in the dynamic media category? Royalty-free, there's still not a huge library available yet. There are still some technical obstacles preventing easy digital distribution; these mostly concern format and file size, but these issues will continue to evaporate with the march to full-DTV convergence. For now, the bulk of what's available on CD-ROM are basic elements for compositing such as explosions, fire, water, fabrics, and so on, with a few archival disks beginning to pop up. These are smart investments for their evergreen qualities mentioned earlier; the odds of needing a good cloud sequence sometime in one's career are reasonably high. For the compositor, these element collections are a nice start. They are sequential files or QuickTime movies, transferred directly from film, ready to be incorporated into a digital production. They are general enough to be reusable several times, and the content is very time-consuming to shoot independently.

There are also production companies on the Web selling footage in bulk on tape rather than per shot. This is hit-and-miss,

⇨ ⇨ ⇨   THE FOOTAGE EXCHANGE

(footex@pigsfly.com): An example of a guerrilla approach to footage and the Web can be found at http://www.pigsfly.com. The following is the mission statement of FootEX (the footage exchange):

I have started this list because it occurred to me that the Internet provides a way for video shooters all over the world to share their own (out the window) location with other producers. You might live in the cold north and need shots of the tropics. FootEx is perfect.

There are NO charges allowed for ANY footage listed. You may negotiate who pays for shipping and/or stock but you may NOT charge for the actual footage. If you find someone charging for footage PLEASE report them to us and we will ban them from this list. Report to owner-footex@pigsfly.com.

Here are some rules. PLEASE follow them and this service will work for you.

Do offer video, not film. It is OK if it was shot on film, but we only exchange video.

Do provide a signed release of any footage you send to another list member giving him/her full use rights to your material. If you don't have such a form we have provided one at http:/www.pigsfly/footex.

Don't offer footage that you did NOT shoot!

Don't offer footage on consumer media such as VHS or 8mm.

Don't offer footage with people in it unless you have signed releases you can provide.

Don't USE footage you get from this list without a use release form.

Sometime in the future we will be offering you a web site where you can see clips of the footage.

I hope this service helps solve your footage problems. Drop me a note now and then and let me know what you think.

Ray Smithers, Flying Pig Ranch, ray@pigsfly.com

and the quality varies greatly. With these vendors, verify that the footage was originally shot in 35mm (unless it's archival) and transferred directly to digital tape. Find out a bit about the history of the footage: When was it shot? Who shot it? Did the company commission it, or are they outtakes from another production? Ultimately, you'll have to decide based on a VHS viewing copy or a bit of streaming footage on the web.

In the rights-protected end of the industry, the protocol for accessing their images is still fairly traditional. The typical routine is to describe what you are looking for to your account representative, and they perform a search for you and compile a viewing tape with possible selections in one or two days. Depending on the request, the search and screening reel may have a base cost of up to $100 or so. However, the Web is rapidly being developed for searching and limited previewing. Companies such as FOOTAGE.NET (http://www.footage.net) are stepping up to fill a technological niche of being an aggregator of library data, the Yahoo of stock footage. While browsing images online is currently a bit sparse, you can keyword search many libraries at once and send "ZAP" requests to the dozens of news, archival, documentary, and commercial stock houses that FOOTAGE.NET represents. This can be an excellent first pass to quickly see what might be out there.

The Art of the Reel

And a lot is out there. Lush beauty shots and old newsreels are no longer the bulk of what's available. There's everything from dirigibles to drag queens, shot from many different angles under all kinds of lighting conditions. Subtlety, nuance, and selection cost more. Expect to pay $500–$2500 to license a 10 to 20-second shot depending on its usage. For the larger houses, this license fee provides use of the film negative; it does not include telecine transfer, which many clients prefer to control themselves.

The stock business historically has been based on human relationships and shifting inventory, so rate cards are often only a place to start. Particularly if you are looking for multiple shots and have a nonbroadcast project, you may be surprised to find that there is a lot of pricing flexibility. Also take the time to find out what other projects this shot has been used in, particularly if you plan to use it "as is" without any further digital manipulation.

An Eye for an Eye

It's also important to note that the "stock market" is a two-way street. Because much of the rights-protected business is based on having a fresh, contemporary library, there is a lot of footage churn. Ownership of most contemporary footage is held by the original producer and is merely housed and managed by the stock house.

In addition to ongoing associations with well-known cinematographers, film stock houses are always looking to represent new suppliers of distinctive footage, so if you find yourself with a lot of unique outtakes from a production or have exceptional material in your personal library, you may be interested in seeing if that footage might provide ancillary income (35mm film is preferred, but the more unique the content, the less of an issue format becomes). Alternatively, you may just want to market the footage directly through your own website and maybe some digital media online discussion groups. Though your exposure may be less, you pocket 100% of the licensing fee.

Scanlines

What if you need source images but don't have access or time to shoot or even find stock footage? These are often the moments of sublime guerrilla madness. *L'image impromptu.* One solution is the radical deployment of an ordinary flatbed scanner.

Like many peripheral pieces of computer hardware, flatbed scanners have dropped in price and gone up in quality, and they

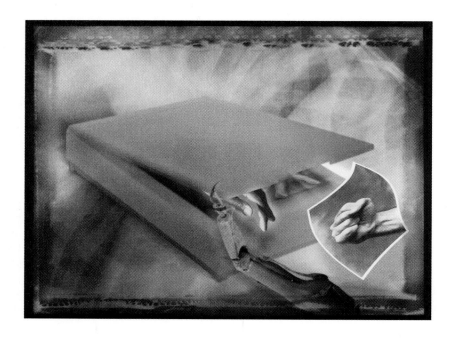

have become virtually indispensable to digital imagemaking. As of this writing, there are now 30-bit scanners for under $100. In the early '90s, color scanning was a tedious affair with three-pass lamps which scanned for red, green, and blue. Today, single-pass, high-resolution scanners are faster and easier to use.

A scanner is an essential piece of gear for acquiring flat art or photographs. It works similar to a Xerox machine except that the scanned image is converted into digital data and stored inside the computer. You can spend a lot of money on a scanner, but unless you are doing serious prepress work for print, I don't think it's essential to spend the extra dough. A good image editing program like Adobe Photoshop or Macromedia Xres or MetaCreations Live Picture will let you correct imperfections in the scan from a cheaper unit (although the moving parts are more likely to give out sooner on a cheaper model).

> **Up Off the Flatbed:** There are several other kinds of scanners. Hand scanners, slide scanners, drum scanners, and even a digital still camera can function in a pinch (especially out in the field away from the studio). The second most useful type of scanner is a slide scanner since there exists a tremendous amount of film positive and negative that is very inexpensive to shoot and easy to transport. Many professional flatbed scanners have a "transparency mode" or special attachment for slides and negs. They work fairly well but usually can't produce the fidelity or max resolution of a slide scanner. Make sure that you have adequate scanning power or, at the very least, access to a nearby service bureau with reasonable pricing.

Scan area, however, is a significant factor, as not all images are 8.5" x 11". I recommend a large-format scanner because it is more flexible (if you've ever tried to tile scans seamlessly together, you know what a pain it is) and even if you are scan-

Copyright Flavio Kampah 1998

ning in smaller pieces of artwork, you can gang up images together and save time (get a cheap standard format scanner for backup and overflow and you'll always have an available scanner within reach). At the cheap end, Adara's Megastar I (12" x 17") has a street price of around $700; at the higher end are the Umax Mirage II and Agfa DuoScan at $2000+ (I know, you can buy another computer for that price, but the extra scan area ends up being very useful and can save your hide with things like maps, small posters, large children's drawings, and oversized books).

For most people the whole point of a scanner is to place a flat image on the glass and capture it, with maximum fidelity, into the

Passing Thought #2806

How to "create" happy accidents ongoingly. A quick note on randomness as opposed to plotting things out. You might want to consider devoting a corner of your studio or computer downtime to "laboratory" experiments that require very little setup and almost no supervision. These might be batch operations with an image manipulation application such as Equilibrium Debabelizer or Terran's MediaCleaner Pro, or perhaps time-lapse photography with a camera hookup;or a compositing/rendering experiment with something like AfterEffects or MediaFusion. That way, every morning, you have something that may or may not be beautiful but you will always have learned something useful.

computer. Indeed, this is a very practical use for such a device. However, to the trained guerrilla eye, the scanner glass can become a living canvas on which to invent unusual images and effects.

The techniques owe great kinship to the kind of inane experiments you might have done with the library copy machine in college. Only now, there won't be a big angry line forming behind you.

Top 5 Tricks to Teach Your Scanner

1. *Smearing:* This involves moving, curling or otherwise distorting the flat image while the scanner lamp is in progress. The effect is kind of "liquid" as the pixels "streak" with the motion of the scanner lamp.

2. *Macroscanning:* Scanning small sections of an image at high resolution to reveal extreme detail. Will usually also reveal characteristics of image surface such as paper or metal texture. Can be used with lap dissolves or "stop-motion" style with lower-resolution scans to simulate a high-power zoom.

3. *Extreme Scanning:* Scanning unusual materials such as reflective surfaces (aluminum foil) and plastic to produce strange, surreal images. Liquids, paints, and gels also produce unusual translucent effects. Keep plenty of Windex handy and don't use your expensive scanner.

4. *Object Scanning:* 3D objects placed on the glass (including body parts like a human face). May need color correction since the scanner lamp doesn't color balance light

reflections resulting from curved surfaces. The effect is distinct from normal photography as only part of the dimensionality is preserved.

5. *Scanimation:* This technique uses the scanner like a single-frame animation system and allows you to incrementally move or replace materials on the scanner glass that, when combined, produce motion. Place some tape or other markings on the edge of the scanner to ensure consistent registration of the artwork.

[handwritten margin note: COMBINE SCANS FOR ANIMATION]

Listen Up

Use a shallow white cardboard box or other seamless white material for covering 3D objects on the flatbed glass if you wish to keep them from picking up additional reflective ambient light.

Scanimation Ideas

○ Have several photographs of the same person in similar but different poses stacked on the flatbed. Continue removing the bottom-most photo quickly during the scan to "blend" the poses together.

[handwritten margin note: MOVING PHOTOS STACKED IMAGES]

○ Place a tightly stretched sheet of plastic wrap over the scanner glass. Then place an organic material such as colored sand, pencil shavings, or thick colored liquids (e.g., hair products or honey) onto the scanner bed. Scan, then move the material around in a random or deliberate man-

[handwritten margin note: OR ORGANIC STUFF OVER PLASTIC WRAP]

ner. Scan again and repeat the process. Combine those frames and loop them as a moving background or some other compositing element.

manipulate film images

o   Take actual processed celluloid or still-image film negative and introduce some physical process such as scratching, burning, staining, tearing, and so on. Register the frames so they can be scanned in proper relationship to one another. Reassemble as a sequence or digital media file.

These are but a few of the mildly dangerous "don't try this at home" approaches that you should definitely try at home. At the very least, you will expand your creative envelope and discover new things that your equipment can do that aren't in any manual. At best, your client will think that you designed some very expensive effect with some super expensive software. Either way, you're ahead.

Again, you may be struck by pangs of guilt or professional hubris that some of these corner-cutting techniques are just hacks, tricks, or cheats; you might feel they compromise artistic originality in the interests of cost or speed. Well, to those delicate sensibilities, I say, "Get over it." It's only the final product that anyone cares about. For the digital guerrilla, much of the creative challenge is in how to make prefab look plain fab.

The Camera

What more poignant philosophical observations can be made about the camera, our surrogate mechanical eye? The camera is,

Is it a digital photo of an asteriod or is it toilet paper? (If you can't afford time on the Hubbell telescope, toilet paper might do the job.)

perhaps, the most profoundly impactful innovation in human communication since the advent of spoken and written language. Its power is, and will continue to be, so vast and far-reaching that it is no longer thought of as a device; it has become embedded into our conscious reality, an extension of our senses. In other words, you should own one. But which one and what to do with it?

I'm not going to create a consumer report chart on digital cameras (it would be outdated by the time you read this; you can find many product reviews at http://www.dv.com or http://www.newmedia.com), but I will outline the important features to look for in addition to price, and you can connect the dots from there.

DV or NEW MEDIA

DV Camera

For some, because of its compressed image, DV will never be professionally acceptable. But for diguerrillas, it's a godsend that supercedes older analog formats in quality and flexibility. It's cheap (relatively), it's digital, and it will continue to become more computer-friendly with the advancing use of FireWire, the digital transfer protocol built into many of these cameras. There's a lot of manufacturer jockeying between Sony, Panasonic, JVC, and Canon for DV supremacy with the DVCAM, DVCPRO, and miniDV formats. The basic choice here is whether you need a good lens for serious shooting (plus timecode and full 4:2:2 bandwidth image) or whether this camera is an auxillary camera for grabbing a few shots here and there that can withstand some small compromises in image quality.

Size matters also. While all the DV cameras are a lot smaller and lighter than heavy broadcast gear, there is still a variety of camera bodies. The Panasonic AG-EZ30 is a light handheld that delivers great pictures. The tiny Panasonic PV-DV910 is the size of a Walkman, half the price, and might be a good choice if you need to shoot unobtrusively. Because of its size, it makes a good interview camera when you are on the go. In fact, with the rise of video streaming on the Web, it doesn't make sense to do audio-only interviews anymore. A video record gives the material a wider range of use.

Mini Studio Camera

There, of course, is still a place for analog-video cameras. A simple camera unit with a decent lens (such as a Cannon XL1 or a video-only studio model), mounted as a downshooter with flat side

Aerial view of the bahamas or a rock from the backyard with some digital tinting. (Not as much fun as going on location but somewhat cheaper.)

lighting, will serve as a basic animation stand and capture station for objects that aren't appropriate for a flatbed scanner. (If you don't want to build your own, Fuji makes the FV-7000 basic system, which includes lighting arms, for under $1000.) If the camera isn't a camcorder, it will need to be connected directly to a video capture card in your computer or a VTR for taping. You will probably want the computer capture option anyway so that, with frame-grabbing software, you can capture images frame by frame.

If you build your own stand (meaning two soft tungsten lights flanking a stand to support the camera above a flat surface), I recommend mounting the camera with an adjustable arm that swivels

90 degrees. That way, you can easily convert the downshooter to a mini-bluescreen stage by hanging a blue background against an adjacent wall with a shelf or platform for supporting the objects.

WebCam

Hey, they are cheap, and they can be used for more than just videoconferencing applications. Get an extension cable and put the camera in an interesting location. Set the software drivers to capture a frame every X seconds and build a QuickTime movie, an AVI file, or a series of frames. It's not high resolution, but the material can have many applications, especially if you're going for that stilted "webcast" look that will be with us until everyone has ultra high-speed Internet connections.

Digital Still Camera

While some of the DV cams take still pictures as well as video, you will still want a still-image digital camera for a variety of uses such as location scouting, quick product shots, and grabbing back-ground textures. They're also under $800. You have to like Sony's Digital Mavicas because of their LCD monitor and their floppy-based storage system. You can shoot 500 images on a charge as long as you have 25 floppies with you. This represents a significant savings over the expensive memory card system that most digital cameras use. Moreover, the floppies go right into your computer's drive without any serial docking/downloading procedure. This is an enormous convenience.

You'll also want a wide-angle lens for your camera (usually between $50 and $100) to capture architectural spaces, groups of people, signs, and so on. The minimum image resolution that you will want is 640 x 480, but you could probably benefit from something like the Casio QV-5000SX with 1280 x 960 pixel resolution and "Movie mode," for 10 fps multiframe exposures. Higher-resolution ("megapixel") cameras allow for cropping the image afterwards without sacrificing the picture quality. Unless you are just an optics junkie, I would pass on the high-end SLR-type models that give you the high-end lenses and ultra high resolution in the $2K–5K range. At that point, you might as well be shooting analog.

35mm Still Camera

Hey, don't throw away that standard 35mm camera just yet. It remains a loyal and productive tool in the right hands (meaning yours). Whether it is a consumer-grade fixed-focus or a more sophisticated SLR, shooting film and processing it on PhotoCD is very useful for capturing a lot of color, resolution, and fidelity. The

> ➤ **Stocking Stuffers:** Nothing that captures an image through a lens should be overlooked as a possible acquisition tool. Lipstick cams, Super8, Bolex 16mm, and even Fisher-Price PIXLvision cameras (no longer manufactured) can be useful in the right application. Perusing the occasional garage sale can turn up a few discarded gems that will give you one more option for acquiring a unique picture.

PhotoCD process is more expensive than a direct camera-to-computer system (about $1–2 per image) but it does provide a rich look that midlevel digital cameras currently don't match. There are more film stock and filter options available for analog cameras, and key product shots or magic-hour landscapes deserve the lush film treatment. A fast motordrive gives you the option of shooting animatable action. Lastly, analog cameras have fewer (that's *fewer*, not *none*) electronic problems on location.

> **DIGUERRILLA WANTED:** We are looking for someone who can write effective advertising copy, operate Betacam cameras, coordinate and provide lighting direction on location and studio shoots, coordinate and provide sound/audio direction on location and studio shoots, and edit using a Media 100XS nonlinear editing system.

Shoot to Kill

So much can be said about the use of a camera that I will confine myself to only a few succinct comments. Whether you are doing the shooting, directing the shoot, or merely at the set or location, there are a few guerrilla practices worth keeping in mind.

Roving Eye

As in the classic Kurosawa film *Rashomon*, every angle tells a different story. Even if you are already planning on covering your scene with two or three cameras, there is an excellent chance that one more lens will capture something the others don't. Don't worry that if the "second unit" camera doesn't cut seamlessly

⇨ ⇨ ⇨ **SKELETON CREW**

There was an independent feature I worked on called Fun *that did very well at Sundance and garnished a lot of attention. And one of the things on that film that really spoke to the whole guerrilla film making effort is, in order to save money on permits they had to keep their crews to less than five people including the actors. A lot of the stuff was handheld, so you just have the camera operator who actually was the DP, you have one guy doing the audio. But what was so great, the DP did such a great job at composing a shot of a single and pull back and move at the key moment in the script to reveal somebody else in the room in that conversation so you got a two shot. He moved the camera in such an intelligent way that when things were appropriate he could go in for a closeup just through camera movement rather than having to cut. It was neat because I was in the editing room going, "Wow, this guy's camera work is great!" It saves you so much time and footage just because he's able to get three shots out of one. And these actresses had such good performances that they were able to maintain it throughout the entire take. Some scenes I would just let the whole tape play. I wouldn't even have to make a cut. That to me is guerrilla filmmaking. (Barry Silver)*

with your primary camera; it doesn't have to be of identical quality. The idea is to have some distinctive additional coverage as backup. A lightweight, inexpensive handheld camera is most flexible (Hi-8, Super8, DV, or 16mm film). The roving camera should have a specific beat (e.g.,. audience reaction shots, extreme close-ups, behind-the-scenes, etc.) that will guide the cameraman's composition. Good instincts and fast reactions are important for this assignment. Not only will there be more selection in the editing room, some of the "secondary" footage may end up inspiring a new approach to structuring the piece.

Reenacting Truth/Improvising Fiction

This might fall into the category of directing rather than shooting, but it bears mentioning either way. For reality-based shoots, there are many instances when, in the flow of events, a critical moment wasn't well covered or was entirely missed. The issue arises in news and documentary circles as to whether the filmmaker should manipulate the event by reenacting some of the action and then call it "reality." Fortunately, this philosophical discussion doesn't apply to diguerrillas. Get the shot by any marginally legal method. If you need to return to the scene for pickups after or if you have to ask someone to walk through a door a second time, don't hesitate. It saves a lot of editing gymnastics if you have the coverage you need. Conversely, if you are shooting something acted from a script, allow yourself the luxury of some improvisation even if it is just a few insignificant gestures before and after the scene gets underway. Improvisations can breathe life into a stale scene and keep actors interested. Often, having the camera rolling in "off camera" situations provides some nice moments that would be nearly impossible to direct. Look for opportunities to give yourself a few more editing options or a less by-the-numbers feel that will impact the final product positively.

Mise-en-Scene for Non-French Speakers

This term is used by overeducated film students and Francophiles to refer to how the picture is composed within the frame. Composition is another area that could be expounded upon for at least a book or two. My five cents worth is this: Go back to some of the keywords that you used in preproduction to describe the intent of the scene (or if you never did that, think about it as you focus the camera), and try to visualize how to create that theme or that contrast within the frame. Will the CEO look just a little more powerful if she's leaning over a balcony with a bunch of cubicles below? Will the baby look just a little more adorable if there's a baby rabbit hopping next to it? Will the attorney look just a bit more sinister if the ashtray full of cigarette butts is in the foreground? What is in the foreground, middleground, and background is decisive in how we read the scene. You don't have to be a master of cinema, just get more useful visual information into the shot without making it seem forced (e.g., a giant distracting trophy sitting right in front of the athlete or massive stacks of cash in the background behind a stock broker). It may just be a question of a different angle or even a different lens.

Composing a Composite

Not only should you compose shots for their ability to convey the maximum amount of information, you should always consider how a particular shot might work as a composite. Even if this is as simple as maintaining an empty area of the screen where a graphic title will super nicely. Maintaining the subject against a large even background such as the sky makes it easier to pull some sort of matte or key later if a different background is more appropriate. Areas of darkness within the frame make it easy to seamlessly drop in an extra element later. Compositing need not be a flashy densely layered affair. Maybe a poster in the background just looks dated and needs replacing. Subtle additions in postproduction can make a good shot perfect.

> **Improving Reality:** Now I shoot totally with the digital process in mind. I'm going for a way to key out certain elements. I compose knowing that part of this frame is completely useless but this other part is the important thing, so I want to make sure I get that and I can move it around. I'm always composing and thinking digitally and I never see a shot that can't be improved. (Cody Harrington)

GIGO-a-Go-Go

Of course, if you are gathering images for extensive processing, the lighting and lens optics are less important than if you are actually shooting primary images. If you are going to use a camera, even in a limited context, learn basic principles of lighting (key, fill, backlight) and which situations might require a manual override of autoexposure settings (e.g., a person with dark skin in a white room, someone standing on a balcony with the sun setting behind them, or white balancing under mixed lighting conditions such as

➤ Decreasing the Video Camera's Electronic "Enhancement":

In my experience *all* video cameras have a degree of electronic "enhancement," The picture output from both old tubes or current CCDs is quite soft and lacks detail. Camera manufacturers design an electronic circuit that reacts to changes in brightness levels in the frame and adds an overshoot in the form of a black or white line to the picture. This is designed to make the picture look sharper. But if this circuit is adjusted too high, the resultant picture just looks "electronic" and unattractive. You will find the adjustment of this circuit named variously as "contour" correction, "aperture" adjustment or "detail" level. They are all the same thing in essence. Viewing your camera on a good monitor, turn this "enhancement" down until you get the picture you like. It might be a small screwdriver adjustment or through a menu in the viewfinder. It might be called "sharpness" in this context. If your camera is a "domestic" (or consumer) camcorder, it might not have any adjustable circuit. In this case employ the following technique to bring about a decrease in "enhancement."

➤ Optically Diffusing the Image:

Many movies are optically diffused to give pictures a "softer" look and to decrease contrast—especially when shooting against the light. Diffusers—flat filters 3 or 4 inches square made of glass or plastic—can be purchased in a range from "subtle" to "overromantic." Depending on "the look" you want for your video, decide which filter is right and shoot the whole film through it. Support the filter using a proper filter holder/lens hood. You should judge each shot since the diffusing effect changes with changes in zoom angle, but in my experience the difference is not great if you shoot everything through the one filter. The added benefit of this filtration is that in many instances it causes the "enhancement" in electronic cameras (as above) to be much less effective—not a bad thing!

The best diffusing filters I've found are made by a company in the U.K. They are called Suprafrost. In the U.S., Tiffen's Pro Mist Filters are nearly as nice.

These techniques will give video a photographic quality that cannot be created in postproduction—and will stop video pictures looking annoyingly "electronic."

—David Crossman, DGGB

fluorescent and tungsten). I will direct you to find what you need to know about technical competence (lighting, depth of field, and audio fidelity) from other sources (http://www.videography.com, for example) including trial and error.

Speaking of error, while the garbage-in/garbage-out rule still applies (good raw material is almost always preferable), there are still times when garbage becomes the main component by default. There's just no way to avoid using crap sometimes. Either your camera malfunctioned, the conditions for shooting were nearly impossible, or your client supplied you with footage shot by an inebriated employee with Parkinson's disease. Come what may, the guerrilla must be versed in the principles of distilling diamonds from donkey dung.

The basic premise, of course, is to use any smoke-and-mirror tactic to convince the viewer (albeit sometimes with a wink) that every image on screen was put there intentionally by trained professionals. No one is really concerned how ridiculous the conditions are behind the curtain; they just want a good product without excuses. Below are some typical videotape-related issues that every digital guerrilla faces at one time or another.

The Seven Irritating Odors of Really Rotten Source Video

(and How to Get Rid of the Stench)

Problem	Possible Solution
Multigenerational dubs. While access to the camera original tape is always preferable, dubs are often the only available source. Analog dubs compromise picture quality with each successive generation. With VHS tapes, second generation already begins to stink.	• Reduce or eliminate chroma. Color bleeding, particularly in the warmer hues, is a noticeable problem. The picture artifacts or noise become less noticeable when chroma is attenuated and contrast is boosted. • Filmic look. Accentuate the grain and contrast (and possibly frame rate) to make the distortion seem intentional. • Reduce picture size. Chroma distortion and artifacts are less obvious when the picture size is reduced. See if you can get away with using other graphics or some alternative framing composition that justifies using a smaller picture on screen.
Glitches, stretches, kinks and static. No matter how well you protect your master tapes, the nylon material itself is fragile and subject to all kinds of horrors as it is dragged through the arms, claws, and flywheels of a camera or VTR. As a correlate to Murphy's Law, electronic disruptions are most likely to occur in your most important shot.	• Add electronic grunge. There are several grunge looks that mask these kinds of signal distortions. One is a kind of "bad satellite feed" look in which you add some additional 2–10 frame "tweaks" at regular intervals such as mosiac filtering of the frame, freeze-frame "hiccups," and vertical hold shifts. • Another grunge motif is the "VideoPhone" look, where the frame rate doesn't sync up with the audio. It is particularly effective when audio is equalized to sound like a phone call, picture is reduced in size, and motion is strobed at 2-12 fps. • Use "film slug," electronic film leader, preferably with identifiable markings such as sprocket holes and grease pencil or academy leader over the offending glitchy frames. This gives us a feeling that we are watching a "work in progress" and can be effective for focusing the attention of the audience on the content and not on special effects.

Glitches, stretches, kinks and static. (continued)	• Intraframe morphing. If the fluidity of the shot is critical, sometimes short morphs between similar frames can give the illusion of having pristine footage. Only use this technique if the glitch is short and you think it will be well worth the effort.
Lighting problems and poor color balance.	• Color correction is possible at various stages of the postproduction process. Try and do most of your adjustment upon input by adjusting the digitizing hardware settings. That way, you can avoid having to deal with color effects later on. Just a reminder, flesh tone is the most viewer-critical part of the spectrum, so adjust for flesh tone and don't worry if background colors are a bit off.
	• If the problem is nastier than a basic hue or saturation adjustment, you could consider a high-end color correction transfer at a post house where they have more control over the spectrum and can isolate different areas. Scene-to-scene correction is expensive.
	• If you don't want to fork out for a scene-to-scene transfer, try reducing the chroma to minimum or all the way down to black-and-white. At this point you can tint it light sepia or blue, and everything will look consistent.
	• If you absolutely need consistent color, remap the palette with an application like Debabelizer. Create a superpalette from a shot with acceptable color, import the media as a QuickTime file, and remap. If there are too few colors in your palette, the image will look somewhat posterized (perhaps an effect you want); if there are too many similar colors, the remapping won't be substantial. However, if every shot in the sequence is remapped with the same palette, there will be an aesthetic consistency.

Shaky camera work.

- After you've finished blaming the cameraman (unless of course it was you, in which case you blame the weather conditions or the earth's gravitational pull), you have a few options. One is applying motion-tracking software (Adobe After Effects, Discreet Logic Flame, Quantel Henry) and stabilizing the shot.
- The other route to go is exaggerate the shakiness by both slowing the shot down and adding a strobe and/or frame blending every X number of frames. It will make the shot seem dramatically jagged and may provide an intentional emotional effect that you can claim you intended to have all along.
- The simplest cheat is not to alter the shot at all but rather contrast the shaky video with something rock-steady that will anchor the frame and make the shaky footage appear to serve some purpose. An example would be overlaying a black mask with a keyhole cutout. The shaky video is viewed through the steady keyhole and becomes much easier to watch because the context better justifies the funky camerawork.

Poor focus.

- You can't really "add focus," but a convolution kernel, like Photoshop's unsharp mask, can pull more detail from the shot at the cost of increasing grain and pixelation a bit. Use with caution.
- If the shot has fallen victim to some consumer autofocus mechanism and keeps adjusting focus during the shot, exaggerate the phenomenon and blur the blurry parts more and ramp them into focus using a key-framed blur filter.
- If the shot is of a consistent focal length but just slightly out of focus, you might want to make the situation into an aesthetic choice. Like most visual attributes, focus is relative to context. If you matte your main subject, say, a talking head, into an even softer focus background, the talking head will appear more focused. To intensify the optical effect, you can matte in more focused elements in front of the talking head and the planes of focus will give a lot of depth to the shot.

Camera reflections, microphones, and unwanted objects in the shot.	• This is more a magician's game of misdirection. If you're lucky, the offending object will be at the edge of the frame and you can just enlarge the frame by 5–10% and it will drop out. Of course, life is never that simple; you need to be clever to hide these kinds of problems. The object is to avoid complicated rotoscoping at all costs.
	• One technique is putting some element into the scene that pulls attention away from the offending area. If there is a window reflecting something undesirable, perhaps you can add a more aesthetically pleasing translucent reflection on top, such as a flock of birds overhead, that overpowers the underlying reflection.
	• If the subject is standing in front of a mirror and you haven't placed the camera at an angle, one possibility is to matte in something nonreflective in front of the mirror at the reflection's location. Perhaps something taped to the mirror like a photo or a note. If the subject doesn't step directly in front of it, the composite is very simple.
Disjointed continuity.	• Either not enough coverage or there were two cameras that weren't identical and the footage doesn't cut together well.
	• For anyone who's had to rush a shoot or had a piece of equipment go down at a crucial moment, there is the familiar feeling of desperation that accompanies viewing a painfully long shot in the editing bay and knowing there is nothing else to cut to. Desperation is just the prelude to inspiration for a true guerrilla. There are a number of ways to "create" more material than you've actually shot without reshooting. The first thing is to identify the real intent of the shot rather than its literal interpretation in the script or storyboard. Would

Disjointed continuity.

it benefit from intercutting titles or stock footage or something that counterposes that shot?

- Or could you cross-cut the under-covered scene with another scene and keep going back and forth to indicate they are happening simultaneously?
- Or would some additional detail added to the scene provide more subtext (e.g., a ringing phone in the background)? Cut to a stock shot of a phone next to an anwering machine. On the soundtrack, you can play an incoming message that is relevant to the action. The same goes for the sound of a television in the background and then cutting to the TV program.
- One last technique is actually breaking up the master shot into component parts. If shot on film, this would ideally be done as part of the telecine process, where sections of the frame (e.g., face, hands, objects) are magnified to fill the screen, giving you a variety of close-ups to cut to. This can also be done at video resolution, but the scaling will introduce more artifacts and necessitate some sort of filtering or blurring to be aesthetically pleasing.

Beyond Acquisition

Beyond merely acquiring images, there are a host of possibilities for manipulating the images being acquired. Even capturing them with a lens or a digital scanner is a form of manipulation. While many of these options are explored or revisited in the chapter dealing with effects, there are other techniques that fall closer to the domain of acquisition and are useful for "reacquiring" or "reinterpreting" material and giving it a distinctive feel.

The following are a few different speed settings for your video blender.

Warning: Some images may get harmed in the making of your project. Some will die so that others may live. The squeamish are advised to stay away from digital video equipment. ■

In Praise of Image Abuse

1. Signal modulation: Or, a funny thing happened on the way to the hard drive. An analog signal from a camera or VTR can be tampered with on its way into the computer. Often this can be accomplished just by manipulating the input parameters of the video capture board. Sending the video signal through a proc amp or other external device can provide interesting results. These include aesthetically desirable noise, unusual color effects, and picture distortions that might be much more difficult to achieve in post.

2. Rephotographing: The idea is to somehow display an existing image and recapture it with some distinctive alteration in image integrity. One example is shooting video images off a television screen or projection screen (including projecting onto moving material such as a billowing sheet); in the process of rephotographing the material, you are free to zoom and pan across the image and otherwise alter its original composition.

3. Photo-roto: Printing out individual frames and creatively reanimating them. This can be a more time-consuming process, but merely printing out the frames on paper and

introducing a three-dimensional process such as physically "crumpling" them can give a distinctive organic look.

4. Time-lapse/stop-motion: These are time-honored techniques for altering the way time is recorded. Actions that span across time can be condensed, or actions that don't actually occur (such as the movement of inanimate objects) can be made to appear as if they occur in real time. These effects require some kind of intervelometer on the camera or a variable frame rate driver for the capture card in your computer. Though many time-related effects can be achieved in postproduction, you will not have as many options with shutter speed and exposure (see chapter 5).

Building Your Own Library

Next to your ideas, your images are your greatest asset. Why should they be used once in a project and then tossed aside? Whether you plan to market your own footage to a library or just keep it around for your own use, it's very important to begin building a personal library of the images that you already own. With CD-R and CD-RW prices at an all-time low (not to mention the arrival of higher-capacity DVD-ROM), it's time to start saving your elements, mattes, and outtakes digitally for a rainy day.

Make it a practice to pull selects for specific archiving purposes before you dump the media from a completed project. Evergreen elements are good, but the obscure stuff that you think you'll never need again (all that footage of that local beach clean-

> ➤ **Evolutionary Production:** The way I really like to work is I come up with an idea but it's kind of a loose idea and then carry a camera around and shoot things that catch my eye and collect images as I go. And I find that the images, after a while, start to tell their own stories. There's no way I could have anticipated that in the storyboard. I might have an idea, I'll put it down but really, the guerrilla-style for me has always been collecting images and coming back and asking, "What do these images say or mean?" I'm left with a whole lot of imagery that I have to go through and catalogue and then try to put through from the matrix of editing, then putting effects on them or I'll start to play with it in 3D and then see how the music works. And then it is what it is. It's really hard to work this way in a commercially sensitive situation, but that's my preferred way of working. (Cody Harrington)

up) is usually the material you'll end up wanting to go back to (Murphy's Law, once again). Select a few variations of a shot (camera angles, screen direction, etc.). It's frustrating if you have a great image, but it doesn't fit into the rest of the project because of the way it's shot. Finally, remember to choose short (potentially loopable) shots for digital archiving; the rest you can archive on videotape in the best format you have available.

This should be obvious, but remember to choose your archiving format carefully. If you have the footage compressed with a proprietary hardware Codec, you'll be limited in how you use the material in the future. Sequential image files or flattened 720 x 486, 29.97 fps QuickTime (either raw or generic-JPEG compressed) is a flexible way to go. Compression should be unde-tectable. Keep small thumbnail proxy movies or "poster" frames on the disk to make browsing easier.

Target Acquired

Having bagged and tagged your images, the adventure is now only beginning. These pictures must now be skillfully shaped into something more than a meandering sequence of frames. The next several chapters describe the long winding march from raw images to triumphant final cut.

Taming the Beast: Command and Control of Your Media

> **❝***All forms of improvisation are alien to me.*
> *If I am ever forced into hasty decisions, I grow sweaty*
> *and rigid with terror. Filming, for me, is an illusion*
> *planned in detail.***❞**
> —*Ingmar Bergman,* The Magic Lantern
>
> **❝***The day on which one starts out is not the time to*
> *start one's preparations.***❞** —*Nigerian proverb*

Media Management Is Dead.
Long live Media Resource Strategy.

There are many aspects of jungle warfare that even the most rabid revolutionary might find a bit dreary. Deploying effective media inventory systems isn't usually the first thing that occupies the mind of a digital guerrilla; these tasks are more akin to digital ditch-digging. If I'm not careful, this could be the most boring

chapter of the guerrilla saga. People tend to consider the administrative side of digital video with indifference or mild disgust. With this in mind, I will do my best to cut through the geeky tedium and take you into the backwater bayous of the digital revolution; we'll navigate the murky territory between acquiring the pictures and fitting them all together. This is typically a domain with the cryptically clinical label of *media management* (or sometimes *asset management*). This term describes the logistical structure for storing, organizing, tracking, and working with digital material. I sometimes imagine a huge warehouse with forklifts and toxic metal industrial containers all nicely barcoded and databased.

While there is nothing inaccurate about this term "media management," it doesn't quite capture the holistic diguerrilla paradigm. In the guerrilla effort, every small decision has an impact on the outcome of the entire campaign. In this context, I think a term like *media resource strategy* (MRS) is more useful. More than merely knowing where your elements are, a resource strategy implies a proactive, hands-on approach; implementing a strategy means being completely in sync with the building blocks of the project. If the diguerrilla is to prevail, they must have an effective resource strategy or face unnecessary bottlenecks and setbacks during the production.

Implementing an MRS in digital video is both simpler and more complex than an analog equivalent. It is simpler because computers excel at navigating tables of data and can therefore help track a great many different media characteristics more easily; it is more complex because there are so many flavors of digital video data that can be combined (graphics, still images, animation, video, audio, MIDI) and need to be massaged for compatibility and optimum performance. This means being aware of hundreds of small technical details, or at least cognizant of which details are of particular importance.

The main strategic resource categories are source data (the tape or original digital file), encoded data (the digitized media), synthesized data (rendered media such as effects and transitions), and metadata (descriptions of how the media is used).

DIGUERRILLA WANTED: Are you a Data Wrangler with artistic yearnings? Motion graphics department at major movie and television marketing company seeks someone with strong technical skills who knows PhotoShop and Illustrator. AfterEffects or Flint familiarity a plus. Duties will range from file management to helping with creative overflow. Great opportunities with dynamic department doing film, broadcast, and main title design.

I intend to address media resource strategy as though you, free-spirited rebel, are skimming this chapter with a predisposed resistance to organizational systems that slow down production and oppress the creative process. If, by chance, you're someone who enters every fiscal transaction into your Quicken Register within 24 hours or someone who memorizes the three-letter identification codes for all commercial airports, then you won't need any encouragement to apply this information. For those not blessed with blissfully anal-retentive personalities, your organizational salvation will come in stages. Pace yourself; do not lose heart. The jungle can be quite dense.

The Thin Line

For the end user, the editing interface, or any software interface for that matter, is actually a very thin curtain of code placed in front of an unruly group of media files. You might think of the graphical user interface (GUI) of an editing or compositing system as mostly a map pointing to video files buried among various drives and servers. A bin or a sequence or a composition is merely a description of placement and procedures that the application applies to a group of video and graphic files. The project files don't really *contain* any raw content in the same way that a word processing file contains all the text it uses. If a word processor worked like a video editor, it would have a master file that told the application to look for the first word in the middle of a file on drive A, the second word at the end of a file on drive B, and so on. Our master word processor file might contain information about fonts and formatting, but it wouldn't contain the words themselves.

The advantage to this pointing and indexing design is speed and efficiency. Only your editorial decisions are being stored, your recipe for shaping the media. Changes are made quickly and easily. The original media files are left unaltered and can always be referred back to in their original condition.

In the coming years, sophisticated visual data tools with automatic scene detection, voice recognition, and OCR features (such as ISLIP's Media Logger) will be routinely integrated into the editing environment so that it can catalog, point to, and process all types of media located anywhere on a high-speed network. A lot of the mundane resource management concerns will be dealt with transparently in the background. Even then, however, it will be essential to understand what is going on behind the scenes. Only a human understands the logic of illogical thinking, which is often at the paradoxical heart of postproduction. For the moment, it's important to understand the strengths and limitations of how digital editing systems organize and track data. With a small amount of precaution and savvy, your workflow will increase and your problem-solving skills will expand.

Code Dependent

Video editing, as we know it today, would not be possible without the Society of Motion Picture and Television Engineers (SMPTE) system of encoding a continuous timing signal on the address track of videotape. The SMPTE system may be a little convoluted, as anyone who's transposed drop frame time code for non-drop frame might attest, but it does function reliably, and it is currently the only standardized way to pinpoint a shot and communicate "metadata" (like which reels and shots were used in what order) between different editing systems.

The lower-cost tape formats—BetacamSP and its grudgingly obsolete predecessor, 3/4" videotape—both have standard SMPTE address tracks. Newer formats like DV support SMPTE timecode in their professional (DVCAM and DVCPRO) versions. VHS and SVHS tape will also hold timecode on an address track, but very few prosumer camcorders and decks write or read the code.

The Numbers Racket

In the future, digital television and noninterlaced broadcast schemes will obviate the need for this kind of "leap year" time-

> ➤ **Drop Talk:** For those of you not familiar with the macabre intricacies of timecode and the NTSC broadcast system, there are two flavors of NTSC SMPTE time code. Most of the time, NTSC video is referred to as running at 30 frames per second, which corresponds to two interlaced fields per frame running at 60 cycles per second. This mathematical parity is great on paper, but it doesn't reflect reality. In reality, the NTSC broadcast signal is 59.94 Hz, which corresponds to a frame rate of 29.97 frames per second (two cycles, or fields per second). In a stroke of schizophrenic wisdom, the SMPTE committee decided to adopt two timecode standards, one just rounds up to 30 fps (non–drop frame) and one pretends to be 30 fps (drop frame) but drops a frame approximately every 33 seconds to keep the time code in sync with absolute time. This standard is called drop frame timecode and is used in the broadcast world to ensure that an hour program is 60 minutes of timecode instead of a couple of seconds short. The European PAL format avoids this math problem by basing itself on a 50 Hz cycle and running at 25 fps. Thus, the timecode is always uniform.

keeping strategy. For now, all editing and logging systems are based on timecode, so if you haven't yet, surrender and make timecode hygiene a part of your video ritual. Even if you don't have an internal timecode generator, there are inexpensive "blackbox" or third-party computer solutions to externally generate SMPTE timecode and record it onto the address track. Whoever does the shooting (or dubbing), make sure they are professional about setting the time code generator on the camera so there is a natural progression and no strange jumps or breaks in the code.

Why is this important? When the editing system searches for a particular shot to digitize, it finds it by locating the timecode address of that particular frame. If there is a break or jump in the code, the VTR can get confused and start spastically shuttling back and forth through the tape. It's kind of like cruising slowly down a dark street looking for a street address and finding the buildings all numbered illogically; you end up stopping traffic.

Many times, I've seen tapes come in with continuous time-code, but every single reel begins with hour 1 (consumer DV camcorders are factory set this way and cannot be adjusted). I'm not sure if this is a case of laziness or ignorance on the part of the videographer. It is much easier to identify tape labeling errors if the tape's timecode coincides with the reel number. If I know that reel 005 begins with timecode 05:00:00:00, then I can spot and easily correct a problem if some shots in my bin are labeled reel 006 but have TC addresses beginning with hour 5. If every tape has the same timecode, a tape labeling error made while logging could mean that the wrong shot will end up in the final assembly, and a lot of manual backtracking will be necessary.

Nontimecoded Material

Most editing systems will accept nontimecoded material. The system assigns arbitrary timecode usually beginning at 00:00:00:00 as the material is digitized. Once digitized, the footage behaves like any other timecoded footage. The only problem is redigitizing the source material later. The system will not

Timecode Tip #1

Aside from the standard protocol of having the reel numbers match their timecode hour, I try to maintain a practice of going to double-digit for B-roll footage. Since most of my projects shoot under 10 hours per camera, I like camera B or the second unit camera to use a reel number starting at 11/hour 11. That way, I instantly know from looking at any EDL or reel whether I'm dealing with primary footage or "B-roll" (another angle or cutaways). Moreover, when shooting two cameras in the same location (but not shooting sync-time code), hour 1 on the primary camera can correspond to hour 11 on the secondary camera. This extra step isn't always appropriate, but it has saved my neck more than once and is a fail-safe against confusing types of footage.

➤ **A Final Variation:** If possible, I save hours 20–23 for transferred footage—in other words, material that originally didn't have timecode, so it was transferred to a time-coded tape. That way, I know that an original master exists somewhere, and I can backtrack if there is a problem with the images. Obviously, when you surpass 24 hours of material, these distinctions won't apply and you will need to rely on other tracking techniques.

be able to go back and find the artificially generated timecode on the source tape since there was no timecode on the source tape or source file. This may not be of urgent interest if you are talking about a simple title super or are mastering your program directly from the current system and have all footage loaded in the computer at maximum quality. Even under that scenario, if the media file becomes corrupted or damaged somehow, you will have to locate the shot on the source tape manually, redigitize, and reedit.

Tactical Options

○ *Poststriping:* This is the oldest method of getting the material timecoded. A timecode signal is generated and recorded onto one of the audio channels of the source videotape (typically channel 2). The timecode signal can then be read by certain VTRs and third-party timecode readers. The advantage is that you can use the original tape without dubbing; the drawbacks are that not all VTRs read channel 2 timecode, one of the audio channels is lost, and the other may get bled through from the signal, heard as a high-pitched squeal more annoying than the loudest fax machine (video without audio is the best candidate for this process).

○ *Bumping up:* The first option is to put the material onto some sort of timecoded tape format, either by dubbing the source tape or laying off the digital file out onto tape and using the timecoded copy as the source tape. The rule of thumb is to "bump up" to the best available format (BetacamSP at a minimum but preferably digital Betacam, D-1, or other digital tape formats that are immune to generational loss).

○ *Auxillary time code.* Some editing systems allow you to punch in (and edit with) your own auxillary timecode which might correspond to another camera or sound that was shot simultaneously or other timecode that is pertinent but wasn't recorded on the address track

○ *Digital media archive:* Make a copy of the digital media file at the highest available resolution and transfer it to CD-ROM, DVD, magneto-optical, JAZ, and so on. A permanent copy is preferable so you won't be tempted to dump the file one day and then have a client call six months later and want changes to that scene. I am distinguishing between the original source media, say, a still Photoshop image or VHS tape, and the digital media file that most systems create when the image is digitized into the editing system. That digital media file, with its randomly generated timecode, can be relinked into the editing project without reimporting the media and having to

---

Tip #96

What I recommend for dealing with nonTC source is to just work with it at high res all the way through. Your TC'd source can be low res and the nonTC'd source can be high res and of course it'll all work fine. Then, when you redigitize, just ignore those files and everything should be at final res.   —Michael Wohl, Apple Computer

reinsert it into your program. This process works best when you are finishing on one type of editing system as most media file formats have proprietary characteristics (e.g. compression standards, file wrapper, organization of media tracks). As a precautionary measure, archive the *original* source file as well in case you do have to switch editing environments and reimport the media.

Tip #97

Though no one ever deliberately wants to transcode media from one compression scheme to another, it is a fact of guerrilla life. Make sure you label your media archive if it has been encoded with a hardware-assisted compression algorithm (Avid, Scitex, Radius, Media 100). Many have a unique software codec, which is a small system file for decompressing the video. If possible, include that file in the archive so if someone on another system needs that footage, they can read the digitized media.

The Guerrilla Library

This whole timecode soliloquy is not merely to make certain that your EDLs are more intelligible; the ulterior motive in instilling a Pavlovian response to timecode is that those numbers are the foundation of building your media library database. The typical guerrilla doesn't have time to codify and categorize every tape in their library. However, there is a vast amount of descriptive data that you are *already* generating when logging material that shouldn't go to waste at the end of a project. Most NLEs (nonlinear editors) will allow you to export the bin or project window into a tabbed text file, which can be imported into a basic flat-file database or spreadsheet program as long as your database fields correspond with the tabbed text.

You probably already are familiar with the benefits of databasing records for addresses or invoices. A database of tape footage and digital media gives you a similar kind of efficiency boost. With a digital media database, you can search in a much more customized fashion—across reels, across projects, across dates, across subject matter—or in any combination. There are numerous "media management" software packages that have been brought to market (such as Imagine Products Executive Producer, Cinebase ISLIP Media Key Builder, Virage Video Catalogger). They range from expensive and complicated to cheap and complicated to cheaper and underpowered. At $10K–50K, the diguerrilla probably won't have a lot of use for these products, particularly since you can get much of the basic functionality out of a database that you might already own, such as Filemaker Pro.

While the guerrilla is prone to just dive into the material and start editing, there are too many productivity benefits not to adopt a few simple procedures in setting up a project for more comprehensive media indexing. Even a system with a relatively sophisticated media tracking, such as Avid's Media Tool, requires some human ingenuity to avoid losing shots and wasting disk space. Specific logging tips will be covered further in chapter 4. However, here are a few basic tips for standardizing the log/database structure.

Data Fields

reel
timecode in/out
active tracks
note

The most important fields are the reel number, timecode IN, timecode OUT, active tracks, and any descriptive notes. This will vary somewhat if your source is a digital file and not a videotape. For archiving purposes, I like to include a few additional fields that most logging programs don't automatically include, such as CLIENT, FORMAT, and CREATION DATE. If there is a permanent digital archive of the file like a CD-ROM, that should also be noted in the log as a source. Helpful but nonessential fields include location (int/ext) and time of day.

client
format
date created
location
two of day

Tip #72 Reel Names

To avoid the problem of having a hundred source reels called 001, I use an alphanumeric system with the project or client's name and a number, keeping the total to eight characters to accommodate the idiosyncrasies of DOS (which is the protocol of most online editing systems). Thus, Yamaha material would become YAMAHA01, YAMAHA02, etc. That way, it's easy to search by project or client, and the reel names will also easily convert to a CMX-style edit list (001,002, etc.)

Consistent Naming Conventions

Efficient clip and reel naming is discussed in the next chapter. For now, I just want to stress consistency. If you sometimes use RAINFOREST and other times use JUNGLE to name a similar clip or reel (or any other data field), you are shooting yourself in the foot for organizational purposes. Even regular laziness, sometimes writing out a word like WASHINGTON and sometimes abbreviating it WSH, doesn't help the cause. I can remember the same shot being digitized three times from a tape because one editor called it SKATEPUNK, one called it INLINE1, and the producer called it KYLE. Computers unfortunately don't sort like your caffeine-addled brain does. Abbreviations are fine, just keep them consistent. If many people are working on the same project, you should create a written glossary of the abbreviations that you anticipate will come up repeatedly. When in doubt, take the extra moment and type it out fully. There will be fewer search errors later.

Anal Detail #312

I recommend using all caps for reel names (even though many systems support more characters, I use only eight to keep them short and DOS-friendly, e.g., BIKRACE1, DOGSHW02) and all lowercase for clip names (bowling1, enter, room, shipdeck, etc.). That way, you can look at a list and tell right away if a reel name has been transposed with a clip name or if a clip name just happens to be named similarly to a reel name.

REELS uc

clips lc

Managing Disk Space

The disk drive capacity will vary greatly depending on the amount of image compression used on the video image. Most editing systems have some sort of warning system when you are about to fill a drive up to capacity with digital media. This is more of a circuit-breaker feature than an intelligent media distribution tool. Taking a moment to loosely plan out drive use can save you hours of copying gigantic files or even redigitizing. Another problem in manually moving digital video files around is that you are changing the directory pathway and confusing the editing application, which still thinks your video is in the old location. Some systems, like the Avid, are fairly sophisticated about tracking data, but others are more vulnerable and will "orphan" relocated files unless you manually relink each master clip with the media file— a hassle that you can do without.

For starters, avoid saving audio and video files on the same disk drive (programs such as Adobe Premiere don't allow you to target audio and video separately, but most professional editors do). By separate drives, I mean entirely different mechanisms, not just separate partitions of the same drive. Even more efficient is targeting graphic and rendered FX files to their own speedy partition; that way, it's easier to identify source files (which are easy to recapture) as opposed to effects or transition files (which are rendered by the system and take more time to recreate).

Audio files, even 16-bit 48 KHz files, are much smaller than video files and don't require anywhere near the throughput capacity. A good practice is to target audio files to a slower, cheaper drive and save the space on the faster drives or the array for only the video files. If you don't have a local area network (LAN), audio files can even be stored on removable media such as a JAZ or magneto-optical drive if you plan on working on them on another audio editing system or updating the audio with new files. Slower drives are also fine for highly compressed video (compressed at a ratio of 6:1 or higher). Video compressed beyond 12:1 can be retrieved from almost any storage medium including many removable media formats. With intelligent space allocation, you can earmark your faster array systems for the higher quality images.

Parental Reminder #59

Clean Your Room: As long as we're talking about drive space, we might as well talk about file and folder organization for a moment. Do you have a system for organizing disparate elements of media? Are all your still graphics in one place? Are your titles easily accessible? What about animated sequences? How do you deal with multiple versions of files? While this might be another obvious point to mention, your project needs both cosmetic and vascular organization. The best way to check if you have an effective file organization system is to see if you can describe it to someone else. If you can't, it's probably not really a "system" but rather the twisted workings of a chaotic mind.

If at all possible, synthesized data such as rendered effects should also be targeted to a separate high-speed drive. These files are particularly precious as they represent not only your creative compositing and effects decisions, but some amount of dedicated computer rendering time as well. Simply put, it's a drag when you lose them. A separate drive will help ensure that you won't casually delete them when you dump a drive full of more-easily restored taped material. Because synth media files are usually smaller, I also recommend a backup either on another mounted drive or removable storage medium.

Listen Up:

Drywall revealed. Some of you may be less familiar with the technology behind formatting a large hard drive. The operating system of the computer places limits on the amount of data it can account for on a single drive volume. Thus, even though there are single drives with a capacity of 9 GB and drive arrays with a capacity of 72+ GB, the operating system needs to address the drive in partitioned chunks (normally 4 GB). Partitioning is like putting up drywall on the drive so only certain sections are available for each volume. As far as data retrieval goes, there is still only the one mechanical reader (for each disk), which must jump around to different sections of the disk based on the partition being addressed. If synchronous files such as audio and video are kept on the same drive but on different volumes, the mechanism has to jump back and forth on the same disk and will not have the same retrieval efficiency as if the audio files were on a completely separate mechanism.

If you follow these few guidelines, your bins and shot lists can easily be imported into a basic master database and act as a library catalogue for footage you own (or have access to), which can be used as a stock resource for other projects. Keyword searches will pull up shots you've logged previously, and you can export them into tabbed text format and import them into a new bin for editing. The master database also acts as a backup system in the event that the original project files are lost or corrupted.

⇨ ⇨ ⇨ **Boolean Alley:**

*A quick note about keyword searches. Some editing applications, including Premiere, support Boolean keyword searches—that is, searches that can combine more than one keyword and use operators in between. SEARCH: **house** AND **int** should yield all the interior house shots if they are labeled correctly. Good Boolean search techniques can really slice through tons of footage to find the three shots you really need. The power of Boolean logic, however, is only as good as your logging and labeling efforts. Even under lousy conditions, you can extract stuff quickly. Searching by certain time-codes, creation dates, or even durations (interviews are longer; B-roll is shorter) can yield some fruit.*

Parental Reminder #47

The project files are much more important than the digital footage itself; most footage can easily be redigitized, but project files have all the information about how the images are put together and are harder to reconstruct. Protect your work by backing up all project files, bins, and EDLs on some sort of removable disk (they will often fit on a floppy) and keep it safely tucked away.

Compression, Resolution, and Other Digital Detours

Upon acquiring your images and bringing them into the computer, you will undoubtedly run into the mathematical labyrinth that has evolved around storing digital images. You will need to consider image size (resolution—normally expressed as H **x** W in pixels), the compression algorithm and ratio, and several other settings for picture and audio.

Resolution is important because it defines the size and shape of the picture. Proprietary editing systems tend to "lock" the image size to the resolution of television, while stand-alone video capture boards have scalable resolution defined by the user. There are three broadcast-style "standards" floating around at the moment. One is the older 640 **x** 480 pixel resolution which evolved from extrapolating a 4:3 image size across a 13" monitor. It is also mathematically efficient for scaling the image down to lower resolutions (e.g., 320 **x** 240, 160 **x** 120). The other common resolutions are 720 **x** 486 and 720 **x** 576, based on the CCIR 601 standard for digital video, which was established by an international standards committee. The last broadcast resolution is still being standardized. It is based on HDTVs 16:9 widescreen format and can either mean that 720 **x** 486 is being stretched to fit widescreen or that the image was shot at a higher resolution specific to the new DTV aspect ratio.

For compositing, it is sometimes helpful to have resolutions higher than that of the standard video frame. Unlike Discreet

➤ **The Bitmap Trap:** You've probably figured out, somewhere along the line, that most digital images are composed of small pixels, either square (as in the case of a computer) or oval (as in the case of broadcast video). It's important to realize that unlike a film negative that holds a lot of detail that we normally don't see, there are a finite amount of pixels in an electronic image, a finite amount of digital information, so that magnifying an image that is meant to display as a frame of video will not really reveal more detail by interpolating information "between" the pixels and thus distorts the image. This becomes quite noticeable beyond a 15% enlargement.

The drawback to buffering larger bitmaps is that system performance bogs down. You'll need to work around this. In the simplest case of a moving background, you may want to prerender the move before compositing the foreground. Or, if you have a large number to create, you may want to physically shoot them under a camera in motion.

The exception to the bitmap architecture is the use of vectors for graphics. Vectors describe shapes mathematically and don't use pixels. Thus they are structurally compact and free from the size limitations of bitmap images. They can be scaled without image degradation.

Currently, only a few video-friendly products handle vector graphics and rasterize them into bitmaps. The ability to continually rasterize a vector image has been one of the features that has made Adobe After Effects such a popular product for animating text. With continuous rasterization, a small vector logo or text can be scaled to 2000% of its original size with none of the "pixelization" inherent in scaling up bitmap images.

Logic's Flame or Quantel's Henry, most Mac and PC compositing software applications will let you buffer an image larger than the viewing screen. This makes it possible to move an image around the screen without hitting the edge of the frame. You can also "zoom in" (actually scaling the image) on a higher-resolution image without encountering the kind of image artifacts that a lower-resolution image begins to interpolate.

Compression is not new to TV. The PAL, NTSC, and SECAM color broadcast systems were all devised to compress the full bandwidth RGB signals from cameras and telecine transfers into a single 5.5 or 4.2 MHz channel. To store an uncompressed broadcast image digitally, it requires just under 1 MB per frame. Digital compression solves the problem of storing and moving 21+ MB per second of media through the system's hardware. By compressing the data, it becomes more manageable and economical. Digital compression, however, is an inexact science. It tries to analyze a stream of images and resolve them into a series of patterns and colors. It makes assumptions about pictures just as stock brokers make assumptions about market behavior when both are random to a large degree. Thus, the more compression applied to an image, the more likely that noticeable amounts of information will be truncated.

The amount of compression defines the quality of the picture. Under ideal conditions, no compression is used so that the image endures no digital degradation. Though we are beginning to see more affordable hardware to support uncompressed digital video, it is not yet commonplace because of the enormous storage and data throughput requirements. By compressing video, representing the picture with less data by tossing out redundant information, more images can be stored and can be displayed with simpler hardware. At full screen resolution, a compression ratio of 2:1 or between 300–400 KB per frame is almost undetectable to the eye but still requires a lot of storage space (over 500 MB per minute of video). By contrast, a compression ratio of 10:1 or 80–90 KB per frame displays a slightly "blocky" degraded image but needs only 170 MB to store a minute of video and has modest hardware throughput requirements. There are currently dozens of varieties of compression algorithms that mathematically compress video to run on a particular piece of hardware, run without specialized hardware, or stream over the Web. The amount of compression applied depends on the particular stage of the production process (rough cut/final cut) and the medium of distribution (broadcast, disk media, Web).

⇨ ⇨ ⇨ **JARGON WATCH**

Sometimes the terms "compression" and "resolution" are used interchangeably. Though you will often see resolution used to describe the amount of compression, for purposes of clarity, I will use resolution to describe the height and width of the picture in pixels and compression or picture quality to describe the mathematical algorithms that determine the picture's total amount of digital data.

It is important to keep these technical specs in mind over the course of the project as you begin to mix and match material from a variety of sources (videotape formats and imported digital files). Depending on your ultimate purpose, there are two general working models that guide resolution and compression. The first is the offline/online broadcast model (moving from high compression to low compression, small files to big files), which creates a working pyramid with all the available material brought into the computer at lower resolution and narrowing towards a final cut that is redigitized with minimal compression for maximum picture quality. The second scenario is a one-pass model that digitizes all material at low compression and streamlines the process for faster finishing.

➤ **Antiquated Terminology 101:** "Offline" and "online" editing are terms still tossed around in the video industry, but they are antiquated and don't really describe the fluid nature of a digital editing environment. Offline editing used to refer to linear editing systems that worked with copies of the master tapes with timecode window burn-ins. These more inexpensive systems were used to generate an EDL and then "conform" the list in an online suite (online meaning "computerized" for semiautomated editing). With nonlinear systems that can handle both low- and high-resolution images and special effects, the distinctions between offline and online editing have become increasingly blurred.

Project Strategy

Aside from nice naming conventions and good backup practices, each project requires its own flavor of resource strategy appropriate to the material. If you have a high shooting ratio, meaning a lot of footage relative to the final length of the piece, one strategy makes sense; if you have a small amount of material for a short piece, another approach might be better.

This simple table may be of assistance in planning out how to handle your project elements more efficiently:

Project	Typical shooting ratio	Other elements	Primary distribution
90-minute documentary	30:1	graphic supers, maps, still photos	theatrical release
30-second commercial	20:1	compositing elements, logo art, animated type	broadcast TV
9-minute promo piece	5:1	product stills, charts, logo art, animated type	VHS tape, Web

Case Study 1: The Documentary

In the case of the 90-minute documentary for which over 30 hours of interviews and location footage has been shot, there are two key issues: (1) how to sift through all the interviews to get the right clips and (2) where to put the huge amount of digital footage. There is also the matter of producing a film negative cut so the actual film can be conformed for theatrical distribution.

The first thing to address is the logging of the source video. You'll want to have access to a large portion of the footage at one time, but the full 45 hours will be problematic if you only have 36 GB of drive space available. Logging the footage will give you a first pass to eliminate much of the inferior material. We'll assume that this documentary has all elements timecoded, and we'll assume that for a project this size that there is at least one editing assistant. You could begin digitizing material into the computer right away, but with that quantity of footage to review, a better plan is to begin logging offline so that the editor can begin editing a portion of the material while the rest of the footage continues to be sifted through.

Offline logging can be accomplished in a number of cost-efficient ways:

1. *Logging with deck control:* An offline logging application such as Executive Producer or AutoLog, that controls a VTR with a 9-pin cable. With a laptop, an NTSC or PAL monitor, and a VTR, you can control the deck from your keyboard, automatically log timecode and shot information, and export the list to a format the editing system will be able to read and batch load. It's the most comfortable way to log because you move through the material faster and you don't have to break your mental rhythm.

2. *Logging without deck control:* This is a bit more cumbersome but equally effective. Using an NTSC or PAL monitor and a VTR (or VCR), you manually shuttle through the tape and note clips to digitize. The advantage

is that no special software application or high-powered computer is necessary. A properly configured spreadsheet or database will do the job. The VTR need not read time-code; you can use a consumer VCR as long as the tapes are dubs of the masters with a timecode window.

3. *Logging without a computer:* This is the oldest method of logging. While it is the easiest to set up (all you need is a VCR and a TV), it creates duplicated effort later as the numbers must be punched into the editing system by hand, creating another potential layer of human error. Window dubs are made of the original masters, and then a paper list of timecode numbers is made as the footage is reviewed.

> ➤ **Keep it loose:** One of the pitfalls of a novice assistant editor is that they log shots too tightly, meaning there isn't a lot of extra head and tail before the significant action in frame. Logging too tightly is problematic for two reasons. The first is that you haven't left enough head room for a dissolve, which requires extra frames for overlapping with the next shot; the second is that it takes longer to log shots that tightly and footage needs to be logged as quickly as possible without foregoing accuracy. Some systems let you add arbitrary "handles" to either side of each clip while digitizing. I prefer to have the footage logged correctly from the onset. A good rule of thumb is to leave at least 45–90 frames on either side of the meat of the clip. If there is a slate board in the shot, leave that in the master clip for identification. Later, you can break this footage down into subclips.

[handwritten margin note: etras — leave 45–90 frames]

Whichever method you choose, logging is time well spent. When done well, it becomes a type of mental editing, and in the process, ideas for shot combinations begin to occur. Note these ideas down briefly in a notation field.

Now that you've eliminated much of the footage from contention, you are ready to batch digitize the material in your log. You now face another decision—at what resolution and compression setting should you digitize the material? Editing systems have different ways of measuring the amount of compression. Avid uses proprietary AVR (Avid Video Resolution) number ratings, which correspond to different data rates; Media 100 uses a kilobytes-per-frame designation; Adobe Premiere uses a megabyte-per-second rating; and other systems use a fractional ratio expression.

Most systems now support varying amounts of compression within the same project. In the documentary example, one common strategy would be to digitize the interview footage with a high compression setting since talking head shots are normally determined by their audio content rather than their visual impact. On the other hand, wide-angle or B-roll shots could be digitized with less compression so the details of the shot are easier to evaluate. (Edge detail is one of the areas impacted by digital compression.) If you have logged your shots beforehand, it will be fairly simple to sort them into various compression groupings.

Photos, maps, and graphics, unless they are sourced from videotape, should be imported at the highest-quality setting so they don't have to be redigitized at a later phase. Since they are,

⇨ ⇨ ⇨ **MONOPHOBIC BEHAVIOR**

While we're on the subject of maximizing disk space, let me add a quick note about audio. I don't really think there's any point in digitizing anything less than full broadcast audio (at least 16-bit, 44 KHz) because the savings in disk space is negligible when compared to the loss in audio quality. However, many times, digitizing both audio tracks is unnecessary, as in the case of interviews. Unless the subject and interviewer were miked separately, the audio on A1 is identical to A2. Editing systems have hardware limitations on how many tracks can be monitored simultaneously, so don't waste tracks with redundant information.

for the most part, still images, they won't take up appreciable amounts of drive space.

Case Study 2: The Commercial

A commercial has less source material and a much shorter window for postproduction. As a result, the media resource strategy should be streamlined for maximum speed. Even if the commercial will be finished on another system, the director and the agency will appreciate seeing the piece as close to finished quality as possible. Bring all elements as long unbroken clips at the highest possible quality. As you review the footage, pull subclips and annotate them appropriately. This will serve the same purpose as logging, but the footage will already be loaded.

If you are tight for storage, a commercial is an easy project to consolidate since after the first few cuts, the footage is fairly locked and the subsequent adjustments are timing and effects oriented. Consolidation tosses away unused footage to conserve drive space while keeping the essential footage. Some shots in the commercial may need special compositing treatment. If you are intending to finish the piece for broadcast, avoid compressing the layer elements of the composite. Have them transferred

➤ **Variations on a Theme:** Of all the programming formats, my experience is that commercial work commonly demands more than one finished version, and digital editing has facilitated that trend further. Typically, more money is spent per second in advertising than in any other kind of project. This kind of attention to every frame often begets some obsessive need for permutation. Not only do agencies routinely want a 30-, 15-, and 10-second version (sometimes a 20-second spot for European television), but everyone from the copywriter to the creative director wants their own cut. Part of a good media resource strategy for commercials is keeping good notes about each edited version, who authorized which changes, and so on. If all you know is that cut 16 came before cut 17, it will be harder to locate which version had the elephants at 50% slo-mo and the New York phone number or which one had the smiling girl that the art director liked.

I try and keep prominent characteristics of each cut noted in a text field adjacent to the sequence icon in case I have to return to an older sequence the following day or the following year. If I don't have notation fields available for the sequences, I use a naming convention that leaves room for at least one keyword in the title (e.g., 01.NYC.seq; 02.smiley.seq) and a suffix that also identifies it as a sequence so it is easier to identify in case it's mixed in with other clips in a bin).

uncompressed to an Exabyte storage tape or some removable medium.

Even at a low compression ratio of 2:1, minute compression artifacts can be an obstacle for creating clean keys and mattes. With a direct digital transfer, you can bring your shots as individual uncompressed frames into a compositing application and begin to layer and add effects without any edge distortion from compression. This is especially important for bluescreen work.

Case Study 3: The Promo Piece

Promo pieces, particularly marketing presentations for corporations, often have a few idiosyncrasies. Sometimes, there is footage shot on a variety of formats: a certain event or interview was shot with a DV camera, some essential factory footage is only available in VHS, some is transferred from 35mm film from a high-end stockholder piece they did last year, and some is original Betacam footage that you shot last weekend. Oh yes, and the client has this idea that it would be fun to use Hollywood film clips interspersed to introduce each area of the company.

So there is the creative issue of how to blend all these different types of images together, and there is also the issue of how to deal effectively with all the nontimecoded sources. My general rule of thumb noted earlier is to bump everything up to a time-coded source. However, it can sometimes be a judgment call; if you are only using one or two clips from a VHS tape and you know you are finishing the piece on the same system, it may be more important to avoid the generational image loss incurred in dubbing the footage. In this case, import the nontimecoded material in at the lowest compression and the timecoded material with higher compression. Make sure you have the reel numbers entered correctly because you'll want to redigitize only the timecoded material later. Target the nontimecoded material to a particular designated hard drive partition so it won't accidentally get deleted.

Digital File Harmony

One would think that digital technology would make all this media intercompatible. After all, it's all inside the computer—isn't it really made of the same binary material? Would that it were so, fellow idealists. I mean, somehow they get every kind of car to use the same gas but not so for video. While it's true that all digital material is numerically represented, there are many ways that the material can be organized and "wrapped." A file's wrapper identifies it as having certain characteristics and organizing principles that, when recognized by an application, can be interpreted and used.

If an application can't utilize a media file in its native format, it might have an import function, which usually means it has a little routine written into it that cracks open the file wrapper, extracts all the relevant data, and creates a new native file that the application can handle more efficiently.

There are dozens of graphic, video, and audio file formats floating around. Some, like JPEG (still images), are recognized by

project progresses and gets increasingly more complicated. It's just no fun scrambling through a tape at the last minute to find a shot when you already have it digitized, but you just can't dig it up. It's no fun running out of disk space and not knowing which files won't be used and can be deleted. It's also no fun thinking that you're done with a project and finding that some shots are at the wrong picture quality settings. Without becoming fanatical, just a little more farsighted, you can dramatically improve productivity and enjoy smoother execution of postproduction processes.

If you manage to integrate some of these databasing and formatting practices, you will find yourself rising to an elevated state of consciousness about your project. By creating a schematic map of the types of data, you will be able to anticipate incompatibilities and eliminate unnecessary conversion steps. You will feel lighter and move faster through the material. You will be able to trace missing files with confidence. You will be able to work with others on the project more seamlessly. You will be master over your media.

Editing Fundamentals:
The Revisionist Revolution

> 66 *Editing a picture correctly means allowing the separate scenes and shots to come together spontaneously, for in a sense they edit themselves; they join up according to their own intrinsic pattern...it is not always easy to sense the pattern of relationships, the articulations between shots, particularly if the scene has been shot inexactly.* 99
>
> —*Andrey Tarkovsky*, Sculpting in Time

Warning: These next two or three chapters may very well be the most practical section in the book. After reading them, you may be gripped by a sense of awesome power and freedom. Do not be alarmed; this is only temporary. Your imagination will always outrun your processing speed, and your creative appetite will outstrip your available drive space. A more familiar sensation, one of overwhelming frustration, will gradually return. Do not despair; all is well. Frustration is fuel for the digital guerrilla. It leads to invention. ■

In this chapter you will be exposed to some of the most powerful aspects of the digital revolution: the ability to manipulate images with a level of control, speed, and economy never before possible in the history of moving pictures. In this chapter you will examine

1. nonlinear thinking applied

2. the fundamentals of visual storytelling

3. some of the rules for constructing good solid video and how they were meant to be broken

New Jack Video

Quite simply, without the advent of digital nonlinear editing and compositing, guerrilla video would still be confined to the low-rent cheesiness of the 1980s (bad music videos, late-night local commercials, and poorly cut, shoestring documentaries). The capacity and affordability of digital post in the '90s greatly opened a creative door for upstart media mavericks. Talent, rather than money or equipment, finally became the decisive factor in video post.

To understand how dramatic the shift in postproduction technique and philosophy has been, we should quickly glance at the analog feudalism of the not-so-distant past. In the '80s, video (and film for that matter) postproduction was a rather mud-slogging affair. Offline editing systems, those used to generate an edit decision list, were essentially a simple interface between a playback VTR and a recorder. Each shot was located on a source tape and recorded over to the edit master in a sequential fashion.

This process resembles typing a novel on an old IBM Selectric. If you made a mistake, or changed your mind, you had to white-out the last bit and retype. If you radically changed your mind, you had to crumple up the paper and feel your ulcer begin to churn. Traditional video editing, though less messy than white-out, has similar shortcomings. Any revision beyond the previous edit requires a lot of backtracking and repetition of labor to rein-sert, or "ripple," the string of edits that succeed the change.

Film editors gloated because they were free of those elec-tronic constraints and could just insert shots easily by physically cutting into the picture and splicing. Though that was true in the-ory, the practice was often equally frustrating. Though the para-digm was nonlinear, the medium itself was not well suited for making many tiny changes. When making decisions about one and two frame edits, the editor often ended up damaging frames from the workprint or glopping the cut-up with too much splic-ing tape. Often, the film had to be reprinted at the lab and recut into the scene.

> **Like Magic:** In the old days...if you liked a cut but wanted to try something new, you'd have to send that cut out, have a print made of it, usually it was black and white, so you save that, that would take a couple of days, then you got it back. Then you'd have to disassemble the whole thing, reconstitute it into reel and then recut it from the beginning again. This whole process to recut a few scenes could take you, three, four, five days. And nowadays I'd sit down with a director and say, "Here you wanna see it?" Boom. There it is. (Barry Silver)

Wide-open, creative editing, where dozens of possibilities are attempted and tweaked, required a lot of patience, time, and money. There were the long, meditative waits to wind tape and locate a shot, preview it, and review the edit in context. Most budget-conscious directors and producers either edited in cam-era—meaning they shot only what they thought they would use—or they came into an editing session with much of the pro-gram worked out on paper from having viewed the dailies. The editing process itself often became yeomanlike construction work with little latitude for modification unless major problems were encountered. Well-organized producers developed good in-cam-era and paper-based shot selection techniques. Though in-camera

> ➤ **Mindshift:** I've always been into computers, I've been programming, sort of, off and on since I was 16 years old. So I sort of have my one leg in the computer world and then got to a point where editing on computer seemed to be such a natural. It was something I envisioned when I was cutting videotape in the mid '80s because I saw word processors were coming out. I bought my first Mac. My Mac Plus. 1 meg of RAM. Woo! Just word processing on a Macintosh, I figured you might as well be able to edit pictures as well. And lo and behold, a few years later there were systems out on the market. (Barry Silver)

> ➤ **Digital de Riguer:** *The paradigm shift in information editing is so complete in my functioning, that it has become unconscious. As I write this book, I barely notice when I rearrange paragraphs, move sentences to other chapters, and modify pieces to fit in their new locations. One may point to this process as being a recipe for incoherency, and if this is your experience while reading, I apologize. Digital technology has had lit-tle to do with this writer's predilection towards disjointed discourse. Lack of proper med-ication might be a more probable explanation.*

and paper-based editing are useful and efficient skills that serve well in any environment, they lack the spontaneity and flexibility that are the hallmarks of the guerrilla approach.

Though it wasn't completely obvious at the time, anyone with exposure to computers in the '80s, could see a train approaching in the distance. The word processing, desktop publishing, and digital audio revolutions took place in quick succession. It was clear that information of all sorts was being, as Nicholas Negroponte was to call it, "atomized" into easily modifiable bits. The editing process, at least in print and audio, was moving from a linear, IBM Selectric paradigm to one of collage.

Digital Collage Artist

Everyone who has had in his hands a piece of film to be edited knows by experience how neutral it remains, even though a part of a planned sequence, until it is joined to another piece, when it suddenly acquires and conveys a sharper and quite different meaning than planned for it at the time of filming.

—*Sergei Eisenstein,* Film Form

I never really understood what Eisenstein was about. He had a book out and I've never really understood it. I saw the pictures he did and I was very impressed with them, but I never really understood what his theory was. And I pity the poor young people who are required to study that.

—*George Cuckor,* Who the Devil Made It

The diguerrilla is, by nature, a collage artist. Creating a collage is all about the position and juxtaposition of individual elements. The individual elements may be powerful unto themselves, but they take on new meanings in the context of the larger picture. The arrangement is only limited by the medium, and modifications are inspired by how the entire piece begins to take shape. From a digital guerrilla perspective, the editing, more than the acquisition or creation of the elements, is the essential art.

These concepts were actually theorized in the early part of the century by intellectual Russian filmmakers like Dziga Vertov and Sergei Eisenstein and later given a French twist by New Wavers like Jean-Luc Godard and Francois Truffaut. Theory aside, however, the actual practice of editing never fully realized the true potential of these ideas until the end of the century.

The collage model is closer to how the creative mind works. It is more free-associative and nonlinear in action, meaning that one can approach the creation of a collage from any point and need not necessarily work beginning-to-end. It also implies a multidimensional component, an accumulation of layered images. This model is particularly suited to guerrilla strategy because of the many variables that a low-budget, low-manpower production will inevitably encounter. These variables form the gap between the preproduction vision and the postproduction reality:

- What do I do with less-than-optimal footage that cannot be reshot either due to logistical or financial considerations?

Collage

- What if the storyboard we/they developed doesn't really work that well in motion?

- What if it feels flat or boring?

- What if I want to introduce new elements spontaneously during the editing process?

While a larger production might have the luxury of reshooting portions, a diguerrilla is normally left with the task of making lemonade out of lemons or, in severe cases, a masterpiece out of manure. In this case, a less inhibited editing process is both a creative weapon and a life-saving defensive maneuver.

Nonlinearity for the Rest of Us

I don't want to get bogged down in a lengthy discussion of the technical history of nonlinear editing. Like a Stanley Kubrick film or the subject of love, there are many interpretations and a lot of obscure tangents that aren't necessarily relevant to enjoying the ride. For our purposes, I'll attempt to keep this discussion focused on what technology has enabled in terms of redefining video post-production.

Through an evolution of expensive, prototypical nonlinear systems such as the EditDroid, Montage, Ediflex, and later Avid systems, the technology that made possible the digital assembly of a moving image has matured and stabilized. Images are "digitized," numerically represented by calculations corresponding to hue, chroma, luminance, frame rate, and other visual characteristics and then stored on a device designed for instantaneous retrieval, normally a computer hard drive. None of this has been particularly radical thinking given that computers had been doing this with text and still images for several years. The breakthrough had to do with the sheer volume of information that moving images represented. There has been a quantum leap in the ability to input and output large amounts of data quickly in synchronized streams.

This "atomized" approach to film and video both frightened and fascinated an industry that hadn't had a significant innovation in 25 years or more. All the same praises and curses that printers and graphic designers had voiced in previous years about text and image were echoed by the film and video community, albeit somewhat louder and crankier, perhaps because film and video people are convinced that they rule the universe under an exclusive licensing agreement with God and Frank Sinatra.

Some of the whining and celebrating sounded like this:

Cheer	Jeer
"Fast-paced montage sequences are much easier to cut."	"I keep losing track of shots and sequences."
"There are so many features."	"There are too many commands to memorize."
"Changes happen so fast!"	"I don't have time to think about what I'm doing. I made better decisions before."

Cheer	Jeer
"I'm free to experiment without screwing anything up."	"Clients want 20 versions of everything."
"It's so much easier than dealing with tape or film."	"The machine is so unreliable. It crashes all the time."
"There are so many nuances and effects that I can try out instantly without waiting for an online session."	"There's too many cheesy effects that people rely on instead of learning how to edit."
"The digitizing process really allows the editor to get familiar with the footage and get organized."	"This whole digitizing process slows everything down."
"This is more conducive for breaking conventional editing rules and inventing new ones."	"People put cuts into shots for no reason, just because it's easy and they think it's more dynamic."
"It's much easier to collaborate on the same project with other artists."	"Too many people get involved in the soup. Everyone thinks they're an artist."

And so the old school moaned and groaned into the future and the new guard rushed to their souped-up computers. Within a year or two, the Avid trademark, like the word Xerox for document copying, became synonymous with the entire concept of nonlinear editing. By the end of 1992, the producers I was encountering in Los Angeles were asking for Avid by name as if the software itself ensured a better finished product. Whichever side of the silicon curtain you stood on, whether your lineage was NTSC or RGB, videotape or hard disk, it was clear that video postproduction was entering a new era.

⇨ ⇨ ⇨ **PROBLEM SOLVING**

The biggest challenge I had was on this Disney film. It was the grain of sand in the clam that led me to create Slingshot™. We were working on this show, and the director really wanted [to edit on the] Media 100—mainly because he bought one and he wanted Disney to pay for it. I'm sure you've never heard of that ever happening in the film business. It's silly stuff that goes on all the time but the director wanted Disney to pay for it, meaning, therefore, they wanted Disney to rent the system from him and use this Media 100 which had just come out with their version for the PCI Macintosh. So it was brand-new software for a brand-new computer platform. PCI machines had only been shipping for about 3 or 4 months. And having been a beta tester for Avid before and for other software. I dove into this software to try to figure out what was wrong with it. Because that's the first thing you need to find out so you can try to figure out work arounds.

The Media 100's very much a video-oriented environment. The two [Avid and Media 100] are subtly different. Something as simple as your out frame. The out frame on film is one number and the out frame on video is another number. It's a simple distinction, but when you're cutting and you don't know which frame you're cutting on for your out frame you've got to sit there and think about it for a second, ok, I'm on Media 100 system, it's the one after so I gotta go back one, that kind of thing.

One of the things we learned is that we were really pushing the limit of the Mac operating system. We'd have hundreds of tiny little files in one folder. And we found that Mac OS sort of chokes after about 400 to 500. They say theoretically you can go up to 1,000 items in a folder, but we found that not to be the case. Because once we got up to 700 it wouldn't even scroll or you couldn't see anything and the system would crash. We found all kinds of wonderful things like that. We found sync problems. I was freaking out because it was my responsibility to have everything in sync and all the tests that I did found that it wasn't. I sent up a f—ing barrage of warning flares. The whole sky was alight. I would have daily meetings with the production manager telling her I could see a train wreck coming and that was just because I had my ear to the ground. And it's true. The system was wholly inadequate for the job at the time.

And Disney kept assuring us that they didn't want to do film, but during the show, Disney changed their mind; they decided they did want film options. So, I panicked, I got on the Internet, I sent out e-mails to every users group I could find. I called people at Avid. I called people at Media 100, they actually flew out here, Media 100 did. Tony Molinari and I got the product development person at that time who said, "Gee guys, we're sorry to hear that. You're on your own though. We don't have any solutions, we don't know any solutions. So, kind of, figure it out."

I said, "Look, I know how to do this. We could probably write an application that would take care of it. But, I don't know C++ code. I don't have the time to do it. I'm busy working on this film and this other film over here. I already have two jobs. What do I need a third for?" And then, so we got together and I said, "We've gotta do this, this is how the math works out. I wrote out a whole paradigm for him [Robert Mathieu] step by step, this is how you analyze it, you take this information, break it down, blah, blah, blah."... a real rough, down-and-dirty application just to solve that particular problem that we had on that one show.

People knew about what we were trying to do and somehow they found out what we had done. So I would get like, 5 or 10 phone calls a week from independent filmmakers, other editors, across the country, some of them in other parts of the world, saying, "We hear what you've done, can I have the application, you know, how much is the software, can I get it?" (Barry Silver)

> ➤ *My first experience on a big feature I nearly got fired because of bugs that I discovered in Avid software. We needed to conform our EDL, it had been edited so far on the Avid, but then we needed to have a work print conformed to it and we discovered a bug in their "group clip" feature. This was a multicamera shoot so there was lots of grouped clips. The postproduction supervisor blamed me for the errors; she was a woman from the old school. She'd been an assistant editor probably for 30 years working for big editors. And to her the idea of cutting things on computer was absurd. She didn't trust it and she felt that these things were the devil, so to speak. She didn't like me very much because I was like, the new school coming in. (Barry Silver)*

Interfacing the Future

Quite rapidly, the fashion rules for digital editing were established and codified. Almost every system, with a few exceptions (the ill-fated VideoFusion for one and the higher-end Quantel Edit-Box for another) followed a similar interface paradigm: the bin (a

place to store shots), the monitor (a place to view shots and mark them), and the timeline (a place to create a sequence of shots). Most of the metaphor was adapted from a flatbed film editing setup, where the editor hung strips of film near the editing bench and then trimmed them into a reel threaded through a viewer as they were needed.

This approach contrasted with the older CMX-style "online" electronic interfaces that treated each edit as an "event" to execute, much like computer programming code, which made the editing process a very technical, mathematical exercise. Timeline editing not only made the computer a truly creative tool for post-production, it made possible entirely new styles of editing.

Guerrillas in Our Midst

As larger post houses began to purchase expensive Avid and Lightworks systems ($70K and up) and train staff editors, a widely dispersed group of creative people began experimenting with cheaper digital alternatives. These people ranged from computer hobbyists to restless graphic designers to multimedia pioneers. They wanted in on the revolution but couldn't abide the bourgeois price tags.

Some began with NewTek's VideoToaster (around $6K), an unusual success considering that it wasn't really a complete editing solution on its own. It was a video switcher controlled by a Commodore Amiga computer and came bundled with a paint program and a surprisingly sophisticated 3D program called

Lightwave. For many, a video camera, a couple VTRs, and a VideoToaster constituted a pirate studio from which to launch an insurgent media assault. For others, it was the costlier VideoFX system from Digital F/X, a box that interfaced with the computer and became a combination switcher, character generator, and crude nonlinear editor.

Basic Concept #213

The Digital Trinity: This triad of technology still forms the nexus of every digital media system and is worth a moment of emphasis. The three elements are a dynamic time-based digital file format (in this example, QuickTime); video capture hardware (usually a card that sits inside a computer); and a software application that talks to the card and tells it how to process the video and recall it for playback.

The most significant early guerrilla faction built a base camp at the junction of three manufacturer's products, Apple's Quick-Time, a JPEG video compression board (usually either Digital-Film from SuperMac, VideoVision from Radius, or MoviePak from RasterOps), and a software-only editing package from Adobe called Premiere.

These sub-$5K (board and software) "editing systems" were also able to run other graphics software on the same machine and allowed many graphic designers and animators to begin produc-

Apple Quicktime
JPEG Board
Adobe Premiere

ing finished video that had a visually arresting style. These systems were realistically only suited for short form work, and thanks to some audacious broadcast designers, an entire niche market began to develop for graphically dense commercials, station bumpers, and program promos.

Amazingly enough, seven years later—P.D. (*post digital*), that's roughly the equivalent of 35 years later by A.E. (*analog era*) standards—there are still a great many people who still have Premiere-based systems, though the CPU and supporting hardware may have changed over time.

World Premiere

To understand the phenomenal success of Adobe Premiere in popularizing nonlinear editing and spurring the diguerrilla movement, let's look at what this application provides in practical terms.

It has all of the requisites for guerrilla use:

- It's cheap (under $600),
- It has a wide range of functionality (editor, compositor, FX generator, titler),
- It's compatible with most of the digital world (resolution independent, hardware independent, QuickTime compliant),
- It's well supported by the manufacturer (Adobe).

Though it has plenty of shortcomings as a professional product—mainly in the area of media management, advanced editing tools, rendering strategy, and occasionally audio sync—it does enough things at a nice price to have become a rite of passage for the vast majority of the DV Nation.

> ➤ **Look Closely:** Despite Premiere 5.x's claim of having moved to single-track transitions, the track architecture underneath is still basically the same as in previous versions, where there are the two primary A/B video tracks and then subsequent "superimposition" tracks. The super tracks have "rubberband" control of opacity right on the timeline, a helpful, easy-to-use feature. While this model is plausibly workable, it isn't as flexible as treating all tracks as truly discrete video sources that can be monitored and combined independently. Premiere assumes a kind of "pyramid" approach to track building that may not be optimum for all editors or projects.
>
> ➤ **http://www.helptalk.com/premier**—Adobe Premiere Support: Ask technical questions about Adobe Premiere, or post solutions of your own. This is where Premiere editors gather to exchange ideas, get advice, get tips, techniques, tutorials, and talk about editing hardware and software issues.

Digital Cutting 101

Whether you are using Premiere or one of numerous software editors including Apple's FinalCut Pro, In-Sync's Razor, DVEdit, Ulead's Media Studio Pro, Avid's Cinema, or a hardware-specific system such as the Avid Media Composer or Media100 or Discreet Logic Edit, there are some basic concepts in common.

After you've installed the software, read the manual, digitized your footage…where do you stand? Have you changed the world yet? Not quite—but here the guerrilla transformation may begin. Echoing an Apple Computer ad campaign, here's where you get to really think different.

The old way of doing things was in a sequence of segmented procedures. First you would cut the pictures together, and then later, in a final assembly edit session, some titles, graphics, and special effects might be added. The new paradigm is about integrating editing procedures and video processing, using images and sound as raw material, to be shaped holistically into the most effective message.

DIGUERRILLA WANTED: We seek an After Effects/Media 100 artist/editor who is capable of compositing CG and directly outputting a 30-second spot from our Media 100 to our Beta SP video deck. All CG/animation to be created in-house on Strata/After Effects/3D Studio Max. We have fully storyboarded the spot and are in need of putting the nuts & bolts of the pieces together. The person should be a fast troubleshooter and aware of video standards.

Telling Stories

There's a narrative visual language that's been built up with the evolution of cinema that our culture has internalized over generations. We know that when we cut from the outside of a suburban home to an interior of a family eating at a table that we are now inside the house we have just seen previously even though there is no concrete evidence of this. We are just interpreting the accepted cinematic language we've been taught.

The diguerrilla needs to know how to use all these conventions and also how, when necessary, to subvert or bypass them. The central question is, How far can cinematic language be stretched before it breaks down? This "stretching" of convention can be driven by artistic vision or dire necessity, sometimes both.

data entry and shot sifting. Each editor will discover his or her own personal methods over the course of time, but I have included a few of my own to illustrate. These methods will work on most systems that support tab-delimited fields of information associated with the clip.

A Few of my Logging/Shot Organization Tips:

○ *Digitize longer clips:* You can break them into subclips later, and it conserves VTR search time.

○ *Balance your shot-to-bin ratio:* There are two annoying extremes that impede productivity. One is having too few bins with too many shots, like a bin called "Interviews" with a hundred shots that you have to scroll through; the other is having too many bins so that you have to keep opening and closing windows to get at what you need. If there are four clips in "logos" and two clips in "phone numbers," combine them into one bin called "LOGOS & PHONE NUMBERS," or better yet "SUPERS," and break subcategories out when the bin gets fuller. The perfect balance is when you can see all the shots in the bin on one screen when the bin window is expanded without scrolling.

○ *Keep clip names very brief but functional:* Once they are loaded into the edit monitor or on the timeline it won't do you much good if *Really Big Elephant1* and *Really Big Elephant2* both show up on the timeline as *Really Big E.* All you really need is something that will trigger your memory of the shot. In this case, *Dumbo1* and *Dumbo2* might work much better (or whatever keyword triggers your brain the fastest).

o *Talking heads:* Interview footage is always an organizational dilemma. I usually break subclips out numerically, like Fred01, Fred02, Fred03, with another column for keywords like "school funding," "sports program," and so on. It often depends if the program has many interviews and will be edited by subject or whether there is a single personality talking about a variety of topics.

o *Process of elimination:* If I am building a montage or any complex piece where I want to be careful not to reuse shots, I often create a bin for used shots and drag them there as they are cut into the timeline. I also use a check mark symbol (√) to denote the same thing.

o *U can nvr abbrev 2 mch:* I prefer symbols to the personalized license plate look. I'm a big believer in one or two keystrokes to convey a lot of information. For instance, I use a star rating system for multiple takes. More stars = better shot. You could also use letter grades (fewer keystrokes). I use conventional film abbreviations for the focal length (CU for close-up, Med for medium shot, and LS for longshot with variations like XCU or MedLS); below is a partial listing of some other personal symbols I use. If I need to collaborate with another editor or assistant, I just create a cheat sheet so they can interpret my notes.

symbol	meaning
!	a master shot or a key shot that I will build from
≈	not a horrible shot but I should only use it if I have to; close but not A-list. (sort of an extension of the star rating system)
$	the money shot; in the new ad pitch example, it would probably be a close-up of the product
%	needs some sort of motion effect applied to it
¢	exterior shot; second unit type shot; usually an establishing shot like a building sign or a familiar shot like the exterior of the White House
@	good audio, bad video; the talent or interviewer is saying something good but the framing is bad or boring
+	montage material
#	needs graphic (super or title)
~	reverse angle of sister shot
^	super or keyed shot
&	something about this shot has built-in transition or cutaway potential; maybe it has a blur pan or a natural change in lighting or a flash frame or a zoom

(handwritten margin notes)
! master
$ money
% needs effect
¢ exterior
@ good aud
+ montage
# needs graphic
~ reverse
^ super
& potential to transi

You may already have plenty of your own hieroglyphics that help you notate material. The important thing is that you have some sort of accurate system that minimizes data entry. If you're lazy about shot organization, you don't know how much time you're wasting looking for material. All the sifting, sorting, and Boolean search functions that may be available in your editing package are useless if the shots aren't well documented.

Diguerrilla Workaround #19c

Little or no space for annotating clips with descriptive text. Keep a word processor or spreadsheet program open simultaneously on your computer. Copy the name of the shot into the word processor and type in your description.

word program for note

It should be obvious to students of human nature that many people are visually oriented rather than textually oriented. Thus many producers don't come into the editing room with a time-code log of their material. They may, however, have fairly sophisticated visual recall of the material they have been watching. So it becomes very important to have important visual cues noted in the comments field of your shot bin. If you are working with an editing package that limits text notation, resort to Diguerrilla Workaround #19c.

It's also wise to become a subclipping fiend. As you become familiar with the footage, you will undoubtedly come across various shots that weren't exactly what you were looking for at the moment but trigger the same sort of biophysical response that prompts you to buy an item from the impulse rack in the supermarket checkout line. Whenever you feel this lightbulb go off above your head, create a subclip out of what you are looking at and put it in a bin for later use. You might be so clueless as to where some of these shots might eventually go that you can make a bin called *Use these somehow*. Again, whatever will trigger you to navigate most efficiently.

use somehow

Subclips should be used strategically along with user marks. Subclips are more like ready-to-wear clothing. You grab them out

143

of the bin, preedited with fairly accurate in/out points, and plop them into the timeline. User marks are more like accessories that accent an outfit. User marks or locators are implemented differently in various systems, but they basically allow the editor to embed some information at a certain time location in the shot such as *talks about childhood* or *turns to leave.* They work like tabs in a word processing document and appear in the timeline or on the clip as small icons. Some systems allow you to scroll through a list of user marks and jump to any point. However the marking system is implemented, it is an excellent way to start shaping the piece and reminding yourself where time-specific events occur. I most often employ user marks with interview footage to let me know what the speaker is saying at a particular moment. I also use marks to cue important audio events such as where music might come up or where a particular sound effect might go. By mastering user marks and subclipping, you will improve the agility of your editing exponentially.

Form, Flow, and Feel

Form and flow are partly predicated on scripting and storyboard, but until you start to see the images combined on screen, it's impossible to be 100% certain that things will work the way they were envisioned. While you are getting shots bagged and tagged, you'll begin to map out a progression. Some editors like to begin immediately tossing clusters of shots onto the timeline and seeing immediately how they work together; others like to group shots into a kind of digital storyboard using the icon view in the bin, which displays shots as thumbnail pictures that can be moved around like cards on a corkboard.

Although I like to work with the timeline right from the beginning, it can also be confusing if a client is in the room watching. They aren't used to watching shots loosely cobbled together, and they inevitably start talking about fine-tuning the timing when you are just trying to lay out a rough sequence. The storyboard method is sometimes easier for the client to grasp conceptually. Then they are just viewing still frames and sorting them like a slide show.

Concept #201-cx

Breathing: Breathing when applied to editing is implementing build and release cycles into the overall rhythm of the piece. A quiet moment after an intense montage; a slow-building music track that foreshadows a mood shift; a gag followed by a visual that you can continue laughing over while you adjust to the next scene...all these are techniques for varying the tone of the piece and allow the viewer to experience and retain more information.

In order to increase creativity and efficiency, you will again be making mental adjustments to your workflow. Remember that nonlinear means that you don't have to work in a specific sequence: you can have dessert before dinner if you want; you can give the answer and then ask the question; you can start with the epilogue and build to the introduction. Even if you are editing the most straightforward 1-2-3 kind of program, you are not obliged to work in a 1-2-3 progression to create it. Use whatever approach stimulates the best expression of the overall message.

FOOD FOR THOUGHT:

Form	Flow
Does your opening initially draw the viewer in?	Does the piece build and reinforce itself?
Is the progression clear and accessible?	Does it move at an appropriate pace?
Is the conclusion/tagline/epilogue strong?	Does it have any sticky or awkward transitions?
Is it too dense or too fluffy?	Does it breathe?
Does the structure help mask any imperfections in production?	Can you watch it twice in a row without cringing? How about five times? (When you get to ten times without cringing you either have a decent piece or you're too tired to care.)

[handwritten margin notes: opening = build / progression = pace / conclusion = transition]

Concept #533-1

Nonlinear as a Way of Thinking: You have the freedom to think and work without time-based constraints. Like avant-garde French filmmaker Jean-Luc Goddard, when asked if his films had a beginning, middle and end, replied, "Yes, but not necessarily in that order."

The advantage of nonlinear thinking applied to nonlinear editing is that you can apply more context to the process. Instead of just filling the timeline with the beginning, followed by the middle, summed up by the end (which is an approach that is often entirely appropriate), you can work from the "key frames" and then "in-between" the action similar to the process of animation. Often the key segments of the piece will dictate timing, tone, and continuity for the rest of the piece. By jumping around in the timeline, the editor often makes important discoveries that impact the final piece. Perhaps a lengthy introduction becomes unneccessary because of the exposition of the core action, or maybe the conclusion of the piece starts to dictate a different ordering of images.

Key frames

In our advertising example, perhaps we skip directly to editing the consumers' reactions to the product—let's say in this case, the new Tristar Cruiser motorcycle—and find that they are so strong that we don't need so many product shots or an introduction. In fact, less is more; just some quick beauty shots peppered in between their reactions seem to keep things moving and tell the story of a superior product without making the viewer feel like they are being "sold." It soon becomes apparent that some customers are more articulate than others, but we want to convey the fact that we've spoken to a lot of people. Instead of plodding along with endless interviews, we extract many quick soundbites from the more verbally challenged customers and begin to layer them on various soundtracks so that there begins to be this col-

Sound
high-end images

lage of satisfied customers. Under that we layer the low rumble of the motorcycle engine and some guitar-based road rock. The visuals display the bike on the road maybe mixed with some historical images of the motorcycle in American pop culture.

While this example isn't necessarily a stylistic breakthrough, it points to an underlying technique, a way of approaching the material. I like to call this technique of condensing many fragments into one cohesive message, *distilling*. Although all of editing can be seen as a distillation process, there are many times where editors throw out a shot completely when there are a few frames or soundbites worth salvaging.

The digital guerrilla often doesn't have the luxury of a 10:1 shooting ratio, and thus every usable frame is precious. Distillation becomes a process of increasing the density of the message without increasing the mass. Thus in our example, we have a breezy, romantic introduction to the Tristar Cruiser, but at the same time, we are underscoring it with a symphony of satisfied customers.

Concept #202-vx

G-spots: G-spots are the visceral moments when a cut, a music cue, an effect, or a gesture can all collide to create a satisfying snap-crackle-pop harmonic convergence that just "feels" right. They often come together by accident. Become adept at sensing when you're close to one. (A side benefit: your significant other will appreciate this new found awareness.)

Concept #202-vm

Cringe frames: Cringe frames just make your neck hair stand up and you want to walk out of the editing suite. They are just those suckola kind of moments in the piece where nothing seems to be working. You obviously don't want cringe frames in your program, but sometimes they can't be avoided, like when this is the only usable take of a key shot. For the time being, just become more sensitive to that dull nausea that you've been trying to suppress and pretend is not there. True guerrilla mastery will come when you can transform cringe frames into G-spots without reshooting. It's even cooler than snatching a pebble from the hand of a Shaolin priest.

We've told the whole backstory of the product in a brief amount of time (nice bike, people like it), now all we have to do is present how our client—TrulyHip Advertising—is going to change their client's current advertising message to sell more motorcycles.

backstory

We've touched a little on form and flow, which emanate from the script and storyboard and the mechanics of editing. The last F-word you should keep in mind is the overall "feel" of the piece. This is the hardest part to convey and the most important. The feel of the piece supersedes any of the individual technical aspects, although they all contribute. Often, creative people use the expression "that works" or "that doesn't work" about a particular point and don't or can't give much more articulation than that. What they are referring to is the place beyond language where feeling is lingua franca. In visual communication, feeling

'feel'

⇨ ⇨ ⇨ **LEAVING WELL ENOUGH ALONE**

In one scene there were two kids riding their bicycle up to a cemetery late at night—the boy is fixated on it 'cause that's where his mother is buried—saying stuff that spooks out the little girl. The director comes in and he's all proud, he goes, "Man, you're gonna love this scene. I covered it so well. I've got 2-shots and I've got close-ups and I've got the wide shot and all that." And I looked at all the dailies and I made two cuts. I took the wide shot and a medium shot and I let the whole thing run. He looked at me at first like, what happened to all my coverage, and then he realized what I had realized when I was just watching the dailies, which was, the scene played; the spookiness that this girl experiences listening to this guy talk...if I had jostled the viewer at all with another angle or given them an opportunity to breathe, because it was kind of claustrophobic, then you'd completely lose the moment. The only way that scene could really play was as just one shot. [The director] looked at me, and I looked at him and he says, "Movie magic." (Barry Silver)

and not formula is the ultimate arbiter of what you should ultimately put up on screen.

Now how do we address this area of guerrilla training? Do we send you to work with Yoda for a year and promise you'll make better video? Well, it does take a certain discipline and practice to get good at identifying your emotional reactions to things. You may not need a Zen master around the house, but you do need to become fluent in the language of images.

Begin by watching good movies, commercials, music videos, infomercials, and so on, critically. What works best about them? It's something beyond the production technique. Then if you have time to experiment a little with a project, start to intentionally edit it in the worst possible way. Then find the best thing about that horrible sequence. There will be something if you look hard enough. Expand that tiny G-spot by reediting until it feels better and better. Try to get that rich six-course meal feeling even if you are editing a 30-second spot. Don't worry if you feel you improve something and then go too far and ruin it; you are strengthening your instincts. These are your most valuable weapons. You will often be second-guessed in an edit bay—everyone has their own two cents to add; but if you have access to your instincts, you will be able to push forward when everyone else is floundering.

The Bag of Tricks

I've tried to give you the abstract theoretical stuff first because there is no revolution without first getting a bit of dogma on your shoe. Editing is a very conceptual process, and you will thank me for the Zen stuff later in life when you have to impress people with what you do for a living. But diguerrillas do not live on philosophy but rather by their wits and their Wacoms™. So let's edit out all the chit-chat and go right to tactical training, shall we?

Let's assume that you've already gone through the manual at this point and know the basics of your editing system. You've got some footage that you've organized and are starting to put some shots down on the timeline. Here are some of the deep dark secrets that the manual will never tell you.

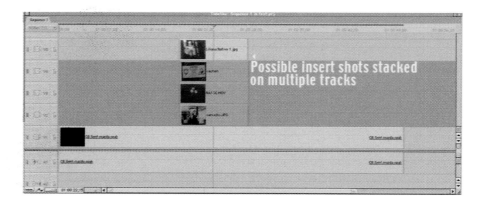

Possible insert shots stacked on multiple tracks

This figure illustrates the use of multiple tracks to audition various shots or takes without having to "commit" to a particular cut. You can preview different variations merely by toggling which tracks are being moritored.

Ten Pretty Darn Useful Nonlinear Editing Tips

1. *Use multitracks for "nondestructive" editing:* Multitrack timeline editing was developed around breaking away from the A/B-roll bottleneck of having only two video sources and being able to layer many sources. The multiple tracks are also useful for "storing" alternative shots and sequences that you might want to use or return to later. I developed this habit when I owned a Video F/X system that used a clip-based timeline instead of a track-based timeline. There was no overwrite function, and old clips would just get buried as they were superseded by later clips. The advantage was that I could recall an old edit very easily by pulling it back up to the top of the heap instead of referring to another version of the sequence. Now I don't have to work that way, but I like some of the efficiency of using the additional tracks kind of like extra bins. Most NLEs (nonlinear editors) monitor only the uppermost track, so by stacking alternate takes and camera angles, you can more easily flop shots or cut away just

by monitoring another track. You don't spend extra time undoing the cuts if they don't pan out so to speak.

2. *Dynamic cutting:* The L-cut, the T-cut, and the G-cut: The first two letters refer to the shapes that the clips make visually when laid out on the timeline (see diagram). The last one refers to the G-spot metaphor for creating a visually satisfying moment. The concept of leading to cut by introducing the sync audio ahead of the video (or vice versa) is not new. It is a well-worn film and documentary technique designed to make editing more transparent to the viewer. Digital editing simply makes the implementation easier and adds more variety. Traditionally, "checkerboard" style editing has been used for shot–reverse shot dialogue scenes where we hear the second character speaking just before we cut to them or to make talking head footage more interesting by intercutting it with more descriptive B-roll footage.

In guerrilla video, L-cuts and T-cuts have many more uses. They are nip and tuck cosmetic surgery techniques for sagging video. Merely leading the audio ahead of the video cut by 15 frames can create a subtle energy boost and offset the predictability of your cuts. Even though the average viewer can't really "predict" when you will cut to

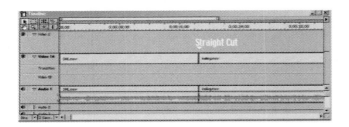

Straight Cut: This figure illustrates a basic straight-cut or butt-edit, where shot A and shot B are adjacent.

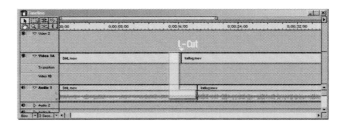

the next shot, they can feel it. Sync tracks with offset in/out points can either mask the artifice of editing and keep the viewer in a more natural flow or intentionally introduce more texture to the scene.

If audio is leading video at the beginning of a new scene, I usually like to cut in right on the fourth "beat" of the dialogue. It also works well if they have a descriptive sentence that is more general and then refer to themselves in the first person (e.g., "…the best thing about running with your friends is the group experience; [CUT IN VIDEO OF SPEAKER] I like to run because it's fun and I feel free…").

L-cuts and T-cuts can also mask jump cuts made to the audio or unsightly moments in the video in a very natural and fluid way. The third kind of dynamic cut I mentioned is the G-cut. The G-cut isn't a specific technique, but rather an instinct; it draws attention to itself like a punctuation mark or a right hand uppercut. A G-cut increases visual tension in a dramatic way. An example would be cutting video to black while the audio continues for a few additional moments, adding emotional resonance to the orphaned audio track: Another example would be adding a few frames of abstract color and noise like a car skidding

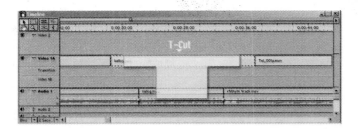

T-Cut:
This figure illustrates an L-cut mirrored on two sides of an edit so that the audio of shot A overlaps the head frames of shot B and the audio of shot C overlaps the tail frames of shot B.

or an electric sizzle up in between two shots to emphasize their juxtaposition. G-cuts can even suddenly eliminate sound altogether so that we can dramatize something visual with additional focus.

You'll know when you've made a real G-cut that really supports the piece, as opposed to just an empty stylistic gesture, when you can watch the cut ten times in a row and get some emotional impact instead of starting to get the tell-tale cringe sensation after the fourth or fifth run-through.

3. *Flip, flop, reverse, stop:* One of the central precepts for editing action is to respect the flow of motion within the frame. If a medium shot of a car is passing left-to-right, editing logic says that the ensuing close-up of the driver should be travelling in the same direction. For any number of reasons, you may find yourself with shots that make sense to cut together but don't have a "motion match." Digital systems allow the editor to flip shots as you would flip a reversed 35mm film slide in a projector so that the action "reads" in the opposite direction.

Again, this is not a new technique, but it has broader guerrilla applications. Flipping shots, as well as flopping

FLIP L/R
FLIP TOP/BOTTOM
STOP = FREEZE

them (reversing them top-to-bottom) can be used effectively to energize the editing and disrupt the predictability of shots. Seeing backwards signage in the background of a shot or having a shot appear unexpectedly upside-down can provide a useful visual jolt, particularly in an action sequence where the coverage is weak and you are in danger of repeating shots too often. This kind of "intentional sloppiness" in joining shots can give the viewers a sense of freedom around the subject matter. This kind of editorial freedom liberates the content from rigid presentation and offers many comic and ironic opportunities.

In a similar vein, reversing motion, actually playing the shot backwards from out-frame to in-frame, can be used both as a transparent effect for making a gesture shift meaning (e.g., opening a door becomes closing a door) or an obvious effect for altering time-reality (e.g., a breaking glass repairs itself). The counterpoint to reverse motion is stop-motion, either a full stop (freeze frame) or truncated motion (strobe). These rivet the viewer's attention on a single frame, which can underscore an action and make the viewer imagine the continuity (e.g., jumping from a building) or create an altered emotional environment because the action has stopped but the soundtrack continues.

4. *Fractured fairy tales—multiple dramatic threads:* Digital editing makes it easier to experiment with different narrative patterns within the same project. The multitrack metaphor can be used to tell the story in more sophisticated and jazzlike form. Because it is possible to cut into

a sequence with another sequence, it becomes an easy task for an editor to manage multiple narrative threads within the same piece. This kind of narration has become prominent with the rise of the music video as a narrative form where the fixed soundtrack provides the overall structure and the visuals have a looser relationship to each other.

In a typical scenario, a live performance by the band might be intercut with an acted story based on the song, which is intercut with some backstage footage of the band on tour or in the studio or some animated sequence. Each set of images is building its own narrative, but they are all interconnected by the soundtrack.

For the guerrilla, this kind of multithreaded structure can be extremely advantageous. A linear structure for a marketing video (introduce product, describe market, show customers, conclude message) might benefit from an interwoven approach, particularly if there is a scarcity of material for any of the individual sections. Cutting away from one story allows the audience to advance it along in their imagination so that when you come back, it can be much further along without showing all the intermediate exposition.

5. *Freestyle transitions:* In the beginning there was the dissolve, and the dissolve begat the wipe. In the guerrilla domain, there are no more rules. In fact, how you transition from one scene to another can carry as much communication as the content itself. We will discuss all the

effect-driven transitions in a later section, but for now, let's mention a few simple cuts-only transition techniques.

The blur pan is the action editor's best friend and makes the camera work look better than it might actually have been. If cut into a moving camera shot, a few frames of blurred movement hide the cut and move the viewer to the next subject as if it were one continuous shot.

The cross zoom can be another device that seamlessly welds disjointed action. A quick flash zoom, dissolved over a few frames with another zoom out can give a powerful undulating quality to the action without jarring the viewer out of the action.

The flash frame is a simple device that mimics the overexposed frame that occurs in most film cameras when the motor is cut, rolling celluloid comes to a stop and overexposes in the shutter gate. Anyone accustomed to watching unedited dailies sees these sometimes colorful blips that flash between shots. This can be a way to transition between shots that vary widely in content or as an alternative to using jump cuts within an interview sequence.

6. *Black is beautiful:* Like they say in the fashion industry, black never goes out of style. The creative use of black leader is one of the simplest and most effective editing devices. The big advantage is that there is an endless supply of it, and you don't need any footage at all. By removing the visuals and having viewers look at a black screen (or a title card), you refocus their attention on either the

soundtrack or give them time to consider what they've just seen prior before moving on to a different action.

Black leader can also be used to mask the absence of missing continuity. If we see a close-up of a woman cut to black leader and hear her walking and getting into a car, we can cut directly to a moving car and avoid showing the intermediate footage (which might not exist anyway).

7. *The hypermontage:* While "montage" is the French word for editing in general, it is often used to denote a combination of short shots that create a particular mood or transitional element. Action is often condensed into a montage to indicate frenzy and intensity.

   The hypermontage is an accelerated manic variation where the maximum amount of visual information is packed into the minimum amount of screen time. Since the frame counts of each individual shot tend to get quite low, it is important to put very recognizable content in the frame. Close-ups, high contrast, simple movement are good ingredients for hypermontages.

   A fast way to build a hypermontage without too much microcutting is to cut a short sequence together and render it as one media file. Then apply a motion effect to the montage and speed it up 200–400%. The resulting sequence assaults the senses and can be accentuated with fast tempo music or counterpointed with leisurely voiceover.

8. *The drama of realism:* While a lot of editing technique

can center around where and what to cut, there is also the whole domain of what not to cut. The illusion of real time can enhance the impact of even a 30-second commercial spot. Quiet pauses, silences, longer takes can all give the viewer a feeling of expanding time instead of condensing it. Particularly if the mood you want to create is contemplative, discover how to make the editing non-intrusive. Perhaps that means leaving a speaker on screen as they grope for the next phrase or leaving a few seconds of time at the end of a spot with no music or voiceover, just ambient sound.

Sometimes the single take can be visually more powerful than the most masterful multiangle camera coverage. In an age of accelerated information, taking your time, when done well, can stand out boldly and invite viewers to dwell inside the world you are creating.

9. *Overwrite editing:* This kind of editing is like burying someone in sand until only their head sticks out. A lengthy master shot is placed on the timeline that provides much of the soundtrack and maybe some of the visuals, and then undesirable pieces of the master shot are covered up with other footage until the sequence plays well visually. The master shot gives the editor a framework while the sequence is being built.

10. *Mismatch, jump cut, and noncontinuous editing:* This is a deliberate counterpoint to the established "rules" of

editing that say that action should "match" from shot A to shot B. I call this kind of gestural editing a *Babe cut*. It's named after Babe Ruth, who allegedly pointed to the spot in the outfield where he was going to hit a home run. It is an umbrella term for eyeline matches, reaction shots, and inserts that are logically implied by the previous shot. For example, if you were to edit the Babe's famous home run, you might cut from his pointing finger to the outfield fence.

Since most viewers see that kind of editing all the time, it can be effective to subvert audience expectations by altering the progression. A mismatch might be cutting from someone swinging a bat to someone sliding home rather than the expected shot of the ball hitting the bat. Mismatches can influence perceived time elapsed and cue the viewer to pay closer attention.

Playing with continuity issues can also make a sequence more unique and dynamic. In our previous motorcycle example, if the bike stays the same, but it is in a different environment with a different rider in every shot, we have disregarded conventional ideas of continuity but kept the viewer focused on the product as well as quickly communicating an underlying message that this bike has many customers.

➤ **A Note About Noodling:** Noodling is the not-so-technical term for fine-tuning a cut, trimming a frame here or there to make it optimal. Some of you like to get a cut right and then move on. I much prefer the leave-it-loose approach while I am mapping out a particular editing direction. It's easier to walk away from a dead end if you haven't invested too much noodling time already. However, you may need to make a few concessions to others in the editing bay who can't envision what the finely tuned cut will look like.

Final Cut

These are the ground rules for guerrilla editing. Always know how much ammo you have and snipe from as many angles as possible. You can't afford to get bogged down with A-B-C, connect-the-dots thinking: Keep shaping the piece. Experiment with temporal and narrative conventions to make your message bolder. Have fun.

In the next chapter we will cover creating the overall look of the piece and how editing interacts with other visual elements.

the answer is merely that it looks cool, you might be headed toward candyland. Everything will become clearer once you have identified a visual hub that supports the whole piece.

> **DIGUERRILLA WANTED:** Looking for 2D and especially 3D designer/animators to work on a large on-air promo package. Reels submitted must contain work that is exciting and bold. Experimental work is also welcome. Fantasy work a plus. Creativity is more important than work experience.

Face it, you will never have the time and budget you really need to do it "right," so it's wise to sharpen your digital guerrilla skills—strike fast, spend less, and do more damage. You must seize what is available and begin. First off, keep the ideas simple. Don't stew in your own juices more than absolutely necessary; you don't need to spend weeks mulling through your subconscious for visions and epiphanies. Diguerrillas don't have time for such bourgeois indulgences. For visual inspiration, there is an entire century of filmed and animated images, a few centuries of commercial print graphics, and a few thousand years of painting from which to spark yourself. If you aren't sufficiently inspired, steal an idea from a friend, colleague, or some demi-god you admire; you simply cannot afford the luxury of artist's block. Once you've distinguished a particular direction, you need to assess whether your source images will need to be processed in any way.

The digital guerrilla will usually attempt to achieve his or her look with corner-cutting and cost-effective means rather than go for painstaking frame-by-frame procedures such as rotoscoping or

> ➤ **Something from Nothing:** The tag line on the script said, "The teacher goes on a trip." So, what did [the director] do? He shot her against a blue screen, stepping up some blue stairs and leaving—I think it was actually shot for another episode or something. What we did was, Ricardo and I, we sat down and started thinking about what we could do, we actually built an actual set, an electrician came in, and we got some stock footage. We wanted to create an airport. We got some stock footage of an airplane turning around, stuck that behind the windows of our virtual set, added texture, we had a couch and there was a railing 'cause it looked like she was holding on to something. And it still didn't look right so we had to add reflections, except the reflections were positive reflections, they weren't of the back side, so it was full of all these weird little things that weren't quite right, but it worked. And we added a couple filters to kind of soften it up a little bit so it didn't look so computer generated. (I guess now they have all these grain filter plug-ins that are pretty cool.) So we created something out of nothing. (Barry Silver)

expensive electronic processing. The guerrilla aesthetic is rooted in the age of reproduction. We beg, we borrow, we steal (aka "make homage to," "are inspired from," "are influenced by"). We live in an era where manipulating the image is as important as capturing it or editing it.

Keys to the Kingdom

There are a smorgasbord of elements involved in creating a visual look, but before diving into the buffet, let's make sure that we know where the plates are stacked. By "plates" I mean the basic digital elements. Many effects such as keying and superimpositions are based on the layering capabilities of digital video. One of the amazing aspects of computer-based postproduction is that the number of video layers are usually only limited by the amount of memory in your computer rather than the number of VTRs that you are controlling simultaneously. Thus having the ability to "stack plates" of images over one another dramatically expands what is possible to put on the screen.

Then there is the business of making things move. Over 80% of digital effects tools are key-frame based. Key framing is a concept drawn from traditional cel animation: The key animator would draw the extreme positions of the characters, and the working class animators would draw the in-betweens. Through technological miracle, economic necessity, and Marxist irony, the machine does much of the proletarian labor today. By setting parameters at key intervals, the computer incrementally adjusts the frames between one setting and another. The more key frames, the more intricate an effect can become. The secret to any sort of effects mastery is understanding the power and limitations of key-frame animation.

Setting lots of key frames takes time and patience. For some effects, such as complicated motion paths, there is simply no other way. However, a lot of graceful movement can be created with one or two key frames and some "easing" in between. If you're in a hurry, this kind of A-to-B animation frees you from having to iron out bumps and kinks in the motion path.

➤ **Happy Accidents:** I had to deliver a storyboard to E! Entertainment Television one day and I was working with my scanner and my scanner was broken. The colors were misaligned. But the funny thing, they were asking me to do a promo in a style that looked like was 3D comics from the '50s. This is a perfect example of a happy accident. Just go for it. We recreated the same effect in the [Quantel] Henry. It worked very well too. (Flavio Kampah, Media Designer/Director)

➤ Good software lets you do things ten different ways or a hundred different ways. Someone can achieve the same effect in many different paths, so there's not just one way to do it, so that opens up the whole world of how to do it most efficiently. One of the paths could be a nightmare, but along that path you could have many happy accidents. In fact, in the way I work, I start to think about an effect and start to play with an animation and I'll have maybe five or six different happy accidents where I learn, "Wow that's what happens when you do that." I put those discoveries on the back burner for future reference. Meanwhile I get to the effect I want, but I would say 50% of my work is happy accidents. It comes out better than I even thought just by using the tools and learning the tools better as you use them. I don't think you can ever learn all the tools now. You can only like dive into a new area that you want to explore and you discover the use of the tool and you have a happy accident. And the client's just blown away like, "Wow, how did you do that?" (Cody Harrington)

➤ I don't think there's really anything that might be called a happy accident. I think it's more that you push at it real hard and you finally come up with an acceptable solution. I think happy accidents are like successful gamblers. The guys that suddenly come into the bar and buy everyone a round because they're the big winners at the track, but you don't know about the fact that they've lost their car and their house because of their previous track record. It's mostly just knowing how to work the tools, and trying to put them together in new and novel ways or trying to push them to their limits. (Doug Barnard)

Building Blocks

These effect categories can be infinitely combined to form the most subtle or mind-bending changes to your basic images:

color correction	tint, chroma, luminosity, contrast, replace color
motion effects	slow motion, 24 fps/30 fps, freeze frames, time lapse
image texture	fields vs. frames, image grain, distortion, focus
lighting effects	2D and 3D lighting
perspective	modify height, width, and depth
shape-based distortion	morphing and warping
filtering	displacements, image processing
motion tracking	stabilizing, synchronizing
rotoscoping	painting frame-by-frame, replacing frame-by-frame
image keying	(bluescreen) chroma, luma, alpha difference

Color correction

motion effects

image texture

morph

filters

painting by frame

Color Correction

Field manual notes: Adjusting color is one of the most basic and most powerful guerrilla tools. The eye automatically responds to color intensity, hue, and contrast with emotional associations. Color correction can add dramatic emotional impact, from making an interview seem more authoritative and journalistic to transforming a smoggy sky to Oz-like blue. And, it's fast. Many inexpensive editing systems offer realtime color effects.

> ➤ **Telecine on Food Stamps:** (converting color neg to positive in Premiere) Well, after figuring out that there's no "magic setting" to do the conversion perfectly, I decided to just play around. In Premiere, I eyeballed it and used "invert," "levels," and then "brightness and contrast" (yes, I know I can get b&c results in levels, but it was just easier this way).
>
> The accuracy of the inversion was somewhat mixed—none of the clips have what you would consider "normal" color, but some ended up more normal than others. However, since this was Super-8 footage and we were going for a little weirdness, the variations and general funkiness worked to our advantage. I wouldn't recommend it if you're looking for "true" color, but if you're a little more flexible, give it a try...we got great stuff! (Neal Evans)

Color correction is your best friend. It takes some of the burden off the quality of how the material was originally shot and allows you to hide a lot of garrish lighting mistakes or accentuate certain thematic elements. It can make your material seem more optimistic (high chroma, reduced pallette) or pessimistic (less chroma, more contrast) or other worldly (tints and color replacement).

Guerrilla apps: The key distinction here is control. Some color correction interfaces are little more advanced than your home television; they only have chroma (color intensity), luminosity (contrast), and individual controls for red, green, and blue.

It's better than nothing, but you will ultimately require more fire-power. Advanced color controls are something so fundamental that once you've baptized yourself, you will return to them over and over. You want access to the color curves, the math that describes the relationship between chroma, luminance, and hue. Curves can emulate the more complex relationships between light and dark

Motion Effects

Field manual notes: Along with color, image speed or frame rate is the most fundamental building block in modifying an image. The illusion of compressing or expanding time by altering the frame rate was one of the most profound discoveries of early cinema and is still equally powerful today.

By compressing 24 hours into 30 seconds using time-lapse photography or expanding a swimmer's dive from 2 seconds to 15 seconds, you are altering the normal context and allowing the viewer to see something in a way they haven't seen it before.

Guerilla apps: Again, the big key here is function-curve control. This is the latest advance in motion effects. Previously, if you wanted to alter the frame rate, you either changed the setting in camera while shooting or repeated or stripped away frames in postproduction. It was difficult to seamlessly alter motion within the same shot except by manually tweaking the camera during filming. With f-curves (After Effects calls this kind of operation "time remapping"), you can now have a single shot seamlessy

altered frame rate

time lapse — or slow moti...

After Effects

173

begin at normal speed, get faster, and slow to a freeze with one continuous f-curve. This opens up tremendous possibilities for creative expression: the frenetic pace of youth slowing to the sluggish gait of old age in one shot, or the agonizing tension of a baseball pitcher's windup accelerating into a realtime 100 mph fastball.

Image texture

Field manual notes: By "image texture," we mean the subtler, "cinematic" aspects of motion and optics. Motion video is not just individual still frames moving by to give the illusion of motion; there are two pictures within each picture, called fields (see scanning sidebar), that give video a very different look to our

---

⇨ ⇨ ⇨ **SCANNING**

In a television display, interlaced scanning is the process of reassembling a picture from a series of electrical signals (video signal). In the NTSC system (current TV picture), 525 scanning lines are used to create a picture (frame). The frame is made up of two fields: field 1 has 262.5 odd lines (1, 3, 5...) and field 2 has 262.5 even lines (2, 4, 6...). The odd lines are scanned (or painted on the screen) in 1/60th of a second, and the even lines follow in the next 1/60th of a second. This presents an entire frame/picture of 525 lines in 1/30th of a second.

In progressive scanning, typically used by computer monitors, all the horizontal scan lines are "painted" on the screen at one time.

Adopted DTV formats include both interlaced and progressive broadcast and display methods.

Types of Motion Effects	Description
standard speed effect	Mathematically increases or decreases the frame rate of the shot, which changes the shot's duration. Some motion filters will allow you to interpolate frames, which will actually produce new "in between" frames instead of merely repeating the existing frames.
strobe	Staccato "choppy" motion. Maintains overall duration of shot but repeats every nth frame with a factor of x. (A strobe setting of 5 would yield 5 frames of frame one followed by 5 frames of frame 6 followed by 5 frames of frame 11...)
trails	Also called lap dissolves. Outgoing frames fade out over incoming frames. (A short decay factor will smooth the stuttering effect caused by exaggerated slow motion; a long decay factor will cause a ghosting surreal effect.)
freeze frame	Holding a single frame of video for an extended length.
time lapse	Extreme time compression usually captured by modifying a camera to expose one frame every second or longer intervals. Can be simulated with a motion effect by taking a long "realtime" shot and speeding it up 1,000–10,000%.
fit-to-fill	Extends a shot the precise number of distributed frames to "fill" a specific duration marked in the timeline.

Handwritten margin notes:
- speed
- strobe
- lap dissolve — decay rate
- speedy 10x to 100x 1 min → 6 sec or 0.6 sec
- fill

eyes than standard film formats that offer less visual information. In addition, a century of photography has given us an unspoken visual familiarity with the chemical grain of film emulsion as well as the focal lengths of prime lenses.

Guerrilla apps: One of the big laments of digital guerrillas is wanting to shoot on film instead of video for the look but only having a budget to shoot video. In the past, producers have in fact paid expensive fees for electronic "film look" processes that made their video look more like film. Now there are products like Digi-Effect's Cinelook/Cinemotion and ADI's Film Pak plug-ins for After Effects that are, in many ways, more sophisticated and are a fraction of the cost.

But if you don't have the time resources to delve into the arcane details of the film mystique, just be aware that frame rate and field removal are the dominant characteristics to be concerned with. We primarily identify film by it's relatively slower

film look —
frame rate +
field removal

> **Plug-in, Tweak-out:** [I believe in using plug-ins] as long as the plug-ins allow customizable attributes, as long as you can go in and tweak the parameters for a unique look. At least it gives you a starting position and then you can build on the effects in your own way. Everyone knows the lens flare, but now Knoll has 50 lens flares that are all customizable parameters and that's the way to use a plug-in. Plus, you never know what's going to happen if you just combine two or three plug-in effects laid on top of one another. Well, you know, that's a unique look. You might see the remnants of one, but it's still using what's at hand artistically. (Cody Harrington)

frame rate and shutter speed; if you're not trying to match a particular film stock, a convincing "poor man's" film look can be created by merely digitizing the footage with only one field (which the majority of compression hardware supports) or by mathematically interpolating the fields together with a "de-interlace" filter and then reducing the frame rate from 30 fps to 24 fps. If you still need a bit of quick tweaking, boost the contrast and chroma 10–20%. If you want to really heighten the illusion, slap a black letterbox over the top and bottom image to mimic the 1:1.66 aspect ratio of 35mm film. With a minimum of effort, your client will believe you went to the expense and trouble of shooting film. Perception is everything.

Lighting Effects

Field manual notes: Lighting is the strongest emotional element of photography. The way a scene is lit cues the viewer about mood, spatial relationships and where to place your attention within the frame. The most effective place to be concerned about lighting is obviously during the shoot itself, but thanks to a bit of digital sleight-of-hand, it is possible, with many limitations, to relight the shot after the fact.

Guerrilla apps: Integrated three-dimensional lighting tools, such as those found in the Discreet Logic Flint, Flame, and Fire products, are currently still priced for the rich and famous. Two-dimensional lighting is easier to get your hands on and can be

Scene lighting

quite potent in the right hands. The most common 2D lighting fil-ter comes with Adobe Photoshop and is accessible through After Effects. It allows you to place different kinds of light sources around the flat plane of the image. If you are using an editing package that doesn't have any virtual lighting tools, you can fake some hint of dramatic lighting by overlaying a grayscale animation of light on top of the image. This can be created by shooting strong flashlights against a white wall or by rendering a lighting sequence in a 3D animation package. Extracting mattes from cer-tain organic images such as light fog or water reflection can give another interesting sense of lighting.

Listen Up

If you are using lighting mattes rather than direct filtering of the image, try and use a multiply function rather than just superimposing the matte at partial opacity. That way, the blacks in the matte won't muddy up the image chroma.

Perspective

Field manual notes: Video images are, in digital terms, two-dimensional planes represented by rows of pixels. They can thus be manipulated to squeeze or stretch an image along an x-, y-, or z- axis. This mathematical repositioning is the basis for many clas-sic digital video effects (DVEs) including wipes, crops, and pic-ture-in-picture functions.

Adding some squash or stretch to the image or shifting perspective adds, well, a new dimension to the visual. Why should you be limited to the framing and aspect ratio recorded when the image was shot? What if only a particular section of the frame is of real interest? What if you need to fit more on the screen than one shot and you don't want to superimpose? What if you want to give the impression that the image is projected onto a surface?

Guerrilla apps: The simplest uses of resizing and perspective are in simulating widescreen cinema formats. In the poor man's film-look example, I mentioned that you could superimpose a black letterbox over the image to emulate the widescreen aspect ratio. To give the illusion of Cinemascope and avoid cropping some of the image top to bottom, you can resize the vertical height of the image so that the image resembles the stretched look of Cinemascope images without the proper anthropomorphic projector lens.

Slightly tilting the top of the image back along the *z*-axis can also provide visual drama, as though the image were being projected onto a tilted surface. Tilting the sides of the image back along the *z*-axis introduces the drive-in theater effect and indicates to the viewer that this image isn't the "reality" happening in the frame but rather a piece of media like a movie or a television or some sci-fi hologram that is only a part of what is happening inside the frame.

Abstract perspective is also useful for a wild-style look. Simply rotating the image upside down or sideways or severely stretching the image produces a very disorienting, chaotic feel. Expanding the image beyond a 20–25% scale increase will begin to produce noticeable pixellation artifacts in the image as it attempts to approximate new pixels for which there is no new additional data. This can be used to your advantage if you are trying to create a "low rez" feel in the piece, such as you might get when watching the Jumbotron in Times Square.

Listen Up

Keep in mind that changes in perspective will sometimes leave you with unwanted black areas of the screen where the picture no longer fits the screen exactly, and portions you want to see may be cut off. You need to keep adjusting height, width, and *x-y-z* coordinates in combination to get it all just right. You may also have to add a background, border, or repeat part of the image in order to fill up the screen.

Shape-Based Distortion

Field manual notes: Otherwise known as morphing and warping, this kind of effect takes differing shapes and transforms one into the other incrementally. If the shapes contain a bitmap image, then the images metamorphically blend as one displaces the other.

While morphing uses two or more images, warping is the term for shape distortion within the same image. Morphing and warping have traditionally been based on 2D shapes, but 3D models and formulas can also be applied to produce unusual effects.

While this kind of manipulation is traditionally associated with surreal sci-fi effects, it has many additional applications other than simply turning one face into another.

Guerrilla apps: Quick morphs (12 frames or less) don't need the edge precision that longer morphs do, where imperfections in the warping path can create a mess. Blipmorphs can accent a transition or add a dash of surreality without a lot of effort.

Filtering

Field manual notes: By "filtering," we are referring to mathematical algorithms that actually change the image's pixels according to some artistic technique. The original "plug-in" architecture of Adobe Photoshop was designed for filtering photographic images and mimicked many painting and drawing aesthetics. Now the plug-in filter is an industry unto itself, with many filters resembling small applications within the larger application.

Guerrilla apps: Again, a little goes a long way, especially with aging, overused filters such as charcoal and watercolor. Often filtering only a certain part of the frame—either masked on another layer or operating on only one or two of the RGB channels—can enhance without overpowering. Often I combine a filtered layer of the same footage on top of an untouched layer and either multiply or dial down the opacity to attenuate the effect somewhat. I am partial to filters with a variable random number seed, such as in Xaos Tools' Paint Alchemy among others, because they change the way the filter interacts with the pixels over each frame. Thus,

✓ the filter itself becomes an animation tool and, if used carefully, looks like you painstakingly animated each frame.

> **The Art of Math:** The wave that I've seen is that the software is becoming more and more artist oriented. So that an artist that really has an understanding of color and design and is now able to grab these objects that have the math imbedded in them. As long as you can open up and play with the formula, it allows the artist to understand the math behind it. The problem has always been you have programs that are meant for the artist and they don't get too deep with math. It's always [parameter] sliders or this or that. But to let the artist finally have access to the math in a nonthreatening way where they can just play with the formula and see the results, then they start to associate the math with the visual.

Math is art. Now [software] lets people access it. I'm learning a lot more about math and because I can access the math instead of saying, ok, it's a slider, or I'm grabbing the sine wave object and just placing it in the node. Now I can actually look at the formula and I can actually understand the syntax of what's going on. It's a big industry. Now the artist doesn't have to know anything [technical] but as long as you can get behind that beautiful interface you can go as deep as you want. (Cody Harrington)

Motion tracking

Field manual notes: Motion tracking is what separates garden-variety compositing (logo treatments, bumpers, and show opens) from the truly magical, seamless weaving of photographic and synthetic images. Motion tracking is like having a second camera crew in postproduction that can reshoot images for you that precisely duplicate the camera moves of principal photography. Motion tracking mathematically plots the coordinates of a certain group of pixels as they travel across the screen. It basically is the antithesis of key frame animation because a tracker plots coordinates for every single frame, thus allowing you to lock images to very subtle and irregular moving objects.

Uses for motion tracking include removing or adding camera shake and gate jitter; replacing moving logos, signs, people, and objects with other images; adding a special effect to a moving target (e.g., a glow effect to a flapping butterfly). While motion tracking is still considered a relatively high-end feature, Adobe After // Effects has it in their production bundle at a guerrilla price.

Guerrilla apps: Motion tracking is a way to recycle old images and make them fresh again. Putting a new logo on a passing truck or changing a TV show playing in the background of a shot to avoid a lawsuit are typical copyright cosmetics. Another important use is to match handheld footage with locked-down footage. With a motion tracker, you can either make the smooth footage look jerky or vice versa.

One of the great underexplored uses for a motion tracker is just creating organic motion path data from natural media. A shot of a feather floating down or the tail of a dolphin undulating through water might provide interesting motion paths for other objects in other scenes.

Rotoscoping

Field manual notes: The rotoscope, patented by Max Fleischer studios back in the '30s, was a machine that allowed artists to trace over photographs either to mimic the shape and motion or to better place animation within a live-action scene. Today rotoscoping describes almost any sort of frame-by-frame paint or masking process.

Guerrilla apps: Traditionally roto work has been the real sweatshop ghetto of the digital revolution, but there are now masking and roto aids, such as Auto-Masker for After Effects and Commotion from Puffin Designs, that make life easier. Rotoscoping is largely done to hide things, take out wires, hide backgrounds, and so on. But there are a lot of things you can do with quick and sloppy roto work that add energy and excitement to your images. Just dabbing digital paint randomly on frames gives the footage a free-spirited, arts and crafts look. More "serious" applications include loose hand-painted mattes with lots of feathering that "swim" at the edges. This gives your compositing a soft liquid quality.

Keying and Matting

Field manual notes: Keying is a mathematical way of combining multiple video sources. By specifying a level or brightness (luma key) or a specific color (chroma key), these specified parts of the image are suppressed, and the background image is seen. The harshness of the early electronic video keyers has evolved into a highly sophisticated array of mathematical algorithms for defining edge softness, shadow fidelity, spill suppression, and other advancements that have made keying a more useful process.

Matting is a film term that describes the mask layer used to hold back parts of an image when combining them with another. Mattes can be "pulled" with the kinds of keys mentioned earlier, by rotoscoping, or by using a difference matte. A difference matte uses software to calculate a matte based on the difference between a frame containing the key element and an identical frame without the key element (e.g., a girl in a yard compared with a shot of the yard without the girl).

Keying information can either be extracted as a separate element or stored along with digital images on a discrete color channel known as an alpha channel. Alpha channel information can be used in a number of ways and is the basis for compositing layers of digital images.

Guerrilla apps: Keying is a godsend to guerrillas because it's a lot faster and sometimes more accurate than rotoscoping a matte by hand. Bluescreen or greenscreen shooting techniques have become the cornerstone of live-action effects work because when shot correctly and digitally processed with a good keying algorithm, such as Ultimatte or Primatte software, they produce the cleanest, most faithful mattes.

However, a guerrilla's life is lived in the underbrush, and a clean matte upon which to lay one's backplate is the exception rather than the rule. Fortunately, there are many less-than-perfect keys that work perfectly. Skies, for example, when prominent in a horizon shot are great candidates for a soft luminance key since the sky tends to be much brighter than the foreground. The sky, with its soft texture, tends to be a very forgiving patch of pixels. This sky key can be used to merely change the feel of the weather by placing a different sky on the background plate, or for creating something more surreal.

One of the problems with bad keys is seeing ragged edges or seeing similarly colored parts of the image start to disappear. One way to use these imperfections to better effect is by keying a treated version of the same source material so that the background image matches up perfectly with the foreground image. This technique is good for some interesting coloring effects such as softly keying a light-colored car on top of the same image treated with some texture and attenuation in brightness. The car appears "weathered" and can be dissolved into its shiny new version if necessary.

Look Sharp

These are generic concepts to give a sense of how combined effects can work together. They are meant to be a starting point for your own recipes, not a cookie-cutter approach.

Mood	Possible Elements	Description
Nostalgia	—washed out chroma —sepia tint —high-grain —blown-out whites —soft focus —18–24 fps or slightly strobed slo-mo —slight frame jitter —filmic imperfections such as dirt and scratches	Nostalgia, our emotional relationship to memory, though thoroughly subjective, has been influenced by the changing formats of motion media throughout the century. From black and white, hand-cranked film to Super-8, viewers are visually triggered by the representation of the past as softer and technically cruder. Early motion picture cameras had optical imperfections as well as mechanical idiosyncrasies. The chemical developing process, especially for consumer film, was temperamental and favored certain parts of the color spectrum.
Postmodern	—bright chroma, limited color palette —use of black and white with color —depth of field, unfocused background elements —emphasize primary colors —warped, optical distortion, slight fisheye lens look —subtle use of semitransparent text —key in floating objects	Who really knows what Postmodern means any more, but it does have a high-brow stylized connotation. Here I'm using it to mean very stark compositions that make a strong impact on the eye. We're talking Kandisky meeting Polanski.

Mood	Possible Elements	Description
Cinema verité	—long takes —talking heads —high contrast —innocuous typeface —camera shake —video glitches —"bad" lighting —focus problems	Named for the French school of "true cinema," these were the first real guerrilla filmmakers. From Casavettes to "Cops," this on-the-run, documentary style still gives the impression, correct or otherwise, that the subject matter is being presented "as is" and can sometimes be more compelling than a slicker treatment. Can also be used in combination with more structural design elements for effect.
Webvision	—image in a smaller window surrounded by graphics —consistent "interface" —small text bites that flash on and off the screen —prominent icon or animated logo for consistent branding —fewer wide shots	I use this term to describe an entire infographic look that has evolved in sports broadcasting and 24-hour news networks and on the Web. The need to cram a lot of information on the screen has been both a technical and design challenge. Today's viewers are trained to scan the screen and take what they need. If your project is loaded with data or statistics, you may want to consider designing that information into the images.
Softgrunge	—lots of keys and supers —multiple layers —image degradation —unconventional typeface —organic shapes —bits of "found" stock footage —abstract undulating backgrounds	Real urban skank art, from Beats to Punks to Hip-Hop, has been diluted and absorbed into a kind of gorgeous messy mosaic of styles and colors rule-breaking composition. This is grit without the sting. It's a fun time to be designing because so many design rules are being rewritten. Of course, a lot of crappy-looking compositions are also finding their way into public consumption.

Mood	Possible Elements	Description
Shock Therapy	—blitz montages —abstract images —subliminal flashes —harsh or driving sound-track —radical scene transitions	This category is a little more extreme version of softgrunge. A bit more of an aftertaste. It includes editing rhythms and image processing that are more intentionally dissonant and disturbing.
Corptech	—clean, easy-to-read text graphics —animated infographics —uniform look —smooth scene transitions —balance of talking heads and supporting footage —strong voiceover for emphasis and summary	Thanks largely to the World Wide Web, corporate presentations and graphics have become a lot richer than tossing down bullet points in a Powerpoint file. Gone is the plodding slide show and talking head format; today's corporate look is glossier, livelier, and more information-efficient, delivering more in less time.
Fluffumentary	—interview and "unscripted" footage —wild info graphics —intertitles for structuring —easily digestible bites of information —camera moves over still photographs and important documents	Smoother looking than cinema verité, the fluffumentary is a label that I give to almost all nonfiction material that isn't straight news or traditional documentary (e.g., electronic press kits, "making of" promos, new product launch videos, brandumentaries, new business pitches, etc.). This look alludes toward a kind of "real world" legitimacy while at the same time promotes a carefully articulated agenda.

Mood	Possible Elements	Description
Heartstring	—stirring music —powerful emotional images —slow motion —"optimistic" color correction —narrative "story," human drama emphasis —spare, "romantic" text design —understated effects	Heartstring illicits a more orchestrated sentimental emotional response like a Spielberg movie or a picture you carry in your wallet. It relies on tapping into the collective "soft spot" of the audience with images that sound like they were plucked from the Hallmark greeting card rack: childhood, true love, paternal love, personal dreams, or personal loss. This look is much more about getting the viewer to identify with your images; designed to push your audience's buttons and have a gut response without falling into ineffective cliches.

The visual elements in combination are still only a part of the overall look. With moving images, timing is the decisive factor. The addition of a time component throws in a whole new design dimension. When will another element appear? At what intensity over what time period? Though I am not a musician, the image that comes to mind is that of a symphonic score. What each instrument is playing is important, of course, but even more critical is when their part comes in, when they will solo, when they will play sotto voce, and when there will be a crescendo. Like a composer, you can't merely concentrate on the few bars in front of you; it must be in the context of the entire fabric of the visual symphony.

Combining, Canning, Customizing

The whole point of discussing postproduction effects as an integrated strategy instead of a laundry list of separate effects is to stimulate thinking beyond a random pastiche and toward a well thought out approach taking into account the communication content, the audience, fixed media assets, and time frame.

For example, you might like a really frenzied graphic look and it may be absolutely relevant to the subject matter, but a densely layered 10-minute piece might not be practical if there is a short schedule with many changes along the way and you will end up choking your CPU by rendering all these layers of image data.

Or your client might want to have a rich, glossy look, but you've been supplied dog-food video to work with and some Neanderthal graphics that are supposed to be scanned off a second-generation fax. Under these circumstances, the guerrilla spirit might take over and spontaneously come up with a strategy, but here are some generic prescriptions for reality-checking your project.

Quick Turnaround

For quick turnaround, the "reduce, recycle, reuse" mantra of the environmental movement is applicable to the diguerrilla as well. While merely reducing the number of layers and amount of footage is an obvious tactic (do we really need four different kinds of cloud patterns, or can we be smart about using one or two?), there are many other methods for streamlining the process.

Technique	Description	Fine print
precomposing	grouping layers that will appear as a single element (e.g., a complex background or an animated text sequence) and prerendering that as one finished layer	Remember that you are essentially "locking together" certain groups of layers so make sure they don't contain an element that will be the subject of a lot of creative discussion like a bird flying across screen. Good candidates for precomposing are landscapes and backgrounds that don't move and precomps of any kind of atmospheric texture (snow, pixels, smoke, rain, splotches, etc.).
spot welding	picking strategic points to hide imperfections with a bit of camouflage	Often, there isn't time to really paint out an unusable part of a frame where there was a mistake in photography or a bad matte or some such unsightly scourge. Think Band-Aid: What can you throw into the frame that is simple and looks intentional? If the eyesore is at the edge of a frame, it can be easily cropped out. If it is in the middle of the frame, you will need to get in there with the blowtorch and try to composite a tree branch, a text graphic, a streetlamp, whatever will draw the least amount of attention.
low-res "render-vous"	low-res layering and proxies	Many applications have good management tools for using low-resolution proxies to design a composition without spending the time rendering the full resolution image. Other applications make the user do his own proxy swapping. This can be tricky if you need to see a lot of detail as in a zoom. However, the use of proxies is invaluable, especially when certain elements are not yet available.

Technique	Description	Fine print
presets, loops, and tiles	automating parts of the look with ready-to-wear algorithms and images	Presets are just a grouping of parameters for an effect or a motion path that has been saved because they can be reused in various situations. Many applications come with dozens of factory presets. The most useful presets are your own because they will be distinctive, and if you ever have to go back into a project months later, you will know exactly what you did to the images. Loops and tiles can help you turn a little bit of media into a lot. A loop is a seamlessly repeating piece of video or animation; a tile is a still image that can be laid side-by-side with itself without producing a noticeable seam. Both are indispensable as building blocks.
the analog strain	using nondigital methods to get an image	Nondigital image generation methods can be essential for creating lots of images quickly. Pointing a camera at a piece of glass with water droplets running down it can usually produce better background footage faster than an animation package trying to do the same thing.

➤ **Following Procedure:** When I was at ABC, I started learning from Eric Daniels, who's a great animator. He taught me how to use [Sight Effects] Prisms and it got me thinking in a whole new way about how to be efficient with 3D by using procedural animation. And that whole metaphor of "procedurality" in animation or the production process is the most efficient way of working that I've ever discovered.

It's like object-oriented animation where you can have [reusable] objects. Once you animate something, you can always (reuse) that object into another animation. Say you have a formula, a sine wave passing through a particle system that's taken you some time to create, you can always use that same formula in any other animation. So you don't have to rewrite that or rethink it. With Prisms or Houdini now it's totally based on that procedure. You can take that node and put it in between two objects and with a little tweaking it looks different. It's like if you had ten nodes in the animation, ten different processes that effected a geometry, all you might do is change the one little aspect of the first node and it would ripple its way down. You wouldn't have to rebuild the geometry, as opposed to the early days of any other package, where you always had to rebuild the geometry if a client wanted to tweak this or that. You'd have to rebuild it from scratch. The procedural approach essentially lets you tweak one little parameter up the chain of procedures and it ripples down.

Right now I have hundreds of 3D animations that would work in any scene. And that's a just drag and drop, more or less, mentality. At ABC where we had different promos due every three days, that was the only system that really proved itself. With other [less modular] software packages, it was really hard to make a deadline. I think now everyone is starting to get it.

It's a templating process. You can always reuse what you do and when the client comes to you with an effect that they want, you can think back and what you've done, or what other people have done and then put it up on the Web and you can think of how to do this effect. Well, it's so complex sometimes to figure it out yourself if you're not mathematically inclined that you can just look at someone else's file and grab what you need and then tweak it and you're there. It's a way of thinking. It took me at least three months to change the way I was thinking about 3D. Once I changed the way I thought and the way I built things, it was a whole new world really. It saved so much time and it just makes the whole effects business more accessible. (Cody Harrington)

⇨ ⇨ ⇨ **MONKEYS AND GUERRILLAS**

There was this scene where a little boy runs to pick up a telephone and as he's running he's supposed to morph into a monkey. Well, morphing is really difficult if you don't have your subject in the same place doing the same motion, you know, and try to get a monkey to act. It just doesn't work. And to top it all off they didn't lock the camera off, they shot the kid, then they moved the camera a little bit, then they shot the monkey. Even the backgrounds didn't match. So we basically, had to morph. We created a three-dimensional gorilla foot that came down and squished the little kid, when he squished him we shift the frame so it made it look like there was a little earthquake there and it popped up and there was the monkey there. So it took care of the camera shift, took care of the fact that they weren't in the right place at the right time and still got the story idea across. (Barry Silver)

AltNeuland

Here and there, I've been dropping hints that a lot of what passes as an innovative postproduction technique is really just an adaptation of something that's been around for a while as an analog technique. There is a lot to be learned from traditional and experimental animators who have already tried to do many effects you might come up with without the benefit of digital tools. For instance, in the old days, if you wanted to intentionally degrade your image, such as in a film like Woody Allen's *Zelig* (1983), you might just physically scratch on the celluloid itself and then rephotograph it. It seems a crude way to work when compared with the software solutions of digital technology (no undo button), but there is a variety of useful techniques that can be mixed into a digital environment that have enormous time and cost-saving benefits.

> ➤ **Technorganic:** You're always trying to avoid being subsumed by the technology. You grab a tool, you use what's needed. I like a real natural feel to my work. Like when I'm actually building things in the real world I really enjoy using natural elements. Like with the kayak I just finished building. It's redwood strips, but it's got high-tech epoxy on the outside 'cause I don't want that thing to sink. So, I think that's a good analogy to do things. Use natural stuff to get a natural feel, but don't shun whatever technology can help out. (Doug Barnard)

Downshooting and Optical Printing

Optical printing is a technique of rephotographing film to add some sort of effect or superimposition. A downshooter is slang for a traditional animation camera rig that is suspended over a flat lit surface and shoots the images as they are laid down under the camera. Many posthouses still keep a downshooter camera rig around to shoot flat graphic titles and logos.

Rephotographing, in a digital context, can expand your tool set without buying more software. All you need is a modestly priced video camera with a decent lens. The advantage to using a camera is that everything is being acquired in real time so there is no rendering involved.

Projecting images onto unusual surfaces and shooting them can provide an entirely different emotional impact than the original material had by itself. By just using a video projector, some billowy fabric, and an electric fan, your image can have an ethereal quality that would take more effort to create digitally.

Rephotographing or scanning individual registered frames, sometimes called the photo-roto technique, is another way to create an unusual look that transforms the image itself into a malleable object. Frames from the original material are printed out in some fashion and are reanimated back into motion as three-dimensional objects. They can be crumpled, cut, burned, soaked, or wrapped onto any surface while being rephotographed, frame by frame. The viewer becomes conscious that these are individual pictures being shown in succession.

Stop Motion

Stop-motion photography is frame-by-frame photography of three-dimensional subject matter. It is normally used to animate an inanimate object. After each frame or two is exposed, either the camera or the subject is moved incrementally and the process is repeated. When played back at normal running speed, the illusion of movement is created. Claymation and time-lapse photography are good examples of techniques that employ stop-motion photography.

Some Guerrilla Applications
for Stop-Motion Photography

○ *Mini-telecine:* This technique is a great hack for a no-budget 35mm shoot. It requires an autowind, continuous-shooting 35mm camera. Choose a short distinctive action such as a bowler striding toward the lane or a loopable action such as someone doing a simple dance step. Shoot an entire roll of 36 exposures and have them processed to PhotoCD. A PhotoCD can hold 100 images so you can almost squeeze three rolls of film onto one disk. The result will be a stylized sequence whose "jerkiness" of motion will depend on the speed of the action and the speed of the autowind (usually between 1/25 and 1/2 second). You can soften the jerkiness by adding a trailing motion effect.

You will probably want to batch process the sequence using a conversion tool such as Equilibrium's Debabelizer from the PhotoCD file format into a QuickTime file or a series of Targa or PICT files for use in video. One nice aspect of the PhotoCD technique besides the pristine film look is the variety of resolutions that the format provides. You can use a variation on this recipe and use oversized images and then zoom or pan over the image during compositing. The total cost including film should be between $1.00–$2.00/frame.

- *Shuffling: Redistributing frames in random order:* Can create very radical or subtle effects depending on how much the subject in the frame is moving.

- *Faux time lapse:* This is a use of stop-motion combined with replacement animation. Say you want to show something like an apple being consumed into thin air or a wall being graffiti-ed. You lock down the camera like you would for time-lapse photography, but you keep adjusting the subject matter and shooting only the frames you want (unwanted frames can also be removed later). Also works well when played backwards when the object goes from a distressed state back to its original pristine condition.

- *Offsetting (nontraditional strobe effects):* This is a variation on the mathematical manipulation of frames such as the effect created by traditional strobing. A 1/3-second strobe shows every 10th frame for a duration of 10 frames, making the motion appear staccato and stylized. Other offsets include doing a procedure to every nth frame for a desired effect. Ideas: Just using black every nth frame for a frame or more (this creates a flickering visual tension as images are being hidden from the viewer; it usually makes them pay closer attention to the content of the frame); making every nth frame a different size for an undulating effect; making every nth frame a slightly different take of the same shot or the same shot offset many frames.

o   *Time-shifting:* There was once this "Star Trek" episode where this group of aliens lived in such an accelerated dimension that the crew members of the Enterprise seemed to be standing still. It's an interesting concept that might visually express the notion that we don't all move to the same rhythm in life. In this technique, your subject is moving very slowly, perhaps licking an ice-cream cone, and people and other objects in the background and foreground are moving at normal speed. When speeded up, your subject will be moving at normal speed while everything else zooms past.

An inverse use of this technique can be used when your subject is lip-synching to a prerecorded track such as in a music video. Play the recorded track back at double speed and have the subject mimic the track at double speed; shoot the scene double the normal frame rate (or slow down a normal frame rate 50% in post). The result will be that the subject is in slow motion but the lips and the soundtrack appear normal. This usually works for short sequences before the subject drifts out of synch with the track. (Technically this isn't stop motion, but I thought you should know about it anyway.)

Look or Luck

With so much specialized software on the market for special effects, you may be lulled into a kind of laziness. The client wants the look from that music video; fine, just pull the shrinkwrap from the latest effects package or download a plug-in and there you go. In some cases, this may even be the best route. However, it still demands your eyes, experience, and spider sense to make it all come together. It is ultimately you who is still driving the software. The look is a function of how well you drive. The diguerrilla is, to my thinking, more of a clever cabbie who knows every side street rather than the stretch limo that rumbles straight into midtown traffic.

Lastly, you may be struck by pangs of guilt or sentimental anxiety that some of these corner-cutting techniques are hacks or cheats; you might feel they compromise artistic originality in the interests of time. Well, to those sensibilities, I say, "Get over it." For the guerrilla, much of the creativity is how to make prefab look plain fab.

Digital Audio:
Bring the Noise

> **"** *Sometimes a scream is better than a thesis.* **"**
> —*Ralph Waldo Emerson*

✓

I avoided writing this chapter until the end because audio feels like a vast unexplored jungle to me, alluring and forbidding at the same time. I know intuitively that sound is fundamental to great video; all I have to do is turn down the volume when I'm watching television to realize the primacy of sound. I have great respect for the creative potential of audio, yet I also feel that I still have an infantile understanding of what is possible. I have neither the musical nor scientific training to dissect sound academically. My approach is therefore more instinctual and improvisational than in other production disciplines. However, like a native river guide who knows the route by sense, I've developed a reliable acoustic memory, which is something you will acquire the more you work with sound. You will learn to "feel" your way through a mix. This

aural intuition is, for me, a secret weapon—one that I am still learning to master. In this chapter, we will begin to listen to the pictures and discover just how powerfully they can speak.

Guerrilla production, in most cases, gives audio short shrift. Almost invariably, the effort and emphasis are on creative treatment of visuals, and audio is given a kind of sober pragmatism at the end. Usually, if the narration and dialogue can be heard clearly and everyone isn't too annoyed with the music, we can move on. There is a bit of private remorse knowing that a project has been completed with killer images, dynamic editing, arresting graphics—and merely adequate audio. But what can you do, says the always-jabbering voice in your head, there are only a few dozen hours in a day.

This scenario, unfortunately, is far too common. Picture gets all the hoopla and attention, and audio slips back into the shadows, or is wholly dominated by music. Only when something has gone wrong is serious notice taken. But this is conventional thinking; the diguerrilla knows better and should be ready to exploit the opportunities that audio presents.

Digital Audio: A Strategic Briefing

In the abstract, digital audio is the same binary material as digital video—a file of information describes the sound wave so that it can be copied and kept on a computer storage device. Technically, however, it's a lot easier to deal with than video. It is a leaner type of information, generally occupying far less space than video even at the highest fidelity. There are no colors and screen pixels to keep track of, only volume, frequency, sample rate, and stereophonic data.

Because of its less complicated structure, the obstacles to representing audio digitally were conquered well before those of digital video. By the time the first QuickTime movie sputtered onto a computer desktop, there were already sophisticated computer-driven systems for creating and editing different types of digital sound. In the 1980s, independently produced music exploded out of bedrooms and garages across the world largely due to the availability of inexpensive digital audio equipment and upstart guerrilla production efforts.

Today, a garden-variety personal computer, with little or no hardware enhancement, is capable of manipulating full-bandwidth digital audio with an extremely high degree of sophistication. Most of the technical obstacles in dealing with digital audio have been deftly handled. Those working with multimedia and the Web have probably already discovered the technical and economic advantages of working with audio—it's cheaper to work with than video, it takes up less digital "space," and it's easier to maintain the quality across varying distribution formats and bandwidths.

Creatively, audio can be full of subtle pleasures and intriguing challenges. Working with sound provides an opportunity to create a more fully realized "world" on screen without having to necessarily show it visually. Much of the creativity in working with sound comes from what I call "subtexturing" images—giving them more depth and impact when viewed with the final audio mix. Sound design, when practiced with the same level of inspiration as visual design, produces stunning results.

The Alchemy of Sound Design

Psychologically, the viewer interacts with sound in a different way than with picture. Picture is a "make me believe it" paradigm wherein the viewer is constantly making barely conscious decisions about what they are seeing and deciding if they "buy it." The sound designer must forget assumptions inherent in the way we perceive and start listening to the character of the sound as opposed to the source of the sound. Sound doesn't always need to be typecast; sometimes a buzz saw doesn't have to play a buzz saw. Sound has perceptive "elasticity," which can be manipulated for different emotive results.

An image is a statement of some kind of on-screen reality that the viewer is asked to accept. Sound, on the other hand, is a suggestion, a trigger to bring the viewer's internal world and map it onto the image. Sound seeps into the viewer's receptors with far less evaluation. In fact, the viewer is much more willing to participate and help create the illusion in their imagination.

A simple example might be some low-lit footage of dusk in a tree-lined park. By itself, a nice image but not particularly remarkable or visually striking. By adding just a few sounds, some sparsely chirping birds and a few lonely crickets, the shot now has one particular emotional reality, perhaps one of tranquility. Layer in a soothing music track, not too overbearing, perhaps a bit of flute and piano and a touch of oboe, and the emotional reality has shifted again; maybe there's a bit of melancholy in the mix now. Finally, overlay a gravelly grandfatherly narrator's voice talking about some childhood memory, and the cumulative result is some dreamy nostalgic effect.

Take the same image. Add a busier suburban feel—some light traffic, an airplane overhead, dogs barking in the distance, children's voices and bicycles. Someone screaming at a crying kid to get in the house. You've created a different kind of place from the same image—someplace less sentimental. Mix in some ambient music, perhaps some long high notes from an electric guitar and a bit of shimmer from a drum kit's high hat, the mood becomes a bit more tense, fraught with the stress of modern life. Off screen, two kids are talking about how there is absolutely nothing to do in this boring town. The soundtrack has transformed a benign park into a symbol of suburban frustration.

> **The Glitz Buffer Overload:** Some things are overdone and it's really hard to put the brakes on. I've mucked things up really bad and I've gone back to very simple versions of it. Even with music. You can overlayer or overdo music and that's a real good learning tool for what you can do with visuals. You can just get muddy, just start sounding muddy. Simple is the best. But you have to be a good designer or work with a good designer, otherwise it really starts to look [or sound] pretty hokey. (Cody Harrington)

This is the mission of sound design: guiding, beseeching, arm-twisting the viewer to "read" an image the way you intend it to be read. Sound locates the viewer in time and space. It is a landscape rich with possibilities, accessible to diguerrillas through the economics of digital technology. It is your secret weapon.

Tracks, Hacks, and Cul-de-Sacs

Before we stroll too far down the yellow-brick road of artistic freedom and aesthetic whimsy, let us ground this conversation in the tools and techniques of audio design and production.

Sound and Fury

The basic practices are similar to the digital image side of the equation with the possible exception of the mix. You begin by gathering elements. In a live-action shoot, you are often provided with location sound (also called production tracks), the audio that was recorded during the shoot consisting of environment (or ambience) and dialogue. Depending on the production, a news story for example, the production tracks may be the only audio you will use. However, a sound designer sees the production tracks as only a base from which to build. In fact, though you want the best location sound possible, sometimes the production tracks may be so poorly recorded and so full of ambient noise that they are unusable. Then you may be forced to "loop" or replace dialogue.

As you start to assemble a rough cut of video and production audio, you will begin to notice a number of sounds that could be

---

Tangent #1138

Dialogue replacement is a time-consuming process and is sometimes harder than shooting the original footage because the voice talent has to match the performance and rhythm on screen. For short spurts of dialogue, a guerrilla can probably get away with looping the picture a few times and recording a few takes in their own studio, hoping to get lucky with performance and sync. If you have a lot of dialogue replacement and you absolutely can't reshoot, you probably will have to pony up the cost of a real ADR (automated dialogue replacement) studio, and it will still be painstaking. Unless, of course, you're happy with the Italian cinema look of partially synchronous dialogue, then you can try it yourself.

---

accentuated or were never in the scene to begin with but might significantly add to the overall result. For example, a siren in the distance on an urban street immediately signals trouble. These are considered sound "effects" because they are put in for their effect and are not part of the original production tracks. Sound effects range from environmental sounds like rain and crickets to human sounds like footsteps and sniffles to made-up sounds like phasers and fairy dust.

Typically there are three ways to acquire these sounds. One is through a sound library that has an archive to browse through much like a library of stock images. However, unlike stock images where a less-than-perfect choice will stand out like a sore bitmap, sounds are a lot more malleable and adapt easier when transplanted into your project. The second method is to record them yourself out in the field with a portable DAT recorder, minidisc recorder or other recording device. The third method is to "Foley" the sounds, meaning that they are recorded in a studio with conditions emulating the necessary sound environment. The Foley artist, one adept at fooling your ear with all sorts of auditory tricks, has been around since the age of radio. There are times when nothing else will do and this old analog skill is as precious as fire-starting was in our cave-dwelling days.

How important is it to own a decent sound library even if you aren't a sound specialist? I say, *muy muy importante*. A good digital sound library is byte-for-byte a better long-term investment than an image library (though I recommend both). For starters, it's a relatively cheap investment. Sounds don't have the same price tag generally as images. In fact, a lot of the cheesy bargain-bin sound effects CDs that you find at your local record store have a good percentage of clean, well-recorded, useful sound effects. Even a few good sounds make it well worth the $8–9 investment; they carry a royalty-free license, and they can be reused many times (a car door slam will have a long life, whereas if you keep using the same cloud image in every production, it is more likely to be noticed). Generally, there will be three or four categories of sounds you will need on an ongoing basis: weather/nature ambiences, people ambiences (various crowds and urban environments), everyday sounds (home, office, school), and exaggerated sounds (cartoonish, sci-fi, explosions, etc.), but specialized needs will arise for individual projects.

⇨ ⇨ ⇨ **FOLEY EXAMPLES**   *Sound Effects*

Arrow: *Through the air:* Swish a stick through the air. *Hitting a target:* Throw darts into a dart board.

Blows: *On the head:* (1) Strike a pumpkin with a mallet. (2) Strike a melon with a garden hose. (3) Strike a baseball glove with a garden hose. *On the chin:* (1) Lightly dampen a large powder puff and slap it on the wrist close to the mic. (2) Hold a piece of sponge rubber and strike with the fist. (3) Slip on a thin rubber glove and strike the bare hand with the gloved hand.

Brook: Gently blow through a straw into a glass of water.

Collision: Drop a knife into a slightly tipped tub, shake broken glass in a box, and crush wooden boxes.

Creaking floor: Twist an old desk drawer.

Elevator: Any speed controlled motor (sewing machine).

Elevator door: Roll a roller skate along a short plank. Let it strike a metal plate for closing.

Falling body: (1) Simulate with arms and elbows dropping onto a table simultaneously; then let forearms drop together. (2) Drop a sack of sand to the floor.

Fire: Crumple cellophane slowly or vigorously; playback slower.

Fist blows: Hit a large, wet rubber or cellulose sponge.

Footsteps in snow: Fill chamois bag with cornstarch. Knead bag in footstep rhythm.

Railroad locomotive: Rub a stiff brush over coarse sandpaper glued to a resonating box.

Rain: Sand or salt sprinkled onto a paper held over a microphone. Add rice to simulate hail.

Shot: Slap a leather or plastic pillow or a cardboard box with a wooden dowel or yardstick. Close a book sharply. Keep mic from air blasts.

Surf: Roll BB shot around an oval hat box.

Sword: Clash and scrape knives or iron rods together.

Walking in mud: Make walking sound with hands in soggy newspaper.

You also will accumulate a lot of good sounds from your productions. Because you are editing digitally, it is easy to pull those evergreen sounds and catalog them on a disk. A CD-ROM can hold hundreds of 10- to 60-second soundbites. Just bear in mind that, just like with video, you want to store them in the best file format possible, even if you think you will mostly be recompressing these sounds for use in multimedia and Web-related projects. Storing the sound in a QuickTime, WAVE, or AIFF format (though in my subjective experience, SoundDesigner™ files suffer the least amounts of data corruption and are compatible with a number of editing systems) with at least 16-bit, 44 KHz bandwidth (and 20-bit, 48 KHz for music if possible; stereo is not usually necessary for sound effects unless there are special dynamics involved) will give you the most flexibility for use down the road, even if the files take up a bit more disk space. These file formats are widely accepted across diverging platforms and applications.

Record or import the sounds with the least number of analog/digital conversions. In other words, avoid transferring the audio through analog cables whenever possible. If you record onto digital audio tape, attempt to bring the audio into your editing system through the digital S/PIDF or EBU or FireWire connectors instead of the analog RCA or XLR jacks. If you're pulling the sound off a CD, use software to transfer the audio file directly to your hard drive from the CD-ROM drive instead of playing it on a CD player and running analog RCA cables to your editing system's inputs. Audio, in general, is more forgiving than video in that it takes longer to notice the noise building up from analog transfers. But don't count on this. Practice aural hygiene and keep those files pristine.

It's more convenient to have a lot of different sounds at your fingertips in a digital format than it is to hunt around various catalog sources at the last minute or browse through an audio studio's library at their hourly rate. You will save time because you will be familiar with your own library and able to be more efficient about finding the right sound. Finally, you'll be more creative because you'll be willing to throw that air compressor sound into the mix because you know exactly where it is, and it will only take an extra minute to see if it works or not. If you're struggling to find the sounds, you will in some sense begin to censor yourself because of the time and expense constraints.

We Like Mics

Sound recording on location is a guerrilla endeavor by its very nature. Unless you are recording on a sound stage, the environment will normally be hostile to getting clean sound. Ambient noise, electrical hum, and sound reflections can all become enormous problems. A good sound recordist is constantly rigging up blankets and strange foam panel inventions to try and get closer to audio heaven, total isolation. There are so many variables in recording clean sound—microphone quality, cable quality, sound level, proximity, sibilance, interference, etc.—that you must for-

Listen and Learn #117

Nonstandard Sound Acquisition: A lot of material written about sound recording expounds upon acoustic theory, microphone technology, and cable shielding. But what if you don't have time to go to a location and record an interview? What if you need some immediate report? One quick and dirty digital technique is to use phone answering software available for most personal computers such as Megaphone from Cypress Research Corporation. These applications are extremely cheap ($20–50, or they are sometimes included with a modem purchase) and work just like an answering machine except the messages are digital sound files and can be converted from their native format (usually WAVE or SND at 8-bit, 11 KHz) to any necessary format.

Don't want to dedicate a phone line and turn an expensive computer into a fax machine? JFAX.COM, a digital fax service, also provides digital voice messaging. For $13 per month, they provide you with a personal phone number in any city and send the faxes and voicemail messages as attachments to your email address. Now you can have guerrilla sound elements easily delivered to you anywhere in the world. These won't be tour-de-force recordings, but sometimes content and convenience outweigh other factors. Besides, you used to spend time with an equalizer trying to get that telephone sound; now you get it instantly.

If you're not happy with the quality of the answering machine software, you can tap your phone with an audio coupler from Radio Shack (Part #273-1374) and run the phone signal through your mixing board to balance it and into your digital audio workstation. A 0.1 microfarad capacitor (#272-1069) protects the transformer from the constant voltage that's always on a phone line, and keeps the coupler from interfering with normal dialing and hanging up. If you're getting parts from a more comprehensive supplier, a capacitor with a 100-volt rating will provide a safety margin.

give my stepping over all of them (I will assume that you will either do the best you can or hire someone that knows better) so that I may leap to the very heart of the matter.

In the beginning there was the word, but no one could hear the word because they used the wrong microphone. If your audio is being acquired through an inappropriate device, it is virtually impossible, even with the best digital technology available, to get the right sound. Even if audio is not your bread and butter, a few good microphones are a tremendous guerrilla investment. They all have unique recording characteristics, and they don't become obsolete (old mics, like the large "ribbon" mics used in the golden age of radio, are usually very much in demand because of their distinctive acoustic response).

Basic Survival Kit:

○ *Lavallier (or tie clip mic):* The necessary evil. They're not the best sounding mics, but they are so darn convenient; they get you right up near the mouth of the speaker without being noticed visually. Get the wireless kind, even though they are sometimes a pain in the fanny pack because of occasional signal interference and battery drain. They are the classic interview microphone or location host microphone because the main subject is free to roam around without worrying about cables or going off-mike. Their drawbacks include a lot of distortion if the subject becomes too active and the microphone starts rubbing on their clothing. Multiple speakers must be separated by some space so that sound spill is minimized.

- ○ *Cardiod:* A more directional microphone. There is a whole range of cardiods, from the fairly low-sensitivity TV reporter style to more sensitive music recording designs. If you're only investing in a single microphone as your "studio mic," make it one with a nice beefy sound for voiceovers; a voiceover on a cheap PA microphone can just about kill a project. Be sure to invest a small amount in a screen to help with pops and hisses from your talent.

- ○ *Hypercardiod:* Also known as a shotgun mic. These are very directional mics that are classically used in "boom" situations where a mic is suspended on a grid or pole, out of camera view, above the action. It's the best way to record multiple-speakers with one microphone and usually has a more natural location sound than the flatness of a lavallier.

There are also other specialized microphones that you may want to rent for specific situations—mics built into plates and other mics that can be placed into an environment for clandestine recording. The essential challenge for the guerrilla is weighing convenience, portability, and manpower against the rules of pristine sound recording. Will you even have the budget for a separate sound recordist? Do you even know enough about the parameters of the shoot to predict what conditions prevail? (Who knew that B-1 bomber drills would be going on in that area all day?)

Six Factors That Influence Mic Selection and Placement:

1. Is the mic in or out of the picture?

2. What is the focal length of the shot?

3. How many people in the shot must be heard?

4. Where are the people situated?

5. What is the extent of movement?

6. Is the sound stereo?

The point is not to get stuck with the limited sound from the mic attached to the camera as your only location source. Do whatever you must to get more sound coverage. Treat the location as an FBI stakeout where you want to hear everything with a minimum amount of running around. As always, the diguerrilla is prepared with cheap redundant solutions:

AVND CAMERA MIC ONLY

Stakeout Procedure

○   *Wear a wire.* If you can't get wireless lavallier mics, or if there's interference in the signal, put some standard lavs going into portable DAT players and place them on the speakers. Whereas audio cassettes run at all kinds of different speeds and are therefore mostly unreliable for sync work, a DAT runs at a constant rate; there may be possible sync problems, but none that can't be overcome. Use this procedure in addition to a boom mic. At the very least, you will have some backup wild sound to supplement the boom track.

BACKUP LAVS

○ *Plant bugs.* When you're casing the location, quickly decide on places where mics could be put in stationary place, and either be hidden or be a natural part of the scene. For example, a slim microphone, near a computer, looks perfectly natural today in the age of computer telephony. Desktop microphones are quite easy to hide, particularly in a medium shot. Place short shotguns and sensitive cardiods in light fixtures and vases and any other discreet spot where action might take place. If you are running a few mics, bring a small field mixer to balance input; send the signals to different audio channels on your videotape or separate recording devices so that they can be properly mixed.

○ *Tap available sources.* If the location already has sound amplification going on, plug into the existing infrastructure. So many events (a public speech, a concert, a wedding, etc.) already have a public address system set up and at least some crude mixing console available. Find a way to plug in and record off the available board or run your own microphone through the existing setup. At the very least, get your portable DAT recorder up to the podium and near the speaker.

Track Attack

Way before the digitally inspired concept of "video tracks," there was analog multitrack recording for audio. Audio, more frequently than video (complex video composites notwithstanding), requires a number of tracks to play all the necessarily audible elements simultaneously. Musicians and sound designers went from early 2-track and 4-track systems and eventually topped out at 48 tracks because manufacturers couldn't cram any more channels onto the recording tape. That problem has been overcome by gang-syncing multiple machines together and building mammoth mixing boards. However, the basic idea has remained the same— lay portions of sound down on various tracks and then perform a mixdown to two channels (or more if the project is for surround sound) where the volumes of all the tracks are adjusted relative to one another to attain the most satisfying combination.

The drawbacks of working with multitrack recording tape are the same as videotape; you can't just slip a bit of sound down a few frames without erasing and rerecording and hopefully not recording on top of an adjacent sound on the the same track. With a digital track, all the advantages of physically cutting and splicing are available along with all the advantages of nondestructive, multiple-undo editing.

With digital multitrack recording the editor also has a better visual picture of how their mix is laid out. In the old days, and in certain old-school mixing studios today, the recording mixer used a "mixing score"—a long trail of paper with all the tracks and timings drawn out as a map for the mix. Now all you have to do is look at your screen, and the sounds are laid out and labeled for easy access.

The first thing to know about audio tracks is this: you never have enough. It was true when there were two channels available, and it's true when you have 128. Your appetite for sound expands and contracts with the capacity of your refrigerator, so to speak. Even so, for now, we'll go along with the basic premise that more is better than less.

However, if your editing system still only allows you four or eight (many allow you to have an infinite number of tracks, but you can only *hear* a certain number at the same time), you will need to resort to the venerable craft of track bouncing, otherwise known as submixing or premixing. Submixing is like having a pre-measured pancake mix on hand instead of having to make it from scratch. In other words, if you have a scene taking place at the city zoo, you may want to premix all the animal noises and people noises that will be in the background together so that all that ambient noise occupies one track instead of many.

Premixes are very convenient, especially for complicated environments and elaborate mixes. The downside of a premix is that you're committed to their relative relationship. A digital mixdown actually writes one continuous file with all the sounds in it. While you can change the overall audio level of that submix, you will no longer have access to any individual sounds within that file.

This can be a drawback if you are inexperienced at mixing. Sometimes all your subtle effects get lost, and the whole ambience begins to sound "muddy" when you layer other elements, such as dialogue and music, on top. This isn't because your elements are poorly recorded; it's because you haven't optimized your mix.

The average human ear only hears a limited bandwidth of frequencies, cycles of vibrating sound waves. In real life, when there are a lot of competing sounds in a live space, our brain can choose to filter or focus on the most important one (your child crying for example). However, when recorded together and played through stereo speakers, competing frequencies "dull" the cumulative effect. Add to that the fact that the viewer's attention is divided between sound and picture, and you begin to understand that a mix isn't just combining sound at the right level but placing it in the right context.

The Yin-Yang Thang

While I don't expect a digital guerrilla to be measuring sound frequencies and figuring out precisely which sounds might cancel each other out (you will get extra points though), you need to gain an intuitive awareness of the composition and balance of sound even if you think you don't have a musician's ear.

It's all about contrast—contrasts in volume but, even more decisively, contrasts in audio frequency. If you have a low-murmuring crowd noise (low frequency), a steam whistle (high frequency) will stand out as a bright, brilliant sound. In comparison, if that steam whistle is playing against the screeching brakes of a freight train, they will be fighting for the same general area of bandwidth, and the same steam whistle will "feel" duller.

Besides the frequency spectrum, there is the illusion of sound space—that there is a spatial location of sound. Part of this is created again through volume (distant sounds are fainter, foreground sounds are louder) and also depends on the speaker the sound plays through. Though there are four-channel and six-channel video display systems, let us keep our mission simple and limit the conversation to two-channel stereo sound. Every digital editing system today supports stereo mixing and allows interactive panning of right and left channel sound. Stereo sound is more important in video than it ever was because of hi-fi VCRs, stereo televisions, and multimedia computers. If you leave the panning faders in the middle position, you are essentially mixing mono sound and merely sending it through two speakers—not a crime, mind you, but perhaps a missed opportunity to subtly add some more excitement to your piece. To get more sound depth, you will want to creatively use channel panning.

Warning: Some of these suggestions will sound crude or even abhorrent to experienced sound editors; others will sound obvious but are worth mentioning. But hey, this is guerrilla video—it's not always pretty, kiddo. The intention here is to try to do as much work as possible, with picture, all in one editor and only save the really nasty stuff for a separate sound workstation. Of course, as your budget expands, you may want to do much more separate audio work and create that aural masterpiece. ■

Sound Design Hack Sheet

1. *Track families:* Group related tracks together. It's not easy to do submixes or "debug" your mix if dialogue is sitting

on the same track with effects or music is sharing a track with narration. For those of you who had analog film-making training, this will be obvious because you try to aim for three submixes (dialogue, SFX, and music). While this scheme doesn't need to be adhered to religiously in a digital environment (sometimes you just need to cram an extra sound in an empty spot on a track), it is an excellent rule of thumb. Make at least one of your masters with the three submixes on different channels; if your master tape has only two channels available, combine music and effects onto channel 2 and leave channel 1 for dialogue. Even though you'll end up with a mono mix in the end, it makes it easier to redub a project in another language for international distribution.

2. *Scour out mud:* We'll assume that your individual elements are recorded cleanly, but the mix is sounding murky. First, isolate what you believe is causing the mud and identify the key sound that is not projecting as clearly as you would like. It used to be that the main postproduction sound processing tool was the equalizer, designed to modulate various portions of a sound's frequency. A classic example is turning a normally recorded voice into a telephone voice by lopping off the high and low ends of the spectrum. Equalizing software and mixer circuitry is still an essential tool, but today even inexpensive sound editing packages like SoundEdit16 and SoundForge have pitch modulation software. This allows you to raise or lower the entire frequency bandwidth

223

without changing the timing and getting the "chipmunk" effect. By changing the pitch of one sound, like making the din of a restaurant rumble a bit lower, it can separate from other sounds, like a ringing phone, and feel brighter and more distinct.

Moreover, with a waveform editor, you can edit at the 1/100th and sometimes 1/1000th of a sample level instead of the 1/30th of a sample level available to you in a nonlinear video editing package. This allows you to do microsurgery on the waveforms to cut out millisecond pops and, if necessary, graft a tiny piece of neighboring sound to fill the hole. If you are concerned about maintaining sync, be careful that you are not affecting the duration of the soundfile.

3. *Flash in the pan:* Sound effects and dialogue, in general, benefit quite a bit from skillful panning. A two-shot where each individual is miked separately or reversing one-shots that depict a conversation, benefit from a judicious amount of channel separation. Only in special circumstances should you pan a sound 100% left or right as in the case of unique accent sounds, like a frog croaking in a swamp panned left and an owl panned right. Normally, pushing 60–80% in one direction will get you enough separation without feeling awkwardly polar. Tracking the sound moving target, such as a person walking across screen, can heighten the emotional impact, but be careful that the pan doesn't draw attention to itself. If the subject moves a couple feet to the refrigerator, it will be comical

for his voice to ricochet from one side of the screen to another.

4. *Hide your cuts:* While a visual cut is obvious and expected, a noticeable audio cut, unless deployed for a specific, jarring purpose, is usually interpreted as a mistake. To hide cuts on noisy production dialogue track, have some stock ambience or "room tone" on hand. This is a bit of sound from location with no one talking or moving and no planes flying overhead. It has the same ambient characteristics as the rest of the track. You can use this as filler in between moments of dialogue so that the noisy track stays constant and doesn't seem to cut in and out. If the location recordist wasn't diligent about recording "room tone," you will have to be crafty about extracting a piece of silence somewhere in the track and making it fit.

The fast and dirty fix if the ambience and the dialogue don't seem to match up perfectly: try short 3–6 frame crossfades to smooth the transitions. If it still sounds choppy, try overlaying an appropriate sound effect near the cut—a horn honking or a car going by if the dialogue is outdoors, or a faint fax machine in an office, or whatever you think you might get away with and distract the viewer's ear from the rough section.

5. *Sound collage:* Often, a shot will require additional sound that really can't be identified precisely. The client might just ask for "something creepy" or "make it more festive" or ambient sounds for a surreal environment. This is when you reach into your special folder marked "cool

[handwritten margin note:] ROOM TONE

[handwritten margin note:] SHORT CROSSFADE (3-6 FRAMES)

sounds" and start building interesting mixtures. Cool sounds don't have to be exotic; they don't have to be rare throat-singing from Tuva played backwards. They can be the sound of an electric shaver slowed down with the pitch shifted.

A sound collage is guided mainly by feel and how much time you have to mess around. Get to know what your sound editing package will do. (This is not the same as your video editing package, which has limited sound manipulation tools. You need a specific sound application that will actually let you filter and microadjust the sound sample.) You will develop shorthand tricks for recycling common sounds into unique sounds by filtering and manipulating speed, pitch, and the frequency spectrum, and by editing the waveform itself.

Make two groups of cool sounds. One should be interesting sound "beds," a kind of foundation ambience like "the humming of the engine room" or "the weird underwater xylophone ambience"; the other group should have accent sounds to overlay such as "funky static," "transformer arcs," "irregular heartbeat," or "psycho sonar." If at all possible, edit your accent sounds so that they can be "looped" and sound seamless. This is done by making sure the waveform completes a full cycle of the sound and matches up to the first frame seamlessly.

6. *Open your mouth:* I'm sure that at least at one point in your life (probably embarrassingly recently), you've picked up a microphone and just started making weird noises into

it just to see what it would sound like over the P.A. system. Well, consider that this sort of tomfoolery is how many sound effects are made. Either by using the vocal chords or by using pure breath, or a combination of both, you can produce an almost endless variety of sounds that can then be warped, distorted, and edited together to create all kinds of unusual effects such as industrial machines, insects, and nature sounds. For best results, use a low-sensitivity microphone so that you can use more air pressure without distorting the signal. Playing with your own vocal sounds is a great way to get comfortable with what your filters, pitch trackers, ring modulators, and other effects will do. The best part is, you already own the source sound generator; it's rack mounted right above your chin.

7. *Wild sound:* "Wild" sound is a term that evolved from doing location recording without any particular synchronization system. Usually its use is confined to location ambience and possible Foley work. In a diguerrilla context, wild sound is, well, wilder. Technically, sound is much more efficient to acquire across a variety of situations; you don't need any light, you don't need to focus, and sound recording devices, pound-for-pound, are cheaper, lighter, and less conspicuous than video recorders.

Consequently, you can get a lot of things on DAT, minidisc, MP3, or cassette tape that you normally couldn't get on videotape. In documentary situations, people may even say things on audiotape that they wouldn't say on video. Even if your subject is not physically accessible to shoot, you can record a phone interview: Even if it's pitch black, you can get the sound of the policemen talking to one another and speaking over their radio. Even if the guard says, "No pictures please," there is usually no prohibition against gathering sound.

I don't mean to directly encourage espionage tactics if they cross criminal or copyright infringement boundaries, but in many instances, with a little creative acquisition, your sound may be more compelling than the picture and may inspire you to rethink your visual approach.

8. *Expanding offscreen sound:* Offscreen sound is usually thought of as sound that helps extend the edges of the frame on screen; it's the sound of what you might see if the camera moved a bit to the right or left. An empty alley with the sound of a howling cat implies that just offscreen somewhere we would find that noisy cat. In classical editing, the audience is usually given a payoff for believing in the offscreen sound—we cut next to a shot of the cat. But for a diguerrilla, the formula of having picture drive sound is only one way to skin that alley cat. Sound can also drive picture in exciting ways. If there are a group of people sitting and talking, you may find that the obvious way of editing, cutting to the person speaking with an occasional reaction shot, is not the best option.

Whether the motivation is creative or technical—the cameraman may have been slow to respond; the person speaking may be boring; the sound levels may be off—there is an awful lot you can do with the sound of *what you don't see*. With the talking group, you may have lots of shots of the rest of the people who are listening and reacting. By cleverly resequencing these reactions to keep the conversation moving (you will need more than just two angles to pull this example off), you may only need to show a second or two of lip-sync to establish the person talking. Then you are free to cut to all sorts of wild sound dialogue that you may have never filmed or may be from a completely different group of people. The trick is to give the audience just a tiny hint of what they expect, a shot of the thing making the sound, and then create enough motivated action around it. Voila! You are now free of the constraints of synch-sound and can redesign the tracks to your liking.

Short sync

Lastly, you can use offscreen sound for *counterpoint*. Maybe you add sounds that haven't the remotest link to the picture for comic or impressionistic effect (e.g., seeing a picture of the president with a laugh-track underneath undermines credibility).

Try This at Home #2

You may get so excited by the possibilities of offscreen sound that you design picture specifically to create more sound possibilities. A medium-close shot of someone's torso pacing back and forth and twisting the phone cord can sometimes be more revealing than the obvious shot of the talking head. Experiment by creating a video that doesn't use any synchronous location sound but somehow "feels" like it does.

9. *Shrink to fit:* Almost invariably, at some point in the production, you need the audio to be flexible. Perhaps there were some frame count miscalculations in the film video transfer. Or maybe the software you are using has some undocumented sync problems. You might be trying to synchronize sound to a special slow-motion effect, or you just have to squeeze a 31-second spot to fit 30 seconds. Whatever the case, you will want to master the art of "rubberizing" your audio and squashing and stretching it.

    Again, this will need to be performed with software that manipulates the sound file itself, something that is usually not directly part of a nonlinear editing system. The trick is to extend or compress the duration of the track without changing the pitch of the sound unless you want the warbling effect of a sound playing through an underpowered tape recorder. Hopefully your software has filters that maintain pitch automatically, but you may have to filter the file in two passes, one for duration and one for pitch.

    Say the final product shot with the spokesmodel is 5 seconds but you need it to be 4. One alternative that occasionally works might be to speed the video up to 120% or (36 fps). The best way is to ramp the speed change so that the video is running at normal speed by the end of the shot. Then make several microextractions of noncritical sound usually at the decay of the sound wave. These subframe edits, if well placed, will almost pull the dialogue a tiny bit out of sync but then regain sync by the end of the shot. The best part is that you don't have to do any additional sound filtering so that the sound quality matches all the other dialogue in the spot.

10. *Relative silence:* Silence can be a powerful use of audio. Maybe that sounds a little mystical, but if a soundtrack is about contrast and counterpoint, then silence is the true antithesis of sound. Too many programs have wall-to-wall sound; they don't breathe. Silence is used within a program to provide a pause or shift mood; the absence can serve to rivet the viewer on the image and provide emphasis. It's also a lot less work.

However, rather than absolute silence (there is no such thing as absolute silence anyway except maybe when you're dead), we're talking about relative silence. Use a minimal sound, a bit of room tone, tape hiss, a very low frequency, a very subtle ambience, but put something on the track. It will register as silence to the viewer, but it

ambient sound — room tone

Addendum #7a

One-Track mind: Even if you're mixing for surround sound, always test your mix in mono. There will always be a time where a VHS copy is shown on a cheap television monitor and you want to make sure that most of the track gets across. By the same token, you want to make sure that you're not wasting your time on all kinds of subtle audio tweaks when you know the final product will only be played through a low-end speaker. Many digital editing systems allow you to just hit a button to hear the mix in mono; in other situations you may have to route it through the mixing board and toggle a switch to hear the tracks all together.

mono preview

will be a gentler silence than dropping out the sound completely (and the viewer won't wonder if their equipment is malfunctioning).

The Sound of Music

Unless you're doing a music video where the music *is* the soundtrack, you will be working with music as one of many sound elements. What music to use is probably one of the most important decisions you and your client will make; it will set the tone and rhythm of the video. I'm going to trust you to choose the right music, and just concentrate on discussing its best use.

Parental Warning #4—Rights and Wrongs: As I've mentioned throughout the book, be clever but don't steal copyrighted material. It bears repeating here because it is almost instinctual to want to use music that you like in your videos. Unfortunately, that music usually belongs to a record company. Unless you are certain this video will never circulate publicly in any kind of commercial context, use music that is royalty-free or for which you have secured the rights. Thanks. ■

Surge and Dip

The first distinction that will give your productions more power is freeing yourself from the inclination toward long music beds. Having a lot of music in the mix can hide a multitude of other recording and mixing sins, but too much creates other problems. Unless the video is, by nature, musical, music should be an important emotional accent rather than a monotonous audio element. Wall-to-wall music, no matter how good, especially when played under FX and voice tracks, eventually undercuts the power of the piece and tends to disengage the viewer from the content.

One general approach or guideline is "surging and dipping" the music. Frequently, the viewer gets the main emotional impact of the music in a short burst at the beginning, between scenes, or during a montage, and then the music dips down and eventually disappears or cross-fades into something else underneath the other tracks. The surge can be a shorthand way of establishing place and mood at the top of the scene, but it becomes distracting if it's not attenuated.

Even if the track is meant to be subtle in the background, it will benefit from getting a chance to fully register with the viewer before it is mixed further back. The ear then does a better job of interpolating that music throughout the scene because it has become aware of its presence.

Motive and Motif

Why are you using the music you are using? Because you like it? Because it's your client's favorite? That's a good start, but you might want to think it through a bit further. If you are using a variety of types of music, the eclectic mix may well serve some larger theme such as youth, nostalgia, high culture, and so on. Think about what the cumulative effect of the music will be even if you are working on a short-format piece. In longer-format work, you are trying to build different subthemes; you may want to return to the similar music a number of times with different variations ready, using the music more like a symphonic composer to emphasize narrative evolution.

If you are using MIDI-generated music, creating variations is very easy since it's simple to swap out MIDI instruments or adjust tempo. If you are working with library music, make sure that you choose pieces with variation built into them; if you are working with a composer, even if he or she is scoring and timing to a rough cut of your piece, explain that you need other short variations on the composition as musical alternatives. You may find that there's something about a shot that needs a bit more simplicity or a bit more pomp. It's important to have that in your hip pocket.

Rhythm and Ruse

Since music dramatically affects the psychology of viewing, what mood we are associating with the picture, it only follows that music naturally impacts the editing of pictures. Think of the times that George Gershwin's "Rhapsody in Blue" has been used in movies like Woody Allen's *Manhattan* and a United Airlines commercial; the surge of the music dictated strong cuts between majestic shots. If the images don't fit the music with some kind of psychological connection, it usually plays as parody (sad music against slapstick or happy music against tragic images).

Equal in importance to the emotional fit is the rhythmic fit. Where do you make the cut? Cutting right on the beat conveys one kind of mood—driving, kinetic, and powerful; cutting off-beat is moodier, harsher, and even subtly disturbing. Mixing your timing can create interesting tension and play against expectation.

Semi-Rhetorical Questions	Diguerrilla Answers
Does the music always have to fade?	Perhaps suddenly cutting out of the music into the ambience track is exactly what will draw the viewer into the critical part of your message.
Do you have to use one musical cue at a time?	Perhaps two cues cut against each other can provide some clue about the theme of the piece (e.g., showing a contrast between cultures or eras).
What if the only music I have sounds cheesy?	Perhaps less is more. Maybe there are two bars in there that sound okay, and you can work them as a leitmotif. (Remember how far the TV series "Thirty-Something" got with a short guitar riff.)
What if the music is better than the other tracks?	Perhaps you should ignore all the other stuff I've written and try and use it as much as possible. Sometimes a complete message is accomplished with a few images, a bit of music, and some type.

Hell Does Freeze Over

Be prepared to scrap any logical approach in the face of a nasty glitch. An advertising guerrilla was just telling me about a new business pitch that he was working on that was based on a lot of interview footage. Upon reviewing the footage, they realized that 100% of the audio was unusable and their original concept was now toast. This is the time when you have to reach down and pull a radical alternative audio strategy out of your back pocket. In this case, with no time to reshoot, they decided to just mock the whole concept of "man on the street" interviews and dubbed whatever they wanted the person to be saying into the interview. It was a kind of *What's Up, Tiger Lily?* of new business videos, and with the proper presentational context, it was effective in winning the account.

Another diguerrilla had finished a piece that was tightly edited to music, only to find that the music that he had been told was licensed by his client was copyrighted material. With not enough time or budget to find library music and recut, he came upon the idea of using his six-year-old daughter just humming her own little tunes that she routinely made up while riding in the car. The piece, which had to do with a children's retail store anyway, benefited from the new innocent quality of a child's humming, and the client bought off on it.

These are just small examples of the radical thinking that is a diguerrilla's stock in trade. Of course, you will want to have all the redundant operations and fail-safe measures in place, but in the event that the original mission is untenable, with a radical alternative, you will march through the fear and turn defeat into victory. These sweet moments are ultimately the most beautiful kind of music to a diguerrilla's ears.

Infrastructure and Exostructure: Making the Most of Your Time and Technology

> ❝ *The nomadic life of the guerrilla fighter in this stage produces not only a deep sense of fraternity among the men but at times also dangerous rivalries between groups or platoons.* ❞
> —*Che Guevara*

Chapter 3 dealt with resource strategy as it relates to a particular project; this chapter examines resource strategy as it relates to your entire infrastructure, from your personal investment in hardware technology to cost-effectively outsourcing and partnering on different aspects of production deliverables. Perhaps the word "infrastructure" might sound a bit overwrought if you are currently piloting a single PC in a spare room at home. Nevertheless, in a wired world, any production configuration is part

of a larger infrastructure, and using that infrastructure, to your best advantage will make for better business decisions and fewer suicide rides.

Autopsy of a Suicide

I remember as a kid the fire marshall coming to school and explaining the triangle of elements that must be in place for fire to burn. He said there must be fuel, oxygen, and heat, and if you remove any single element, you can then extinguish the fire. A digital video project has its own symbiotic triangle composed of *manpower*, *horsepower*, and *brainpower*; if any of these elements are in short supply, it is likely the project will never properly ignite. When your power supply is really impoverished, the project can become a *suicide ride*. A suicide ride is when you are aware that your production pyramid is not adequately fortified for the job, but for reasons overriding logic (e.g., the rent is due, you promised a friend, you want to maintain a client relationship, your partner agreed to do it while you were at lunch), you find yourself on a six-day cruise across the burning lakes of hell.

⇨ ⇨ ⇨ **PRODUCTION PYRAMID**

Manpower: *Manpower refers not only to having the right amount of human resources on hand but also to the level and range of expertise. Creating moving images is a custom-crafted endeavor that requires a series of experience-based micro-decisions. Having too many underskilled digitrons around can be as destructive to a project as a brilliant artist trying to do everything by himself or herself.*

Horsepower: *This is another way of saying, right tool for the right job. It's great to have the right software, but if it's trying to do computation-intensive tasks on a slower machine, you're as screwed as running crappy software on a network of screaming high-octane processors. Lastly, horsepower also applies to the capacity of the enabling hardware, such as the number of VTRs and monitors available, the kind of networking capability, and the way the studio is configured logistically.*

hardware + software

Brainpower: *This is the most difficult area to measure, but for the diguerrilla, it is frequently the decisive factor that can compensate for certain deficiencies in other areas. Brainpower encompasses both creative talent and administrative ability. Brainpower is what tracks the moving target of production to continuously make key decisions that will impact quality, logistics, and cost.*

We're not talking about the normal diguerrilla tendency to promise just a bit beyond what you've delivered in the past; this we might call confidence or courage or *cajones*. We're talking about taking on a project well beyond the scope of your current capacity; this we might label as self-destructive or, in acute situations, completely psycho.

I recall one situation where we had completed a rather arduous all-night edit session and left a bunch of the transitions unrendered to expedite the edit. We had promised we could turn the project around in a day and were elated that we had finished with three hours to spare before the delivery deadline. Unfortunately, we hadn't paid attention to the number of composites and transitions we were adding; a batch render revealed that the final cut wouldn't be ready for seven hours. In this case, manpower was adequate, but horsepower was insufficient, and brainpower (that which was available being extremely sleep-deprived) was in short supply.

Suicide rides aren't just dictated by time constraints. Anytime you commit to flat-rate payment terms without knowing all the parameters of the project or overcommit your software tools beyond the routine stretch of the guerrilla imagination, you run the risk of ending up DOA (Delivering Odious Assets).

Far and away, my most oft-repeated suicidal episodes have revolved around beta or newly released software. Ignoring sane reasoning, I invariably am intoxicated by the list of new features that are included in the new release and ill-advisedly mention to a client that the system can now continually rasterize or motion-track or whatever the latest bell or whistle happens to be. The next thing I know, I'm trying to use the poorly documented new feature in a production situation, and everyone's palms are sweaty because the system has crashed several times in a row, corrupting an essential file and trashing half a day's work.

Beware new Software features

BetaRule #14

Give new software releases at least 30 days of continuous trial use before validating them for production. If you are going to experiment with a new version during a production, do it as a shadow operation. In other words, take copies of your source files and run the application on a second machine while you continue with the old software on the primary machine.

Having been duly warned that this could happen to you, also know that this *will* happen to you. It is nearly impossible by definition to make guerrilla video and not take a few suicide rides. It is with this knowledge, and by embracing this fear, that you can actually create your own insurance policy.

30 day test

Gear without Fear

The first thing that bears repeating is almost childishly simple, yet it is the easiest principle to forget: You are not your tools. The hardware and software arsenal of the digital revolution can be weapons of liberation or self-destruction. The tools only enable; you are the harbinger of creative breakthrough. Ultimately, no matter how seductive the marketing message, the newest software release will only widen your palette, not define your talent. Remember this like a home address that you can return to; otherwise, you will always be stumbling blindly through an expensive maze of technology.

> **Software Lite:** [In 1991] I was working with this 3D software called Presenter Professional, put out by this company called VIDI. And at the time it was like a total garage operation. So, tech support at the time was that I called up one of these guys and just started talking and we'd shoot the breeze for a while and I'd get my problem solved, or most likely told, "Gee, uh no, the software really can't do that." That was during the time when software didn't do too much. And you had to really sculpt your idea in terms of what the tools could do. (Doug Barnard)

The second thing to remember is that present is obsolete. The Zen master knows there is only this fleeting moment of now... and now...and now and, well, you get the idea. Nowhere is this more aptly illustrated than in the digital realm, where as soon as you get the bubble wrap off your swanky new hardware, it has already been superseded in a testing laboratory in some high-tech industrial park with tinted glass. By purchasing your workstation or camera package, you have made an investment in the future of

> **In a Rut:** I suddenly discovered myself at a real software cul-de-sac with the software that I was using and because I had specialized in Presenter Professional I hadn't really gotten any other ideas as to how things would work so I just really had to retrain myself, reinvent the whole thing. I bought my [older] SGI. What a mistake that was. Definitely buying old technology is not a good idea. Best to buy new technology that's cheap, that maybe won't do exactly what you want it to do but also try to get the savviest idea of what's going on by whatever sources you can. (Doug Barnard)

communication, but almost in the same breath, you've begun living in the past.

Having said all that, we can now discuss the value of good tools. For the diguerrilla, the object is to squeeze the most out of your gear for the longest period without sacrificing productivity. If you're going to sink hard-earned or hard-borrowed money into your own equipment, what should be your guidelines and expectations on maximizing a return on your investment? When is it smarter to rent equipment? This will depend on whether you are a boutique production service studio trying to stay in the space race with large deeply capitalized postproduction houses or a freelance broadcast designer working on your own. You also may find yourself in transition from one kind of operation to another. By identifying where you are in the digital solar system, you will be better prepared to allocate your equipment dollars appropriately.

buy or rent?

Max Headroom

This strategy is designed to maximize the life of your machine in your studio. You pay a premium for the highest-capacity multiprocessor machine of the moment and configure it for multiple uses (e.g., video compression board for editing and audio DSP card or chipset for audio editing). Make sure the CPU tower has an abundance of slots for add-on boards so that your investment can expand and multitask.

expandable hardware

Effective "maxxing" requires a bit of knowledge and clairvoyance about the future of the computer industry. What operating systems, processing chipsets, and computer architectures are being developed right around the corner? How easy will an upgrade be? Do the manufacturers who make your hardware and software components have a good track record about upgrade paths? Also ask yourself hypothetically, if I didn't upgrade at all in the next year, would this workstation still be useful to me in my work?

Retro Bargains

Retro bargains come from buying slightly behind the technology curve. Since prices tend to crash when a faster processor or newer computer architecture comes out, there are many cases where buying last year's (or last month's) model will serve you extremely well. For example, if you isolate certain tasks such as logging, scanning, or still frame/paintbox work, these tasks don't require nearly the same kind of horsepower that 3D animation or 2D compositing require. You can save 30–70% by buying a slower but adequate machine and can invest some of the savings into extra RAM and storage.

MASH Studio

The MASH (Media Agnostic Storage Hub) studio is well networked and data-centric. In other words, the most important thing is quickly moving the media and project files around to the best available machine. The "Hub" can either be a centralized server or distributed workstations or both. More attention is given to removeable media options so that the entire project can be transported to another machine running the same digital post solution. The MASH concept works exceptionally well when there are several similar models of the same system with compatible file structures. In the case of Avid technology, it might be nice to do a preliminary edit at high image quality on a relatively inexpensive system like the Xpress and then just transport the drives and project files to a Media Composer 9000 with 3D effects (not necessarily your own) to add the finishing touches. This kind of configuration works best when all the machines in the studio have the same sort of removeable drive towers and peripheral devices. It also minimizes lost production time when a system goes down.

Portable media

Gravy Train

This is the closest you get to a sure thing. You have a contract to do a long-term project (e.g., a TV series, a package of 12 infomercials, etc.). You know that your cash flow is stable for an extended period. At the beginning of the project, calculate how much of the budget is already earmarked for equipment rental and direct it toward new purchases or upgrading.

Planned upgrades

If things are already going smoothly, there is no need to stockpile the latest hardware because you've already been awarded the contract. During the length of the contract, incremental upgrades should minimize production disruptions and keep profits liquid. Key productivity enhancements or additional systems to handle overflow are high-yield investments for high-volume work. The decisive factor is making these incremental upgrades judiciously.

You don't want to be stuck with a bunch of aging equipment at the end of the project, nor do you want to have eaten up all your profits on an insatiable buying spree. At the end of the project, you can assess which equipment should be phased out and which new equipment would be worth investing in for the next Gravy Train project.

Lean and Mean

This approach is the least capital-intensive and works well for independent producers who prefer to build equipment costs into the price of each production. The only direct investment is made in a system for tracking and organizing the production. All other equipment and services are rented as needed for each production. This means a good laptop or a midrange desktop machine with a scanner and removeable storage such as a ZIP or JAZ drive will do the trick. An inexpensive color printer is very helpful for printing storyboards and other preproduction documentation. Don't skimp on RAM, as you will want to run many applications at once (e.g., a spreadsheet, a logging program, an Internet browser, and perhaps an image-editing program like Photoshop). The most important application for this system to run is a database full of all the contractors and vendors you will need to complete the project. This piece of equipment will remain functional for many years and return its investment many times over.

The downside to stripping down is that you don't have a lot of margin for error. Your budgets are based on getting in and out of a job quickly, assembling a crack team out of thin air, and turning around the project without a hitch. Being "on the clock" for every inch of the project can sometimes force you into cost/quality decisions you would rather avoid. The current guerrilla trend is to be trim-and-surly rather than downright lean-and-mean. What that means is that you invest in some slice of the production process and pay for other services when necessary; you buy production equipment that doesn't have a high price barrier but has a lot of creative return. For many, this means a reliable, low-priced nonlinear editing system or audio studio; for others, a good camera package; for still others, it's an affordable animation workstation. No matter what the project, a producer with some in-house resources has some creative and budgetary flexibility that a strictly laptop producer doesn't. Beware, guerrilla producers: It's easy to go from trim to tubby. Once bitten by the technology bug, it can become an obsession, and your simple offline bay can grow to resemble a NASA shuttle project. Keep a cool head and measure the costs and benefits carefully.

Timesharing

Like the vacation condominium concept, timesharing or shared ownership of equipment has pros and cons. The pros are very attractive: access to more and better gear without bearing the entire brunt of the cost. The cons are more subtle and insidious: how responsible and flexible are the people you are buying in with? Who will be accountable for maintenance and scheduling? Are profits shared equally? Though some timesharing schemes are just too good to pass up, many end in tears. In my experience, the best arrangements are more like bilateral trade agreements with sweetheart rates. For example, you have VTRs and extra storage, and I have a nonlinear editing setup; we agree to rent each other's gear at 30% off. It's cleaner, there's a real revenue exchange, everyone knows what's what, and the chances of getting burned in the exchange are minimized.

shared gear

Lease Caprice and Rent Lament

If you tend to have stable, long-term, high-volume production work (even if the budgets are modest), you might be tempted to lease equipment to synchronize inflow and outflow and enjoy some possible tax benefits. If you have sporadic, high-paying work, you might be inclined to rent equipment as needed. These are standard business practices; however, in digital production, they can be lethal and should be considered carefully.

Leasing

For big-ticket items, a lease usually can't be avoided. However, manufacturers and resellers are often quick to get you into a lease to meet their sales numbers when it might not be appropriate for your business model. If you absolutely need it and can't afford to finance it creatively in guerrilla fashion, try to make your lease quick and painful instead of slow and painful. Put as much money down as possible and get the shortest-term lease you can stomach, ideally 18 months to three years. If you can't put up with steep monthly payments for that period, reconsider the purchase. You will be tempted to put very little money down and then extend payments as far as possible. But this isn't a car you are buying that will still go 70 miles an hour in five years; this is a piece of technology that you know for certain will be archaic and significantly less useful in three years (or less). You will suffer making payments on a dead carcass. Lastly, if possible, negotiate into the lease that upgrades and restructuring are anticipated and that your leasing company will cooperate with helping you keep your gear current. If they drag their feet about restructuring the lease, you may be forced to perform out-of-pocket upgrades on equipment that the leasing company might claim ownership of in the event of a dispute.

lease savvy —
3 year life of
technology

Renting

Renting is best suited for commodity items such as VTRs, cameras, and media storage needed on a short-term basis. They are in good supply, prices—particularly in urban areas—are competitive, and you don't have to deal with maintenance. High-performance computers tend to rent for high rates relative to actual worth. Paying a premium rental price is worthwhile to use a specialized piece of equipment, especially if you know that this is a rare situation that doesn't often come up. For instance, it might be worth it to rent a timecode DAT machine and 9-pin converter/controller box for that odd production where audio was recorded separately on DAT. If rates are extremely high, check and see if you can outsource this as a service rather than a rental (e.g., digitize this timecode DAT for me to Avid media format). For most other wild-sound situations, your prosumer DAT machine or CD-R audio works just fine.

> **Do the Math:** The things you want to know about rental equipment are if the price includes delivery and basic installation or whether that is a separate fee. A simple example: if a UVW 1800 Betacam deck rents for a bargain at $250/week but has a $75 delivery fee each way, you may be better off with a sturdier PVW-2800 for $400/week and no delivery fee.

Revolving Door

If absolutely necessary, there is a way to keep up with the Joneses without completely draining your resources. If your workflow is steady and your competitive edge relies heavily on having the fastest desktop computing power available (e.g., for 3D animation and composite-heavy work), it can often be more economical to short-cycle your gear. Short-cycling creates your own upgrade path by playing with the flow of the market. An example might be buying a new CPU and selling it every 3–6 months if

> ➤ **Renting Software:** This is one of the black arts not often discussed around the campfire, but it is effective in the heat of production when you need another workstation running an animation or compositing application but don't have an extra license. Some resellers will rent software (usually with hardware key or other elaborate piracy protection), but they won't advertise this service; you need to hint at it or make noises about trying before you buy. The other source is your informal diguerrilla network; it's a good way to keep the cash in the community and build allies. Usually a freelancer with her own gear will part with software for a soft rate when they are on downtime or want to take a vacation.

your workflow justifies it. Time the sale before your system steeply depreciates and when the new purchase model is just starting to be discounted. You may lose 10–30% in the resale process, but that loss will be cheaper than renting the same machine for that period of time. And you will always have the latest equipment at your disposal.

It has also become easier to simply upgrade your processor speed and not have to trade in the entire CPU tower, thus avoiding the inconvenience of setting up a new machine, formatting a hard drive, and installing the software all over again. Don't underestimate the cost of this kind of "sys config" downtime.

*loss of 10–30%
is less than
renting*

Shelf Life

Since part of the guerrilla instinct is to get the most bang for the buck (though fortunately most draw the line at grand theft), entrepreneurial digi-talent often piece together their rigs from separate components instead of opting for a turnkey solution. This has obvious financial advantages. However, your bottom line shouldn't solely be calculated in up-front costs. This chart looks at the amortizing potential of a sampling of various equipment.

Long term (3–5 years)	Mid term (1–3 years)	Short term (under a year)
large-capacity hard drives	video compression board/audio DSP board	CPU
flatbed scanner	additional RAM	current version software
RGB & NTSC/PAL digital/analog monitor	analog NTSC/PAL monitor	effects accelerator board
audio mixer & speakers	CD-R drive	modem
digital Betacam VTR	BetacamSP VTR, DV camera, DVD drive	Hi-8 VTR
professional digital camcorder	prosumer DV camera	digital still camera

Lease	Rent
There's absolutely no point in leasing them unless your company refuses to own assets outright. Otherwise, there is no economic advantage.	Again, there is relatively little rental market for this kind of system, but it might be worthwhile if you can negotiate a very, very cheap deal.
Don't do it unless we're talking about a serious high-end camera and you are very committed to the shooting end of production.	Camera rental is a mainstay in the video rental business. A lot of still-camera stores are getting into the act on the DV video side as well. Renting cameras is a great way to try out a camera before you buy (usually only prosumer and professional models are available for rental), and of course, if you need a Betacam package for a weekend, $500 beats the $50,000 purchase price.

is—right under my Ron Popeel, Miracle Bass Master—*Caveat emptor.* In plain English, "Buyer beware." But given all the caveats placed upon you, the bargain-hunting *emptor,* there are some sweet hardware deals out there that deserve the attention of your wandering eye.

The basic rule of thumb is, the less moving parts, the better. CPUs, RAM, circuit boards, mixers, cables, microphones, digital still cameras, and workstation furnishings, if in working order, are the safest bets. Hard drives, speakers, removeable drives, monitors, and video cameras are harder to diagnose but can pay off if they are well cared for and have low mileage. Unless I really know the ownership history well or the price is so cheap that any use at all makes it worthwhile, I normally stay away from scanners, VTRs, CD-ROM drives, and DAT recorders (machines with delicate moving parts and mechanical read/write devices).

When to Hold, When to Fold

Just as important as knowing which equipment to buy, lease, or rent is knowing which equipment *not* to buy, lease or rent—in other words, which production tasks are not worth taking on; which require specialized equipment you aren't willing to invest in; which demand a kind of arcane technical expertise that is, for good reason, outside your skill set. When figuring all this out, cost is not the only factor. Hassle is equally important. We can refer to this as *real cost,* which totals price, time and effort together. Though the guerrilla is wont to cut corners by any possible means, there is no point in cutting your own throat in the process.

The Digital Imaging Bureau

Though these digital prepress shops began in the '80s serving the desktop publishing crowd, they now boast a wide variety of services that have digital video applications. (http://www.encoding.com, for example, is set up as an online service bureau to prepare video Internet streaming). For starters, they might do on-site PhotoCD processing, which is superior and more time efficient than scanning photo negatives with a slide or flatbed scanner. They can also perform oversized printing if you need a sign or logo for some shoot or need to repurpose an image in some unusual way (e.g., printing video frames). They can produce high-resolution color prints with exceptional color fidelity. Finally, they can perform a high-fidelity drum scan of material that you may not have the capacity to scan such as slides and oversized artwork.

The best digital imaging bureaus are open 24 hours, can receive files electronically over the Internet, and can turn around jobs quickly. As with any technical service provider, it is important to create a relationship with someone who can track your job to answer questions and provide you with important information about how to prep and deliver your material.

The Post House

This is distinct from what I call a "post boutique," which specializes in a few services, usually offline editing or graphics or audio. A full-service post house is more like a department store for video postproduction, providing services from telecine to MPEG compression, from DVD authoring to realtime compositing and online editing. The best of these facilities provide the latest advanced digital technology way before it becomes affordable to the average diguerrilla.

The most common use for a post house is for procedures involving very expensive hardware and complex processing—the most obvious being telecine transfers from film to video. The machines required to transfer a celluloid negative into an electronic image, because of their intricate mechanical design, will continue to command a premium price. Until there is a cheaper acquisition format with the subtle color and light response of motion picture film, those demanding the most pristine visuals will continue to shoot the old-fashioned way on celluloid.

As discussed earlier, there are many aesthetic decisions that can be made at the telecine transfer that will greatly affect the rest of the project. Color correction while you still have access to the film negative is one critical area. Another is the rate of transfer, 1:1 (meaning that each film frame corresponds to one video frame, which is useful for effects work) or 3:2 pulldown (conforming the film's frame rate from 24fps to 29.97fps of videotape). A competent post house can help guide you in the areas where your logic may be a bit fuzzy.

Another area where a post house provides invaluable services is in mastering D-1 or D-2 video material. As of this writing, this format is currently the preferred for mastering and broadcast. Many agencies and producers request that projects be finished in an uncompressed digital format to preserve quality. For those with their own offline digital system, a post house can conform an edit decision list from the original masters to D-1 complete with color correction and switcher effects.

For animators or compositors, the post house can provide direct digital transfer of your files to a digital disk recorder for further manipulation or layoff to D-1 tape. They can also reverse the process and convert D-1 video frames into individual digital files. Check with the post house; they may be able to provide individual files on common removeable media (e.g., JAZ disks) instead of the traditional TAR-formatted Exabyte tape.

Lastly, a post house can provide the latest in realtime processing, such as the Quantel Henry or Discreet Logic Flame, for creating or tweaking an effect that would otherwise take an enormous amount of time. These suites are most economically used for a very specific effect on which you know your client wants to make changes interactively. Be prepared to get them in and out quickly as the hourly rate can bleed your project very quickly.

The Audio Studio

Digital audio is not the mystery it once was. Professional quality audio and audio editing software is inexpensive and relatively easy to learn. However, there are many instances where you may want to draw the line and use the expertise of a facility specializing in sound recording and mixing. What's more, competition among audio studios in urban areas is generally more fierce than video post houses, and excellent bargains can be negotiated.

Recording: You may have a quiet place and a decent mike around your studio, but it might not measure up to the zero-ambience acoustics of a professional recording suite. With a good recording engineer, and some organization before the session, you can knock out a lengthy voiceover or dialogue replacement in a few hours with better fidelity than you could've done back at home base in an entire day.

Recording Tip #13

Ask the studio if they can provide digital files as well as a tape (DAT, DA-88, Alesis, etc.). Supply a removeable format disk that they can deal with (JAZ, ZIP, SYJET, etc.) and make sure that you can work with the files their system creates (SDII, AIFF, WAV, etc.). That way you walk away ready to edit the dailies and only need to refer to the original source tape as a backup.

Sweetening, music, sound FX: You may have a fairly decent sound effects library, and you may even have a good sense of how your sounds should be EQ-ed and layered together, but a good engineer at an audio facility will probably whip the pants off you in the speed department. They should have access to a vast library of music and sound effects, and there may be many subtle sounds that a cheaper library won't deliver. It's also how you play with the sound. It may be that the engineer is using the same CD of swamp critter sounds that you have, but she knows how to combine them better than you do, how to dull certain sounds and layer them back in the mix, and how to brighten certain sounds and balance the stereo so that it feels just a little more natural and real. Lastly, there may be some sound file surgery you can't handle on your own, such as that time during the shoot when someone dropped a glass during the perfect take and you've been trying to filter out the crash and keep the dialogue. A good sound engineer *might* be able to pull it off for less than you think.

My rule of thumb is to get as far as you can with the sound mix, perhaps even performing some premixes to speed the process, and then bring your elements with you to another sound studio. If the studio is using the same editing system, such as Digidesign's ProTools audio system, you can bring in your preliminary sound composition files and not miss a beat, so to speak.

Mixing: If you have a good pair of ears, you are well on your way to handling your own mixing. Seventy-five percent of mixing is just being able to hear all the audio elements working together and identify which one is overly dominant or underrepresented. Someone who specializes in mixing usually works with a great set of speakers that pick up audio "debris" in the mix that you might have missed. They might also be able to provide an artful cascade of multitrack cross-fades that gives your program an elegance it had lacked before. A great mix is one of those intangibles that you often can't put your finger on. It may only be subtly different than a merely competent homespun mix. However, the viewer can feel the extra care and mastery.

So if your program has a lot more audio elements than you normally handle, and you feel it getting a bit muddy with all the dialogue, voiceover, sound effects, and music, consider bringing your project elsewhere for the final mix.

Duplication House

You may have a few VTRs around the studio with a nice patch bay for easily dubbing from one format to another, but this task quickly becomes a handful if you need 20 copies of something right away. Since the purpose of a duplication house is to specialize in speedy volume duplication, they are usually going to outperform your capacity with less real cost, particularly in the area of quality control, making sure there are no glitches in the tape and that audio and video levels are consistent.

A good dub house will work with you to keep your costs down by allowing you to supply your own wholesale video stock. Some will even help make themselves invisible by printing on your company's tape labels and saving you this administrative task.

Not all duplication houses are created equal. Be careful, and don't entrust this mundane but vital task to just anyone. This is your end distribution product after all. Make certain that they are using the best dubbing path available—component video or serial digital whenever possible—and monitoring signal dilligently.

I personally use two kinds of dub facilities, an A-list and B-list facility. The B-list facility is for the kinds of duplication where visual quality is less important than price and speed (quickie viewing copies, window dubs). The A-list facility is for mastering and final distribution.

Guerrilla Video Economics

Another related development in the diguerrilla battle to stay competitive and technologically current are the beginnings of digital cooperatives, associations, housekeeping agreements, and other kinds of Internet-conducted subcontracting.

No longer does the diguerrilla need to work in isolation, confined to his or her garage or warehouse backroom. Traditional post facilities with additional space have recognized the value of having digital talent around without having to pay their salaries. They have essentially become a boarding house for small digital sharecropping operations. The larger facility provides low-cost space, network connectivity, and discounted equipment access to the diguerrilla in exchange for the rental income and the added value of offering their niche services to facility customers.

> ➤ **Tribal Customs:** I think that the modularity of the tools that are available now is so good that you can get a core group of fanatics together and say, "Joe, you go out and you get all the source video. And Jane, you get the source audio. And I'll start cutting all the rough stuff together. That's what we'll do today. Tomorrow we'll all change jobs so that we all get a piece of the pie." So in a lot of ways it's good because I think that the person that just sits all by themselves in their basement that's completely filled with gear is ultimately gonna be totally out of touch. So unless their own personal ravings are entertaining, or educational, or even things that people care to find out about, then they're going to be out of touch with life. (Doug Barnard)

Increasingly popular are cooperatives where all the digital entrepreneurs coexist in a space on a shared lease and create a media production ecosystem with symbiotic services and certain shared resources. These digital collectives, like any roommate situation, can be either tremendously helpful or full of unwanted hassles and unhealthy competition. The best of these digital beehives has a nice blend of talent in mutually beneficial areas of expertise. In other words, a 3D artist, a compositing artist, an editor, and a sound engineer set up shop together with maybe a couple of good freelance producers. If the mix is right, it can result in a happy marriage—joint ownership of an integrated company or a steady flow of freelance work in all directions.

Going Soft

Another area to consider in getting the most from your investment is creating your own software tools. With the evolution of sophisticated commercial software, most of us have been relieved of the unpleasantries of building a text-based render file or issuing syntax-based line commands. However, with the increase of do-it-yourself languages such HTML on the web, LINGO in Macromedia Director, and AppleScript for the MacOS, there are compelling reasons for the diguerrilla to labor over a few lines of ASCII code.

Building your own software or scripts will provide three important advantages to your operation. The first is that you will begin to understand on a very deep level, how your computer operates and why software engineers build things the way they do; secondly, you will gain an edge over your competition by providing some extra effect or time-saving batch tool that increases efficiency; thirdly, if you begin to network with software manufacturers and start using their SDKs (Software Development Toolkits) to produce plug-ins, export modules, conversion tools, etc., you may gain some sort of "developer" status and become part of the inner circle of 3rd party associates who are provided software and hardware at very healthy developer discounts.

> ⇨ ⇨ ⇨ **SUGGESTED IDIOMS TO GET STARTED:**
>
> Active Scripting, Microsoft
>
> AppleScript, Apple
>
> MovieScript Sonoran Blue
>
> VideoScript VideoScript, Inc.

Stripped and Equipped

The point of this chapter has been to dispel the myth that in a war of survival, the fittest are always the best outfitted. True, you can't squeeze blood from a stone, but even an anemic computer or video device may still have a pint or two to give. Squeezing every drop from his arsenal without bleeding himself dry, the diguerrilla is not afraid to combine the keenest machines with the klunkiest in perfect cacaphony. To make purchases that yield high ROI (return on investment), you should be up on manufacturer product lines, trade magazines, and grapevine gossip. You should also know thyself and thy business. And this is the subject of future chapters.

8

CHAPTER

Webs, Nets, Sats, and ROMs: The New Media Story

From the moment in 1991 when Apple Computer demonstrated that it was practical to represent moving images digitally on a personal computer, those with keen prescience or unbridled fanaticism understood that a new era in communication was sputtering into existence. I really wasn't one of them. In the early '90s, multimedia, as it was evangelized, was more pipe dream than pipeline, more about bandwagons than bandwidth. At the time, a hiccupping little grainy rectangle on a computer screen seemed like a cute novelty rather than a breakthrough on par with the printing press or gunpowder.

It wasn't until I saw a beta version of Macromind Director that I knew that there was a road, perhaps a little sparse on pavement, that might just lead somewhere interesting. But who knew that little road would become a "superhighway" to a new media Jerusalem. Curiously, the ill-fitting term "multimedia," conjuring up images of 1970s slide and music presentations, was tagged onto this new kind of digital content by software evangelists.

With the development of an inexpensive digital delivery format, the CD-ROM, a fledgling new media concept was given an economic opportunity. While the CD-ROM market became an important testing ground for interactive media applications (most notably for marketing, games, and education), few foresaw that this was a stepping stone into a wild new paradigm combining interactivity with connectivity. The rapid ascendancy of the Internet caught everyone off guard. Today, now that I can use an Internet phone with live video that's cheaper and more flexible than a standard phone, or "webcast" a video stream to millions of people without the assistance of a television network, it is clear that the evolution of the modern Internet was the missing piece of the new media puzzle.

The Net is now driving the next wave of the media revolution. The reasoning is this: As motion pictures made possible the concept of mass entertainment, radio and television made possible the concept of an even more massive distribution of information, the *broadcast*. Digital interactive information (DI^2, *die-square* or DI^2nfo)— a potentially more accurate label than the quaintly passé term "multimedia"—shifts the distribution mechanics from simply delivering passive information to a mass market. Today's new media mandate uses digital media to facilitate global communication.

⇨ ⇨ ⇨ **SWEET HOME CHICAGO**

[In the early '80s] If you were just an artist and you're trying to be a guerrilla film-maker, you're not gonna go very far unless you really had the inside connect, or inside track. This was before people had $50,000 they could put on the credit card to finish a movie or something. So, after college I kind of got lost in the matrix of feature film making and just being part of a crew. And I eventually became a key grip and ran crews for these different features.

I got the first Apple II that came out because I was into music. I saw that there was finally a computer that you could plug a keyboard into so I got an Apple II. And a friend of mine, Bill Hansen, got a job at Apple and started turning me on to the different computer technologies. So I used it for music and I built a whole MIDI studio based on the Mac when it first came out.

Bill called me one day and I was [gripping] on a music video for the Booya Tribe (one of the worst experiences of my life). I checked my messages, and he said, "Come to Chicago and do this animation for a couple weeks." He knew that I could put together a pretty good presentation. We've always entertained friends with incredible multimedia slide performances and music and stuff and we just had that as our own little personal art. But now you could do these things in the corporate world for presentations [with computers]. And so I went to Chicago and learned [Macromedia] Director. It was like cel-based animation with automatic tweening and I thought that was really great. Of course it was very low-res and everything else and it all depended on the speed of the computer. But that got me into this whole new world of computer animation. (Cody Harrington)

This is the era of digital convergence or hypermedia or broad-band communications or whatever other techie label you might prefer. I favor the expressions "digital thinking" or "metacommunication" because they begin to describe the possibility, in human terms, of digital information in a networked world. In this environment, the nonlinear concept that we discussed in chapter 4 becomes part of the viewing experience as well.

You may be someone who works exclusively with traditional video formats (broadcast media or nonbroadcast tape-based media) and don't see the tectonic confluence between broadcasting, webcasting, and narrowcasting. You may be one of the many who still regards any image transmission below the quality of broadcast video to be little more than an amusing techie toy. While it is true that interactive delivery is in its infancy, the communication quake is well underway. If you haven't yet felt the rumblings beneath your feet, I still suggest you at least skim this chapter and get a feel for what's shaking just outside your digital video ghetto.

> **Digital Pastures:** I think that the interactive media is finally starting to mature, that we're getting away from pornography and twitch games, that there's going to be much more of a market in edu-tainment. There'll be more digital pastures to graze. Because I don't care how many cable channels you have, eventually they all get boring. So, you want something that has a little bit more than just TV, but a little bit less than doing work or having to research something. (Doug Barnard)

Prelude to the TVfoneFAXnetPUTER

Whatever manufacturing cartels emerge to supposedly smooth out the superhighway with next-gen info-processing equipment, we are already in the midst, albeit a crudely improvised pastiche, of this metacom future. Many of us routinely multitask in front of a computer, creating documents and images while videoconferencing, exchanging email, digital faxes, and pulling information from the World Wide Web, all while talking on a speaker phone to some other similarly wired individual(s).

Much has been written about the new "virtuality" of the workplace because of metacommunication. In fact, this chapter was written while I was in South America receiving faxes, voicemail, email, and digital images as if I were still back at home in Los Angeles. Last night, instead of writing like a diehard diguerrilla committed to his deadline (down here the mantra is *mañana*), I sent flowers to my mother for her birthday while having a live text chat with a friend in Israel who noticed that I was awake and online, from 10,000 miles away. I then forwarded the buffered chat to a mutual friend so they could be in the loop on the latest global gossip. For those willing to deal with a few of the current pitfalls—like the lamentable fact that my home library isn't online and the lengthy downloads sending sizable digital movies through the narrow rickety telco pipes of the Southern Hemisphere—the sense of power and freedom far outweigh the hassles.

Rah, Rah, Sis-Boom-Bah

But enough about doing cybererrands and chitchatting virtually. I will limit my techno pep rally since, by now, you either love or loathe the relentless infostream currently raging all around you. I will leave it to your discretion as to how much information and interactivity you can bear. More importantly, this chapter looks at how this kind of digital thinking influences professional production and malleable uses of digital video.

Just a few years ago, there was a lot of discussion and hyperbole about how interactive storytelling would forever change the face of entertainment and how movies and television would ultimately pale in comparison to the new interactive cinema. While i-movies have yet to become the new form of popular entertainment, by addressing the underlying question—what defines commercial entertainment in a digital world—traditional categories and formats are changing.

From games to retail shopping to computer-based training, new ways of presenting and interacting with video are creating a ripe new frontier for the diguerrilla. In an electronic universe, framed by a computer screen, the image is still king, and moving images are often the only way to adequately communicate an event, a process, or a product in action.

Repurposing: Creative Recycling

The simplest use for digital video in a DI^2 environment is a repackaging of traditionally distributed video. Instead of building a narrative for the viewer to follow as in traditional video, the interactive viewer is more often creating their own narrative by choice, interest level, and amount of time allotted to the experience (normally it's short and sweet). For the diguerrilla, this means a kind of deconstruction of the editing process into bite-sized stand-alone chunks that can be linked by various associations and information threads.

One common structure is setting up a database of related video clips that can be sliced and diced by the user's preferences (chronology, individual, rank, etc.) such as sports highlights or fashion coverage. In this scenario, the carefully edited half-hour TV coverage of a stage of the Tour de France is broken down into components and restructured as a mosaic of footage that can be browsed by rider, by highlight, chronologically, or geographically.

Another commercial application might be product presentation video selected by user criteria such as viewing various travel destinations based on particular preferences (price, activities, weather, language, distance). In this scenario, detailed stock footage of various locations is broken down and repackaged to give prospective travellers site-specific visuals that wouldn't be as targeted or information-rich were this a traditional general-market promo video.

Aside from an open database structure (i.e., describe what you want and we'll find it), there is also a guided interactive structure that is useful for distance learning, training, games, and any experience that follows a hierarchical process (start at zero and work your way through). In this structure, video is broken into components that assume a certain previous level of background or prowess and thus don't need a traditional narrative exposition; in other words, you can get right to the point and deliver the appropriate piece of information.

For example, in a traditional training video describing the mechanics and safety features of a Boeing 767, the producer would have to assume, in advance, a particular viewership. The same footage, broken into appropriate modules, when structured as digital interactive information, may be hierarchically programmed so that passengers might want to view the initial basic level, flight attendants might be required to go through levels 1 and 2, pilots 1 through 3 (which might include emergency troubleshooting procedures), and aviation maintenance engineers might be required to master levels 1 through 4 (which might include detailed technical information on the aircraft's design and mechanical structure).

The underlying strategy in all these examples is discovering how to tell a coherent story in small cellular bites. In an info-surfing world, many people have already learned how to digest information in this manner. The content creator merely needs to organize material to fit a browse-and-pause audience.

Digital Thinking in Action

Besides repackaging images for a new medium, there is content that is conceived from inception for interactive use. This content requires an even bolder strike into the frontier of media production, but then where else would a diguerrilla want to be?

The primary creative question is, How exactly do you design and produce this kind of content so that it seems fresh, seamless, and appropriate in so many different contexts? And the primary economic question is, How do you charge for this?

We'll address these issues in a moment, but in order to place the media into proper context, let's first run through a few of the distinctive metacommunication media formats that have already emerged.

The Webcast

The webcast, or interactive feed, consists of streaming digital video over a digital network. It can be a live (or "live-format") event, a live location feed (e.g., traffic and weather) or prerecorded content. The difference between a webcast and traditional broadcast, besides the all-digital delivery, is that a webcast can be user-impacted. For example, if multiple cameras are deployed, the user might determine which feed they would like to watch (if not all of them simultaneously). Moreover, instantaneous user feedback can be uploaded (purchases, opinion polls, educational testing, etc.).

The Interstitial

This is a concept borrowed from traditional broadcasting, putting a commercial in the middle of the main DI^2 content, say, a game for instance. Unlike television, however, it can be given an interactive twist, and the viewer can purchase or request more information during the ad. Digital video and animation can contain "hot spots" or interactive triggers that initiate other content or some user transaction. One advantage to this type of commercial is that the interstitial can be programmed to "take over" the user's screen, disabling the impulse to switch channels during the commercial. If programmed adeptly, there should be no load time associated with interstitials because they can be front-loaded at the beginning of the game or program. Eventually, a hybrid of the banner ad and the interstitial will emerge as a fully interactive webmercial. Not so revolutionary, but inevitable nevertheless.

The I-doc

The "interactive documentary" is a term I use to connote any use of archival material as a historical or journalistic document. An I-doc can be strictly an educational tool such as numerous webumentaries or CD-ROMs that document a particular era, event, or subject with text, sound, and video. The I-doc breaks free of the conventional documentary format by letting the user browse the areas of the subject they are most interested in and associate information through hyperlinked options. Moreover, the video used in an I-doc can be broken down and accessed in a variety of ways.

The CD+

Currently the CD+ is kind of a subcategory of the I-doc, but I mention it as a niche market that uses video heavily. The CD+ is primarily an audio CD that uses extra space on the disk for digital information about the performers and the music. Consumers with computers are treated to extra interactive information to enrich their experience of the product. The CD+ is definitely a transitional niche product that should transform once DVD and other cheap, large-capacity storage formats take hold in the entertainment and education markets. Expect all kinds of "plus" programming as advertisers perfect the art of cross-promoting and narrowcasting.

The Video Game

Perhaps the most widely distributed form of interactive entertainment, video games use varying amounts of digital video and animation, particularly between levels of play to accent the narrative of the game. They are distributed over the Internet and across various game console and PC platforms.

The Cyberschool

The concept of "distance learning" is a modified evolution of the correspondence course or the closed-circuit classroom, though infinitely more flexible. The use of video is still nascent in the "Click2Learn" era, but this area may turn out to be faster growing than the retail sector in terms of video use. In an international classroom, pictures are even more essential for conveying information.

Weaving a Web of Video

In traditional video postproduction, good footage is often sacrificed to the proverbial cutting room floor because of time and space considerations. In an interactive context, much of this ancil-

➤ **Web Video Aesthetics:** There are reams of technical information circulating about video on the web for which you will find many useful URLs noted in the appendix. Here, it is important to quickly note only what kinds of video images will translate well to the web. Since we are still in an age where network bandwidth is a precious resource, a lot of image compression is necessary to deliver video at connection speeds of 28k, 56k or even 512k. Therefore, a dynamic montage, moving camera or busy layered graphic that looks great at full-frame, 30fps, will probably turn to pixel mush when scaled and compressed for the web.

Though some dynamic characteristics can be preserved with judicious use of motion blur, until the vast majority of your Net audience is amply wired—simpler, sharper, sparser are the pneumonic trinity for web video design. If necessary, you can always augment your images with accompanying graphics elsewhere on a web page or stream vector graphics or other non-video graphic data as separate media tracks.

lary footage may have an important use if organized into suitable visual modules.

The creative opportunities for nonlinear interactive media are intriguing. The traditional "plot line," connoting a single track that the viewer is pulled along, is superseded by a multithreaded approach in which pieces of information are linked together in a variety of ways that somehow, when accessed from any point, are seamlessly connected.

This presents an interesting challenge for the diguerrilla. Video is not so much sequenced as it is *tiled*. It is somewhat comparable to the concept of "tiling" for graphic artists, where a relatively small image is constructed in a way that the edges seamlessly tile with one another, and an infinite image can be constructed from just a few pixels. The diguerrilla must often shoot and edit video that "tiles" with other clips and elements without appearing clumsy or nonsequential.

A Cellular Editing Model

The model is still evolving on this, but the following is a three-tiered framework that I currently use (as always, feel free to improvise):

1. *Miniaturization:* Make mini-movies or mini-docs with a beginning, middle, and end. Just as each body cell has all our DNA structure contained within it, try to format the subject matter so it appears complete unto itself. This means that the person speaking should have a natural break in their speech, the scene should have an appropriate music cue, and information should be coherently organized so that the viewer can digest each "cell" in almost any order.

2. *Orientation:* If possible, lead with an establishing shot, or montage, that quickly gives the viewer context. If we are breaking down a series of the same talking head or similar repetitive action, say, highlights from presidential public addresses, try showing a wide shot of the podium and maybe a crowd reaction shot so that the viewer has a physical feel for the viewing whether this is the first or last clip shown.

If the footage is more varied, such as "insects of the Amazon" or "plastic surgery examples," then other contextual clues may be important, such as visual scale, time frame (time lapse or real time), and references to related material. Of course, onscreen titles or hyperlinks indicating chronology or identity or other appropriate data are effective as well.

3. *Captivation:* Though these individual cells should be viewable on their own, they should stimulate viewer curiosity to delve deeper into the material (vertically) or broader (horizontally). A "leave 'em hanging" strategy, long applied in television news and episodics, can be adapted for use in this medium. This not only helps maintain viewer interest but serves to give guidance to the viewer who might not yet be aware of what is available and relevant to this experience. Include clues or references to important related information within each video "cell" and use devices that will trigger further viewer intrigue or contemplation. Examples include rhetorical questions in the narration ("You had to wonder what the coach told them at halftime"), visual teases (shot of a keyhole in a locked door, muffled sounds on the other side of a wall, or a blurry figure in the distance), slo-mo or freeze frames with onscreen graphics ("this man later testified before a grand jury on August 6th") and then returning to full-motion, and summing up with a pointer ("this feat had been accomplished only twice before in human history").

> **Three-Dimensional Editing:** If you scratch-and-sniff past the surface of the "cellular stitching" concept, you can envision the next level where streams of sound and picture are brought together on-the-fly depending on the needs of the user. This is already being done on a basic level with multiple language soundtracks. The potential is there to go further and give visual elements different combinations depending on contextual needs. This is more akin to how a 3D character in a game works, with sections of movement, "sprites" or "cells," that come together to provide controllable movement for the user. Game programmers have already started to think like editors; now editors will have to think like game programmers.

Fun on the Frontier

Once the exclusive domain of television networks, the possibility of "network" production and delivery has now been placed directly into the hands of the diguerrilla in the form of interactive media. Naturally, it has been those ventures that operate at the entrepreneurial fringe, namely, the pornography industry, that have most rapidly pioneered alternative uses of digital video and interactivity. Close behind are a number of less controversial applications that have yet to be fully explored. Below is a sampling of some emerging niches for the digital video entrepreneur. Some niches are more meat-and-potatoes; others, more champagne-and-caviar.

- *Conferencing:* Videoconferencing, in its early incarnation, has been pioneered by large multinational companies, but the next generation, facilitated by IP telephony and more flexible software, is finally making video an everyday business communication tool. This is good news for guerrillas on several fronts: First, in selling yourself to clients, you will have cheaper access to a wider market. Clients need to see and hear you, but that flight to Amsterdam is usually impractical in the courting stages. Videoconferencing will help you build personal trust and reduce misunderstandings. Second, since many of your clients will be "pitching" new business with a videoconference call, a new visual presentation aesthetic will have to be created that is clear but more compelling than another Powerpoint snooz-a-thon.

o   *Point of purchase:* Point of purchase (POP) videos have become commonplace in the retail industry to assist in the marketing of products from games to jeans to cosmetics. Now that the POP is shifting to online vending sites, there will have to be a creative overhaul of the POP video for an interactive environment. A savvier, more consumer-aware format will evolve (perhaps in combination with live webcasting) that is as visually sophisticated as television but takes advantage of all the viewer demographics collected from visitors to the website. We are talking about an übermercial, something so well-targeted, useful, and thoughtfully produced that the viewer will prefer this type of marketing to all others.

o   *Dynamic Infographics:* The use of "infographics" have boomed over the last decade to the point where our screens are heaving forth with all kinds of numbers, text, and pictures meant to inform the viewer. Until recently, most of the graphics represented fixed-data information. Expanded computer power and mathematical models adapted from scientific data analysis have made possible the rise of the "dynagraphic," which visually represents a fluid dataset or moving target such as a weather front, the position of boats in a yacht race, or the behavior of a microscopic virus over time. Such is the exponential growth of this niche that a whole book could be written about this convergence of math, animation, and live-data input. Suffice it to say that our use and understanding of complex data fundamentally changes with the use of dynamic visual models. One advantage is the speed of assimilation—we read a visual display of traffic patterns faster than a list of freeways and their current status report. Consequently, there will be an expanding market to design environments, models, and systems for displaying this data.

And while we're making lists, there are a number of old-school, down-and-dirty, lens-for-hire guerrilla video strongholds expanding into new forms with Web technology. With a modicum of HTML and a bit of compression savvy, any part of the human experience that can be videotaped, packaged, and sold is being retooled for the Net:

- wedding videos
- anniversary videos
- baby births
- bar mitzvahs
- graduations

- ○ audition tapes
- ○ high school sports
- ○ dog shows
- ○ memorials
- ○ computer dating videos
- ○ instructional videos
- ○ family reunion videos

While these may not necessarily be the glam areas of video production, they fit many of the guerrilla criteria for low production cost and fast turnaround.

Knee Deep in Cybercrud

The catch, of course, is that for all the wide-open possibilities, interactive production can be more hassle with less financial return than traditional video. If you are just subcontracting, delivering video according to certain technical specifications, you may not be aware of the technical complexities and varying quality of content. But if you produce the entire product, you'll encounter many more elements to juggle than a traditional video format.

Those tasks include designing the architecture of the experience, making sure that the links and the user interface are coherent and engaging, and inviting some sort of transaction or user feedback component. Before diving into these barely charted waters, it is extremely important to educate yourself and clients about the labor intensity of building an interactive gateway for delivering DI^{2}nformation.

The other possible pitfall is a creative quagmire. Sometimes, the project becomes more about the gateway, the technology, the retail transaction, than about the creative content. Diguerrillas who tire easily of building widgets (even when well compensated) are cautioned to be mindful of keeping the creative challenges in step with the technical requirements.

> **DIGUERRILLA WANTED**: Net/cable broadcast and publishing entity seeks Audio/Video Technical Producer. This position requires someone who's excited about what opportunities streaming media brings to the Internet. The candidate should be intimately familiar with Internet-based video and audio delivery systems such as Real's streaming format and Microsoft's Netshow. The position also requires understanding non-streaming video technologies such as QuickTime and AVI. The candidate should be comfortable with all technical aspects of production, including troubleshooting and supporting live broadcasts, and coordinating their efforts with other members of the Web team. Additional responsibilities will include training production assistants and helping others troubleshoot problems. This person should be comfortable understanding how the audio and video elements relate to the sitewide database publishing system. The ideal candidate would be comfortable assuming a leadership role and be excited about bringing Web-based video to a new level. Candidate should have a minimum of two years working in Web publishing and should have a prior background in producing streaming content. Additional experience in television broadcast environment a plus.

The Technical Maze:
Constraints and Possibilities

The first thing you notice when you start to produce interactive content is that the rules keep changing. Unlike broadcast television, which is overseen by the government, the DI^{2}nformation world is merely governed by the forces of capital and technical innovation.

As the Net matures as a commercial environment, a certain consolidation of technical specifications continues to evolve. The following are some of the basic considerations in using video in new media environments.

Prepare to DI^{2}e

Before you shoot, and certainly while you are editing, evaluate the various viewing formats that may be desirable for the project. At an early stage in your edit, you will have a lot of digitized footage available to you. Not everything will go into the broadcast version, but other bits and pieces might go into other versions. Multitasking these related projects will require a higher level of media management and project organization.

Moreover, some shots that look brilliant on a full-screen monitor are barely recognizable at a smaller picture size. Maybe some elements that work fine in one frame composition on a broadcast scale should be broken into two or three separate video elements when delivered in other digital environments. Perhaps audio, a less prominent feature of the broadcast edition, may be enhanced in other media environments because of the better data efficiency possible with audio files.

Without advance planning, you will be left with only a default option offering a short compressed clip from the finished video. This may be adequate for many uses but precludes some value-added possibilities for richer viewing experiences.

Bandwidth Tango

Video cameras are built with a television signal in mind. A full-bandwidth video signal, even with DV format compression, represents what we *currently* consider a lot of digital information (see my article at http://www.apple.com/dv for a basic overview). The World Wide Web, a CD-ROM, even a DVD-ROM don't have the capacity to push that much data around. Hence, the picture must be squeezed in varying degrees to make the "stream" of digital video fit the capacity of the "pipe" containing and transporting it.

You're already aware of the use of compression for editing. In current DI^2nfo delivery systems, compression is also used to transmit the image to the viewer as well. Whether we're talking about Realmedia, QuickTime, Windows Media, or DVD MPEG— all these technologies use mathematical algorithms (codecs) to analyze and quantize pictures into a series of space-saving patterns and colors. These algorithms make assumptions about pictures just as forecasting makes assumptions about weather patterns—though both are imperfect by design.

The nonrandom element is the editor who knows the idiosyncracies of the footage better than the compression program and can cheat a leaner datastream in order to get the best ratio of size/picture quality. These parameters involve spatial compression (removing the redundant data within any given image—good for landscapes), temporal compression (storing only information for the areas that are different from the last key frame—good for talking heads), interlacing, frame rate, frame cropping, color, and image sharpness.

Learning to master this process with products such as Terran's Media Cleaner Pro (http://www.terran.com) or finding a good outsourcing vendor will make the difference between excuses ("Well, it looked great on tape") and execution ("We saw the piece on the Web, and we'd like to order your product").

Face-Lifts

There are many cyber-specific interactive touches that you don't think about when you're dealing with a regular broadcast transmission. Though video is still important in interactive environments, it is not the only player; it is part of a cast of elements that are providing information to the viewer. Hyperlinks, "hot spots," QuickTime VR, vector animations, VRML—these are a few of the programming considerations that might work alongside or *inside* your video.

Apple's QuickTime VR has been a pioneer with the level of interactivity possible within the video frame. The use of "hot links" within the frame, sending the user to another clip, another audio track, another description, or another location on the Internet, adds yet another dimension to video editing (http://www.apple.com/quicktime/authoring). While you may not want to take the time to become an expert in interactive authoring, a working knowledge of the principles is essential for mapping out the project and integrating interactivity into the overall look.

Convergence 101

The brief history of the metacommunications era has been dominated by the search for "the killer app," the most lucrative use of interactive technology. Aside from interactive games, which have a distinct history predating the multimedia bandwagon, the interactive killer app has not yet materialized, and may not ever— certainly not in the way that advertiser-supported programming became the killer application for broadcast television. The flexibility and vastness of the medium may, in the end, merely incubate many specialized niches. Up until now, interactive entertainment has really been a minor subsidiary of traditional entertainment media; online retail has seen rapid growth but is still a marginal part of consumer activity; and the distribution of information and services are usually electronic adjuncts to traditional formats.

In fact, the biggest successes in the new media market are those companies building and maintaining the infrastructure (the hardware, the networks, the physical pieces necessary to be wired in). For example, the email phenomenon generates the most revenue not for the manufacturers of email software but for Internet service providers (ISPs) and for the manufacturers of modems and computers.

So, if DI^2 content is currently a smaller market that demands more planning, why should you bother? Well, because you can't afford not to—it will become part of what you do eventually whether you are aware of it now or not. Just as telcos, Internet developers, cable companies, and broadcast networks are climbing on top of one another to broaden their horizon, the diguerrilla must now be ready for an assault on all media fronts.

There are more ways to display pictures, more ways to deliver pictures, and more ways to sell these pictures. Video on the Web is still a free-for-all, the kind of environment that video mercenaries thrive on. While there are more technical details, there is less equipment overhead. The entry requirements for video on the Web are a DV camera, a FireWire-ready computer, and a DV-savvy editing package. For fresh guerrilla recruits, weighing the investment and potential return of squeeze 'n' stream video, this is low-lying fruit with an enormous future. For seasoned veterans of the campaign, this is another revenue stream that will reward the early adopters handsomely...if you can endure the growing pains of this Br@ve_Nu_wURLd.

The Last 2%:
Delivering Product and
Keeping Clients Happy

> **"** *A riot is a spontaneous outburst.*
> *A war is subject to advance planning.* **"**
> —Richard M. Nixon

So you've mastered the tools of the trade: you know how to script, shoot, and edit your video. You're deep into the project, and things are looking pretty good. There is only one thing left: Finish and deliver. Put the final product in the hands of your client or commercial distribution channel.

➤ **The Effort Bottleneck:** I think it takes like 50% of your effort to get a job to 90% completion, 'cause that last 10% is gonna take the other 50% of your effort on the whole job. Granted I see things from the point of view of the client and they're forking out a pretty healthy sum of money so they should get what they want, but a lot of times they're using their own haziness to the artist's disadvantage.

What I've really learned over the past is trying to really set up a viable payment schedule and not be the one left standing when the music stops. Part of that is the negotiation of business, you can't just hope that someone will treat you right. You've gotta be able to look that client in the eye so that if they try to stiff you, they know it's not going to be fun. (Doug Barnard)

Quickie Disclaimer #6

Buyers of digital video services (aka clients) who are reading this book may jump to the conclusion that this chapter contains strategies to somehow pull the wool over your eyes. This certainly is not the case; the suggestions in this chapter are designed to create open, direct, efficient, and sane communication between the digital video vendor and the digital video client. This chapter is designed to assist in creating a climate for delivering the best possible product under the existing time and budget constraints. It is also designed to keep the client satisfied and provide a sense that the digital video vendor knows how to respond to the client's needs and has been down this road before. If you, the client, aren't satisfied, you won't be coming back. On the other hand, if the vendor isn't smart about turning work around, they won't stay in business. This chapter contains a few simple guidelines for helping both parties prosper.

This is less a chapter about celebrating the end of the production process and more about the relief of getting that final, final, final ("You mean I get paid now?") approval that ultimately puts the project to bed. It's about handling the last 2% of doubt in order to declare victory. It's about not leaving yourself open to last-second snafus and glitches that will sour your client on a job that up until the end was 98% perfect. Up until now, we have primarily dealt with the technical and creative issues in media production; this chapter is specifically about the business of digital video.

> ➤ **The Sum of the Whole:** I realize that filmmaking is such a collaborative art and it's not about one person's vision or another's, it's about working to create a common vision. (Barry Silver)

Visual Language: Communication Between Communicators

Just as the proverbial shoemaker's children are supposed to have holes in their soles, it is often the ironic foible of many visual communicators that they aren't always the best at communicating clearly with their clients.

Visual communicators in general and diguerrillas in particular have a number of unique situations to contend with in business. Aside from the common-sense notions of treating clients with respect and a sense of partnership, there are the inevitable misunderstandings that result when people are using verbal language to describe a product that is essentially composed of pictures.

Communication can become strained because you are translating the ideas into a second language, a verbal language, instead of staying rooted in the original visual language. Usually, the client has one set of pictures in their mind, and you hear what you think they want and try to translate that back into a picture that matches what they had in their mind's eye. Anyone who has ever worked with a patch bay can see that this is not the optimum way to route the information.

So this is the first thing a diguerilla must learn. Don't waste a lot of breath. You'll need the energy for the long haul. If a picture is worth a thousand words, by all means, use pictures. This means possibly using Rip-o-Matics and storyboards at the outset of pre-production, as discussed in chapter 2, and using pictograms and iconic language throughout the production process.

Your clients are probably as busy as you are, and it doesn't pay for either of you to be meeting everyday in person and reviewing tapes. Furthermore, a diguerrilla is happiest when his client isn't over his shoulder demanding bottled water and expensive lunches and obscure changes to the product (some of this is inevitable, but let's keep it to structured input and decent take-out food). Previously, it was impractical to stay completely visual. Faxes, phone calls, and face-to-face meetings formed the basis of client feedback. All these forms of communication are vulnerable to misinterpretation.

➤ **Teaching From a Straightjacket:** It's a continual process of educating the client and even the filmmakers themselves...It's a continual process of the client thinking, "We'll just do it in the computer," so the filmmaking side becomes sloppy. Or if you're trying to motion track something, they'll just shoot with disregard. Like hiding wires on the set—[they think], "Oh we'll just have them fix it in the computer." Well it takes a lot of time to paint out wires. It's always good for whoever's shooting to know a little bit about the other side of it so you have to make sure that if they're gonna be on a commercial shoot or if they're gonna be on a film set that they pay heed to the tools that the individual artist has.

For instance at ABC [on-air promotions], we'd get shots in that were shot without consulting us at all in the digital suite. And we'd have to work around not having any reference points to track with or having to have the Henry artist paint out or make a custom matte where it would have been so simple just to put a blue screen right in the middle of the television or whatnot so you could just key right in to it and track it. So there was just no communication because there were different departments, different unions, and we weren't supposed to talk to them and they weren't supposed to talk to us 'cause it's a compartmentalized kind of working environment. I mean at ABC I would have loved to just go out and shoot stuff. Because it would've been so easy. But we weren't allowed to go out and shoot things. I felt limited like that. I was a digital artist. I had to stay in the 3D suite. You couldn't be a designer. You were a 3D operator. (Cody Harrington)

Random Thought #408

Meetings and Phone Calls: You probably will never get rid of the conference call as a means of communication; in fact, with videoconferencing evolving, it will only evolve into a more sacred ritual. Just remember to have someone take copious notes at meetings and phone calls. (A digital snapshot at meetings is also a nice touch to remind everyone who was there and has practical uses after the project as a little PR tool.) These notes should then be recirculated, hopefully electronically, back to everyone at the meeting and other interested parties. If there are points of agreement or amendments to the project, make sure that everyone checks off having read and authorized what is written. I believe the technical term for this process is "covering your ass."

Talking in Pictures

In the digital age, there is no need to rely on such inferior methods of communication. The tools are all available and chances are your clients are more equipped than they realize to work faster and smarter...like you. In fact, that may even be part of why they hired you. With a little education and proper implementation, you will be communicating more, speaking less, and having fewer disagreements.

The suggestions below are all focused toward one goal: keeping the client comfortable with the process and locking down their decisions so that ambivalence and chaos don't have a chance to scorch the project.

How to Stop Worrying and Learn to Love Your Client

1. *Show images to clients on optimum viewing equipment:* Stop using crappy monitors with cheap speakers to show your work. The client notices, and it influences how they perceive the work. If you cut corners everywhere else, create a little corner of your studio as a viewing room with comfortable seating, good audio, and a nice monitor. A nice touch is to hide the tape machines or computers and operate with remotes so that the viewing experience seems a bit more magical.

2. *Still images:* email and the Web: Almost everyone dealing with digital communication has, by now, gotten themselves an email address. Teach your client about attaching files (and more importantly, compressing files). If they don't have an image editing program, get them a simple one so that they can add text right onto the image. This serves two purposes: it allows them to get their art director power rush, and it serves as visual evidence that the client requested something specific. Sometimes a dedicated Web page on your website (nothing fancy) can act as a digital corkboard for shuffling around stills and posting comments. That way, when the client is composed of several decision makers, they can all hit the site at their convenience.

3. *Moving pictures:* CDs/DVDs/tape: Depending on the project, some sort of work-in-progress demonstration is essential so that the client feels you are on the right track. Even if the client is with you in the editing room during

the day, it's a good idea to give them a tape to take home at the end of each session to review and make notes for the following session. However, be careful with these works-in-progress. You will often be using material as a placeholder or have sections very loosely put together. Unless the client is very familiar with seeing very rough cuts and comps, these can cause additional confusion and delays. Try to show only sections that you have put some real work into; show portions of the program with a specific purpose in mind such as obtaining some sort of approval or direct response from the client.

You may also want to give the client copies of the original source tapes and make sure that they have a timecode window (and a date stamp graphic if at all possible) that you both can refer to during discussions. Talking about the "guy leaning against the Honda" is riskier than talking about the shot at 16:22:31:00. It also invites the client to be organized and specific about their comments instead of saying, "Well, you know, don't we have another shot we could use?" By having the footage, they will suggest specific shots, and you can try them quickly without a long tedious search.

Be sure to date and properly mark all works-in-progress submitted to the client as they will be superseded by subsequent versions.

4. *Advanced communication apps:* If you and your client are fully wired, have good bandwidth, and technological parity, there are a number of useful applications available

for evaluating media interactively from Internet phones and whiteboards, to specific digital annotation tools such as Cinebase's (formerly E-motion's) Creative Partner or Web Partner (http://www.emotion.com), an inexpensive QuickTime/AVI software editing package, or even just clever cut-and-paste use of Apple video player.

These applications will allow clients to embed notes, graphics, audio files, and other visual feedback directly into the media files you send them. Even if we're talking about something streamlined, like an annotated Power-point slide show, this kind of exchange is invaluable in creating clarity between you and your client. Moreover, it allows your client to meditate over the project on his own time, freeing you up to move on to other elements or projects while your client processes the changes.

The Column A/Column B Maneuver

I have cooked in a few restaurants at certain points in my career, and I have an appreciation for the delicate balance that must be found around the notion of giving the customer a choice. The wonderful illusion of a restaurant is that you can sit down and order anything you want to eat. However, before you can do so, the management has carefully sat down and evaluated what those choices will be, based on food costs, the projected prefer-ences of the clientele, and the time involved in preparation.

As a sous chef, I had a certain amount of freedom to be cre-ative with daily specials, but if I chose something with costly ingredients and a long prep time, I was very likely going to take some heat (forgive the unintentional pun).

I never understand restaurants with huge lengthy menus. Customers spend a lot of time perusing them, frustrating their waiters and lengthening the time it takes to turn the table around for another customer. In the same spirit, the diguerrilla must offer the client choice without having them walk back into the kitchen and start poking around in the refrigerator.

When you present options to the client, think them through very carefully. Are these changes ones that you can stand behind? Will the quality be enhanced? Are they simple to implement or is this a massive overhaul? Can you document these changes as resulting directly from conversations and exchanges with the client?

My personal preference is to offer two solutions or recommendations and show at least a sample of what I mean. That means that, based on previous discussions, I'm asking you to choose font A or font B, transition A or transition B, take A or take B. Of course, there will be situations where more than two choices are absolutely necessary, but if you can shoot for two, you are on the right track. Failing to hem in the client's choices will leave you vulnerable to the "Second Gunman" syndrome, the bullet that will seemingly come from nowhere; for example, the brilliant suggestion halfway through the production that the piece should be cut "MTV" style when there was hardly any camera coverage, or that there should be extra effects that no one planned for.

Of course, it depends on what kind of restaurant you are. The diguerrilla tends to serve "blue plate specials" and "prix fixe" menus that have been (hopefully) carefully calculated to deliver a delicious meal on a budget. Other restaurants spend more to make more. Big post houses make their clients believe in technologic magic and do a good job of perpetuating the illusion by distracting the client with cappuccinos and massages while staff artists in $700/hour suites scramble for a solution. The diguerrilla

---

The Top 10 Lies Editors Tell Their Clients

10. It's just a preview shift.
9. It's out of the safe area, you'll never see it on the air.
8. It won't really look like that.
7. I'll fill out the paperwork tomorrow.
6. Why no, I don't mind working Saturday.
5. Oh, don't go by THAT monitor.
4. It works better as a cut.
3. It's on the source tape.
2. I think it looks just fine.
1. "I'll be home soon."

The Top 10 Lies Clients Tell Their Editors

10. It's pretty simple. It should only take an hour.
9. Budget? Don't worry about it.
8. Feel free to be creative with this.
7. I only need a couple of dubs.
6. The client will love it! They won't make any changes.
5. I'm positive we've got that shot on another tape.
4. I've never had this problem anywhere else I've edited.
3. Could I see it just one more time?
2. I thought you'd be able to just paint it out.
1. How hard can it be?

---

must make his lighter, cheaper tools deliver the fabulous product the client expects while ducking stray bullets along the way.

Arm Wrestling

Sometimes you will have no other choice than to tussle with a client over what it is they want and what it is they have budgeted for. In a creative process, reason and logic are the first casualties. What is the best way to dance with your client while resisting the urge to break their ankles?

First, since you know that the project is a marathon run with many critical decisions ahead, you can afford to bend on the small stuff. However, make it clear that you're happy to make this particular change and give them a projection of how long it will take. Try to review changes in context and put the ball in their court: Do you really want to change all the fonts right now when we have to cut in the new music, which will probably affect the whole cutting tempo? Do you really want to reshoot the swamp sunset when we only have half a day to shoot the alligator farm?

I find it helpful to keep a schedule/timeline/project breakdown in visual range while working or meeting with the client. That way, you're not perceived as a curmudgeon who doesn't want to make changes. With the schedule blinking in front of all the players like a lighthouse in the fog, everyone is more likely to work together to bring the ship ashore.

Even if you are being well compensated for changes in the original concept, there is good reason to keep revisions contained.

A psychological "muddied water" effect sets in when there are too many changes and things drag on too long. Both you and your client will begin to lose enthusiasm and be less satisfied with the result, no matter how brilliant it might turn out to be. This is subtle poison for a business relationship and should be actively avoided.

> **DIGUERRILLA WANTED**: Looking for people to assist in 2D and 3D animation for 4 half-hour infomercials we have to finish in 90 to 120 days. The type of stuff we will need is title animations and product demonstration animations. All of our systems will be busy editing the shows so the persons will have to have their own system and be comfortable working via phone and the Internet. We would also like to find users of the same tools we use in-house in case there is need for any last-minute tweaking. We use the standard set of Mac tools, Electric Image, After Effects, and PhotoShop, etc, for graphics and special effects. We edit on Media 100s so delivery of files using the M-100 codec is preferred but not necessary.

Fail-Safe

So now you are following a policy of visually presenting options in front of your client, perhaps something along the lines of a list of proposed issues and fixes, their estimated duration, and their tentative priority. If the client is being unreasonable (more unreasonable than you usually know them to be), have a conversation in a quiet place with the key decision makers and have all deal memos and subsequent communication about the project with you. Refer to this only if absolutely necessary. Reiterate that what they are requesting is indeed possible but not within the parameters of the original agreement. You will be happy to devote more personnel or equipment or whatever it takes but only after they authorize an addendum to the budget. Advise them that they should be clear about what they want because each additional change will be outside of the initial agreement.

Well before things get to this point, the diguerrilla has charted this possible scenario and developed a fail-safe strategy for delivering the final product or exiting the project without bloodshed. Again, the success of any "fail-safe" option depends on how you have communicated with the client from the outset. All communication—particularly the initial deal memo, contract, purchase order, or service invoice—must contain the rules of the game. Without them, there is only the word of the client against yours, and the one with the checkbook, the client, always ends up in the right by default.

The rules of the engagement are essentially where to place the pressure points in a game that, by nature, is filled with pressure. However, these pressure points are better envisioned as acupressure points on a human body, which can be applied for improved health. Usually the pressure points are a series of "what ifs" that affect the budgeting, content, and delivery dates of the project.

Below is a sampling of key "what if" pressure points that should be dealt with in the initial client agreement and followed up with all status reports, check points, and project reviews:

- *Delivery date:* How long do you have to do the project from start to finish? What happens if the client wants to change the delivery date (particularly when the date is earlier than originally planned)?

- *Review dates:* When are the major milestones in the project, and when will the client officially sign off (e.g., completion of storyboard/script, shooting or image acquisition, animation, postproduction)? A signoff usually means, "You like what you see, and we're moving ahead. If you change your mind later, there will be significant financial consequences." What are the guidelines for restructuring the budget and timeline if the client changes their mind after a signoff?

- *Project elements:* What are the physical elements of the project (e.g., footage, logos, animation, audio, etc.), and what elements are being supplied by the client or other subcontractors? If there are other subcontractors such as a music composer, what are the guidelines for working with that person? Do you supply specs necessary to the client and they handle communication with the subcontractor, or is there a direct handoff, with you taking responsibility for ensuring that the elements meet the technical specifications of the project?

  In the elements domain, there is no such thing as too much clarity, particularly when you are dealing with subjective things like visuals. For example, you may stipulate that for something like text backgrounds, the client will have a choice between six candidates or provide one of their own to keep the "Can you show me something else?" fixation to a minimum.

- *Margin:* I am a proponent of being up front with profit margins, particularly on flat-rate projects. This is fairly

Cautionary Note #210

Pro bono, an abbreviation of the Latin, *problemmaticus boneheadicum,* otherwise known in the vernacular as "a freebie," is one of the riskiest kinds of projects for a diguerrilla. Whether the proposal comes from your favorite cousin or a Fortune 500 giant with the promise of much more lucrative work, consider the upsides and downsides of the job carefully.

It's an interesting phenomenon, but media production, probably since it can be used to reach so many people, has an enormous amount of pro bono projects. Though you probably wouldn't think of asking your plumber to come to the house on a Sunday to do a "quick pipe installation for a good cause," it's a routine request in vidbiz. Unless you are living with your parents and have permission to use the spare room for digital video (with full access to the refrigerator as long as you stay out of trouble), you must remember that you are in a for-profit business. The client or the concept or the cause may be very compelling, but you must consider the job with a cold, sober consideration before biting off a big chunk of arsenic.

On the plus side, a pro bono project usually implies a lot of creative freedom since you are doing the work gratis. If the project has high visibility, like a promo for a local museum or large nonprofit, you will be noticed by many people, some of whom will be in a position to use your services. On the downside, you may be saddled with a more-complicated-than-originally-planned job because of the higher profile.

The most attractive kinds of pro bono work combine a short turnaround time, a strong creative concept, and a wide exposure potential. You may just have to do the Greenpeace public service announcement because it fits your ethical outlook and all you want in return is good karma. Fine. Just remember that good karma doesn't always pay the ISP bill.

common practice in the production community, where the profit margin is computed as part of the budget, but less common in the postproduction domain. The client sometimes has a tendency to assume they are being price-gouged if they don't see how the money is spent. By being candid about the profit margin, everyone is clear where there is room to bend and where there isn't.

The client is probably contracting a diguerrilla outfit because they can offer superior services for a better price, so they already know they're getting a bargain. Making the profit side of the transaction straightforward takes a lot of the mystery out of all the technological voodoo that can intimidate the client. The formula is straightforward: this is what my equipment costs, this is what the crew costs, this is what it costs to administrate this project, and this is my profit margin.

Of course, in a flat-budget situation, it is understood that some fixed costs may be marked up or may change during the course of the project, but that overall, you have priced goods and services fairly according to the market. For example, you may charge a certain amount for tape stock, within a reasonable market price, and then find that you can get a much better price from some tape stock source. You could pass the savings along to the client, but I believe that you should profit from your astute shopping as long as the client is still getting a decent price.

- *Delivery Format(s):* Get clear what exactly will be the physical media finally delivered to the client. There will inevitably be the occasional extra VHS dub here and there, but you don't want to have any confusion around what format the master should be on, what kind of a safety copy you will keep, and what additional dubs or copies will cost.

The worst scenario with a client is holding the master hostage because there is a dispute over how many copies or what format the client was promised. Avoid this by putting it in writing and double-checking with the dub house, broadcast outlet, or other distributor to make sure everyone knows that it's a D-1 master or DigiBeta or DVD or whatever other formats are called for.

- *Ownership:* Though normally the client will want to own all images contained in the project, there may be circumstances where it is strategic to own the images and just license them to the client for use in their specific application. You may realize that there could be an opportunity to shoot extra footage for stock purposes or that certain animated maps or other elements may be useful in other projects.

  It may be a critical deal point with your client, particularly if you take on a job with a razor-thin margin (or, in unique cases, the infamous "probono" job). You may be looking ahead to the usefulness of this project for your show reel and the possibility of using portions or elements of the project elsewhere.

Of course, you will adjust the client pressure points depending on the type of financial arrangement you have struck. If they are paying on an hourly basis for each service provided, you can be much more amenable going out on a limb for some client's whim. If you have budgeted a rate for the project, resolving production issues quickly and managing the number of revisions becomes even more critical.

> **DIGUERRILLA WANTED:** We are producing a half-hour series and need a sharp designer/3D artist. We are looking for someone who can design and execute their own work. Must be proficient with Mac/NT with experience in 3D Studio Max, Photoshop, Illustrator, and After Effects. We are looking for a positive, hard-working, and creative team member.

Extreme Meltdown: Chernobyl Syndrome

Thus far, this chapter has tried to anticipate the curveballs that might be thrown by the client. But what about the errors and plays bungled by the home team? No matter how precise your planning and how strong your technical skills, there will be some bonehead mistakes and freak accidents that can jack your pulse up past your IQ.

Imagine the unthinkable. Have you precalculated the time and logistics necessary if a burning lake of hellfire ignites in your studio? How long would it take to reload all the media into an editing environment? How long would it take to rerender the animation? How long would it take to reconstruct one or more days' work? How do you minimize the risk of blowing the delivery date, ruining a client relationship, and destroying your mental health? By monitoring all the key flashpoints where most of the fires start and by having contingency plans in place.

- *Data Safety:* The need for digital data backup systems has been discussed in previous chapters. Here, I add a reminder that having the data is only part of the equation. Getting to the data quickly and not having to retrace through a history of versions is essential in a time-sensitive situation. While a project is "live," have backup material in a very accessible place (on a server, on large-format removeable drives, etc.). Don't put the media in "deep freeze" until you are wrapped.

- *Equipment availability:* So your data is safe. What if your hardware fails, or you need more horsepower? Do you have resources or contingencies for a mission-critical computer to go south at the crucial moment? Do you have a vendor who will rent you ready-to-go equipment if necessary? Do you have good-neighbor arrangements with other companies to help one another out in crisis? What about the ultimate cluster-fuck: a long-term power outage. Are you ready with uninterruptible power supplies and even an emergency relocation if necessary?

- *Tech Specs:* Are you certain you have the correct tech specs for the delivery of the final tape/EDL/CD-ROM/DVD or other media format? Have you checked it for quality control? What quality control measures do you have in place? If it is for broadcast, does it meet broadcast specifications for signal and chroma bandwidth? To let an inferior copy of the final product leave the studio will undo all the hard work.

- *Delivery Strategy:* The product is finally ready; it's even been approved. Now the last 1% is getting the media to its final destination, whether that be cross-town or cross-country. Those final changes took longer than you thought. Are you fully armed with an arsenal of delivery options, from a production assistant with a good sense of direction to a next-day courier to possibly an electronic digital video transmission solution? Sometimes you have minutes when you need hours. Do you know the last possible cargo flight out of your local airport? It may be much cheaper to drive the product there than to call a specialty late-delivery courier service. Are you prepared for a no-excuse, no-prisoner delivery plan?

From Micromanagement to Mellow Management

All this talk about doomsday scenarios leads to the question of who is making all these life-and-death decisions. Can you trust yourself with this kind of responsibility? Here, a brief discussion of guerrilla management is warranted.

First of all, is there such a thing as guerrilla management? Guerrillas work under the shroud of barely controlled chaos; managers cram everything into spreadsheets and write too many memos. The guerrilla manager prunes much of the decision-making tree and gives more authority to independent people doing various parts of the job. The guerrilla manager barks instructions a bit less, asks more questions, listens more, and processes the data—the human data—being generated around the project. While loosening the reins on the one hand, they demand a higher level of accountability on the other. Production personnel need to be chosen for their ability to put out small fires themselves and call for help in the earliest stages of a bigger blaze. Finally, dead wood burns quickly, and a guerrilla manager is not afraid to get rid of personnel who can't perform at the pace, skill, and intelligence level that is required for a successful guerrilla operation.

The layers of micromanagement will vary according to the scale of the project. A large-scale project with lots of subcontractors requires more administration and coordination than a 72-hour, crash-and-burn, shoot-and-compute gig. The diguerrilla, by default, is most often working with a skeleton crew and cannot afford the luxury of a thick cushion of management—producers, associate producers, and account managers—that one might find in a large advertising agency for example. Instead, diguerrillas must rely on a more immediate relationship with the client based on trust, open communication, and a clear understanding of project parameters.

Instead of being buffered by a large staff devoted to managing the needs of the client, your direct personal relationship with the client becomes a key factor. Can you exchange opinions and concerns openly without offending or dislodging their confidence in your ability? Can you resolve disagreements quickly? Does the client value the relationship and the services you are providing? These questions, while important in any business relationship, are critical for a diguerrilla trying to work quickly, without the protective padding of an account executive to take on extra hand-holding duties.

Other Management FAQtors
(Frequently Asked Questions)

When will I know if the job is too big for me to do alone?

Weigh it. Remember the Production Pyramid from chapter 7—manpower, horsepower, brainpower. In general, if you are short on one, you can still handle the job if you know where to subcontract. If you are short in two departments, take the job if you have an cast-iron stomach (your odds are better if you have a shortage of manpower and horsepower but surplus of skilled brainpower). If you're short all three, you're either an extremely successful Hollywood producer or a kamikaze masquerading as a guerrilla (our marbles are loose but they aren't completely gone).

If the job is too big for me to do alone, how do I decide whether to get a partner, choose a vendor, or hire someone?

Excellent question. You might as well have asked, how do I mix the perfect martini? Carefully, very carefully. Generally, vendors or service providers are good for commodity services (tape dubbing, PhotoCD processing, camera rentals, Quick-Time VR authoring, voiceover recording, etc.)—in other words, services that are fairly binary: They are done right or aren't done at all. Hiring freelancers makes sense when you need to augment your own talents yet still closely manage fine points like art direction. In between these two poles you might place partners, or entities with whom you feel you can entrust entire portions of a production like music or effects shots. Those are the relationships that take the most time to cultivate. Also, in my book, partnership is a two-way street; a partner company will tend to throw work *your way* as well so that both benefit from one another's success.

If I do this, what do I look for—equipment, personal characteristics, portfolio?

Another excellent question. What do you look for in a personal relationship? You look for certain obvious qualities, and you look for a lot of intangible ones as well. Generally, an interview is appropriate well before you're desperate to hire someone; review their services, the quality of their work, and your personal impressions. This is the part that makes it more difficult to hire someone who lives out of town, though the interview can also be done over the phone. Recommendations are also important (make sure what they've said about working with that client jibes with what the client says). Lastly, do a tryout. Use an individual or company on a small portion of a job, something not too mission-critical, as a first date. As you gain confidence with their work, you can get more hot and heavy together.

How do I make sure this person and I are on the same page?

Checklists, timelines, and milestone meetings. Not only do you need to be clear with your clients about what is deliverable and by when, the same goes for subcontractors, your employees, and yourself. If there is a breakdown in communication, refer back to these documents and determine where the misunderstanding was and how to handle it most efficiently. Remember to "pad" in all directions; set the expectation bar just a tad higher than you think you should but not so far up there that it takes the wind out of everyone's whoopie cushion. Make delivery dates just a bit earlier than the delivery dates agreed upon with the client. With this small bit of padding, you will be able to better cope with unexpected twists of fate.

➤ **Job Tracking Sheet:** I personally hate timesheets, P.O.s, work orders, job memos, and any other bureaucratic device that takes the artist's attention off of what they are doing and redirects it towards administration. It reminds me of talking to my lawyer over the phone and getting the feeling that he was paying more attention to clocking our conversation than to his client's issue. Kicking and screaming, I was shown the efficacy of job tracking by Michael Glock who is very good at documenting and noting client conversations and requests. Below is an example of an informal job tracking sheet with codes for executables, deliverables, changes, additions and presentations. you can use physical sheets of paper or a database but this extra step will help employees, freelancers, managers, clients, and even your accountant all on the same page.

Job Tracking **Bootstrap Produtions**

Date 12/31/99
PO # 991144
job# 04-1951396-101

Artist: _Maya_

PROJECT Linux training ROM

Attn: Jim Herzberg
IEC
4215 Glencoe Ave, Ste, 100
Marina Del Rey CA 90292
Tel 310-555-4464x306
Fax 310-555-7036

Client Contact   Jim Herzberg
Phone   310-555-4464x306
Week Covered   12/26/99
Delivery Date   1/2/2000

GENERAL DESCRIPTION

Digitize DV footage and edit quicktime movies
pull-blue screen mattes
Add animated titles
Burn CD-ROM Mac HFS

X=executable as per original agreement
C=change in plan/schedule
A=additional element/procedure not in original deal
P=Present to client

ITEMS

Code	Date	DESCRIPTION	AS PER	DELIVERABLE	APPROVAL	HOURS
X	12/2?	Load DV footage	JH			2.5
X	12/2?	Design Titles	JH	pending JH/MK		2.5
C	12/2?	change font add animated	MK	pending		2.0
X	12/2?	pull blue screen mattes	JH			4.0
P	12/29	present title animation		✓	MK	
C	12/29	change bevel and title color	JH			2.0
A	12/29	Create virtual backgrounds	MK	pending		7.5
X	12/30	Edit footage	JH			11.0
P	12/31	present backgrounds rough		✓	JH/MK	
C	12/31	Change background #2	MK			2.5
X	12/31	Composite elements				6.0
X	12/31	burn CD with comp elements	JH	X	JH/MK pending	1.0

TOTAL HOURS 43.0

Comments

pending final approval

Release Print:
The Skills to Survive

> 66 *We must remember that the heroism of the guerrilla fighter consists of the scope of the planned goal and the enormous number of sacrifices that must be made in order to achieve it.* 99
> —*Guerrilla Warfare:* A Method *(1963)*

To be a revolutionary takes real fire in your belly. For every moment of digital glory, there are hundreds of moments of frustration, uncertainty, and ill-fortune. The diguerrilla takes it upon himself to be a step ahead of the curve creatively while sometimes scaling the backside of the technology curve (did someone say, "special upgrade price"?). Time and again, you are asked to innovate the form of visual communication as you are handed nearly unwatchable raw material.

When the diguerrilla succeeds in rising above the mediocrity of amateur footage, cheap-looking fonts, and cheesy transitions to

> **Proving Yourself:** Being a freelancer, you always have to have that big surprise. It always has to be just a little bit better than what they think that somebody in house could have done. So you have to constantly be proving yourself. I've always been one for just grabbing different tools to do different things with, and just to try to get a different look or to try to push the envelope a little bit. (Doug Barnard)

create something fresh and dynamic using off-the-shelf software and modestly powered hardware, it appears to the uninitiated that some form of black magic has been conjured up.

Of course the magic is a mixture of hard work, creativity, and technical sleight of hand. But only you and I need to know that. This book is certainly not about magic cures. If anything, this book

> **Worlds Collide:** There are two worlds of people. The ones that understand film and video production, and the people that have been brought up on the computer. It's very hard to find people that have bridged those two worlds. And I think that's the real art of it. People trying to bridge reality with computer graphics and make them work together. (Cody Harrington)

is more about dexterity, adaptability, and improvisation as a professional way of life rather than relying solely on technical mastery. What's more, your tribal alchemy and "Hail Mary" raindances cannot be confined to the dimly lit seclusion of your studio lair—in order to flourish, you must also make rain out in the battlefield.

Live Long and Pander: Shameless Self-Promotion

All tech and no shtick makes Jack a poor boy. In other words, even if you're the MacGuyver of digital imaging, you won't have the juice (literally) to run your CPUs without a client base. In the last chapter, we spoke about keeping them happy and meeting their expectations, but where do these mysterious clients come from?

In a strange way, clients do grow on trees. Once in a while you may just be lucky enough to be standing under a tree when the fruit drops, but more likely, you will have to plant a seedling and nurture it to maturity.

Since most diguerrillas have neither the time nor budget for all this "water the seedling" crap (something akin to a traditional "marketing campaign"), the same kind of guerrilla tactics learned in production should be applied to marketing.

1. *Make yourself an expert:* By definition, no self-respecting diguerrilla ever completely knows what they're doing. You're too busy juggling apps and projects to become omnipotent at any one thing. However, part of Zen mastery is knowing that one is always a beginner of sorts. The digital guerrilla is an expert at knowing how to do things

they don't know how to do (you don't have to tell your clients this, by the way).

Even though you and I know that you'll never know every friggin' trick in the manual (even if you helped write the manual), you should still find ways to project your strengths in the form of expertise. Expertise is a narcotic; people all over the world are doped into a stupor by the sweet smell of an expert.

Find the areas, the microniches, the gimmicks that you have a good handle on and find a way to get the word out. Are you good at creating QuickTime VR? Are you an alchemist of compression? Are you a genius at shooting cheap, underwater footage? Put your expertise in your propaganda kit and at the footer of your emails (i.e. "digital holography" or "advanced morphing specialist"). Find a way to get recognized. Get on a panel at a digital video trade show (even if you have to invent the panel and find the other panelists). Write an article or a long open letter for a digital media magazine. Be an avid, outspoken participant in newsgroups and listserver discussions as well as a visible figure at professional user group meetings. Even write a book if you absolutely have to (though you may live to regret it).

2. *Awards and Festivals:* Getting an award, whether it's an Oscar, a Clio, or a Bozo, seems to have some sort of an aura-scrubbing effect similar to being an expert. There are plenty of festivals for both digital and traditional media material in almost every conceivable category. While they

don't produce instant clients, they do the trick of getting your work out there and often have unexpectedly pleasant side effects. Besides, the certificates make the walls of your studio reek of legitimacy.

> ➤ **Diguerrilla Fest:** One of the pioneer digital film festivals is RESfest, run by and for digital guerrillas. For more information about RESfest and tickets, see their website at http://www.resfest.com or call their infoline: (415)267-4848.

⇨ ⇨ ⇨ **DIGITAL DISTRIBUTION**

http://www.ifilm.net, http://thesync.com, http://proteintv.com—these are examples of websites that specialize in serving up short films, animations, and other experimental pieces. Most of them tend to be aimed at a young, post MTV market, but they are paving the way for getting work seen and heard and don't think that Hollywood, Madison Avenue, and Silicon Valley aren't taking notice.

3. *Create cheap buzz:* Buzz is kind of the flip side of the expertise game. It's the art of getting other people to talk about you. There is the school that believes, especially in Hollywood, that any publicity is good publicity, but being notorious in the digital video world is not necessarily a good thing. ("Oh, there's the guy who dropped a $25,000 camera off a roof. Let's hire him.") Buzz can be getting a story written about you or your company, usually associ-

ated with a particular project so that your client gets a little stroke for doing business with you. Another form of buzz is just having a really original (and cheap) marketing campaign that gets everyone's attention.

I recall one particular art director who had a new thing going every month or so...all interesting and fairly inexpensive. One was the use of woven green paper that mimicked the look of a lot of business checks. A lot of Publisher's Clearing House type outfits use pseudochecks to grab your attention, but they all are easily spotted as fakes. This looked understated enough to pass as a real check from the envelope. Of course I opened it first. The great thing was, the content of the letter was clever enough so that I never felt manipulated by the gag. It was followed the next month with a can of cat food relabeled for self-promotion. Finally, I had to give the guy a call even though I didn't have a job at the moment. I just had to find out who was behind the clever campaign. He told me he was getting much better response than a typical brochure and letter mailing.

Another form of buzz can be hitching a ride on a bigger train. Large corporate-sponsored events often receive non-monetary contributions from smaller players such as artwork on invitations or ambient video projections in exchange for a promotional presence. As I've mentioned in previous chapters, be careful about what you agree to do for free; however, a well-placed bit of artwork can generate a great deal of attention.

4. *No impact soliciting:* Most "artistes" don't like to "soil" themselves doing sales. The whole industry of agents and professional representation rests on this premise. Diguerrillas may have the attitude but not the foolishness to dismiss the importance of marketing. Even so, instead of merely plugging oneself directly, it can sometimes be a lot more palatable to be speaking to various potential clients on behalf of a worthwhile third-party project for which you are seeking help or advice. This we call "priming." Whereas buzz is sprayed randomly, priming is targeted precisely.

    Priming is more like a quick lunch date as opposed to the pressure of a whole evening on the town. For instance, say you've somehow volunteered to take on a Public Service Announcement project for a well-regarded organization, let's say a local literacy project. Rather than do your own creative development, it may in some instances be more beneficial in the long run to approach an advertising agency that you've been thinking about working with and ask if some of their creatives might want to put in some pro bono time on working up a concept. If they like the cause or the client, then you have the potential of forming a relationship that can extend well beyond the PSA spot. The advertising agency is afforded the luxury of getting to know you and building trust without having the pressure of a budget and their own client's reputation on the line.

    Priming is also good when you just want advice. It's flattering to be asked for advice, especially creative advice. Maybe you just want to get some input from a software company on a spec project you have, or better yet, a paying project you have that has a bit of a high-tech motif. If all it will cost you is the price of lunch and you can get this marketing director's brain pumping, they will be anxious to see what you have come up with and will already be considering working with you when they see it.

5. *Biz barter:* Business barter is a practice that has become very commonplace in the 1990s (perhaps not as commonplace as in the 1390s but popular nonetheless). It's a more direct approach than the warm fuzziness of priming and may be more appropriate for shorter-term objectives.

The idea is to create a win-win alliance that exchanges goods and services without the exchange of hard currency. Why is this good, you may ask? My landlord won't accept a 10-second bumper on the first of the month. A good barter situation gives you the opportunity to create a piece of media for your showreel for a real client and receive something of use in return.

For example, there may be a company or organization or event that has a need to produce a visual message. They are a legit outfit, but for whatever reasons, usually ones you can relate to, they don't have the cash to produce a promospot. However, they are willing to trade services or products in order to have you produce the spot. An old associate of mine used to subsidize Carribean vacations by shooting local spots for auto rental and hotel venues that he used.

There are two pitfalls to the biz barter. One is not negotiating an equitable swap or one that is directly beneficial
to you (don't produce a florist spot unless you need flowers). The other is that you don't put your heart into it.
Remember, the initial barter is only part of the plan. You
want to do such a good job that the next (paying) client
thinks this was a decently budgeted project. Not only
that, the barter partner may grow and want a more ambitious project down the road.

6. *Use the back door:* As a diguerrilla, downtime is your
enemy. The longer it takes to woo a client, the more surly
your landlord gets. A guerrilla instinctively senses when
there's a shortcut (don't you always spot that grocery
store checker headed to open up a new checkstand a few
seconds before anyone else?); if you have an angle, work
it. Beg your hair stylist to talk to their television producer
client on your behalf. Does your girlfriend work for a big
architecture firm that needs better presentation video?
Have you been spinning your wheels with some assistant
to the product manager when you know someone who
plays golf with him regularly? The diguerrilla will use
every nepotistic, incestuous, hair-brained ploy to get an
"in" with a decision-maker.

   You simply don't have the time for a long courtship. Make
   your meetings count. Make your presentations memo-
   rable. Make your bid irresistible.

7. *The usual suspects:* We can't overlook the two basic
tools of self-promotion in this business besides the gift of

gab and a nice smile: The website and the showreel. Again, this may all be good common sense, but I've seen enough poorly crafted showreels to realize that the art of presenting oneself isn't talked about enough.

We've talked about using the website as a client communication tool, but you'll probably want to devote at least a few pages to marketing information since it's the first place people check when they want to find out more information about an individual or a company. It's a great tool: It's globally accessible and open 24 hours. However, eyeballs on the Web are twitchy; make your Web pages count. Don't just rehash a brochure. Keep it elegant and simple: Use animated GIFs judiciously, keep text brief, and cut to the chase. Clients want to sample a bit of what they're hiring you for. Have your material easily accessible and intuitively organized. Graphics and title design can be represented with JPEG stills; shooting and editing prowess are better documented with QuickTime movies or other streaming media.

As for the showreel, the video sampling of your work, it is the single most important promotion tool. Put a lot of thought into making your reel; it should be a concentrated expression of your talent and ability. By "concentrated," I mean that long, exhaustive reels that contain everything you've ever done are not a very good way to present yourself. A long tape is more an archive reel than a showreel and might be used as a secondary source if a client needs to see additional work. The showreel itself should probably not be more than 6–7 minutes (though if it is cut extremely well, a 10-minute reel can feel like 5 minutes). It should show the best, freshest, and most diverse work you have (better a very short tape with excellent work than one padded with mediocre work) and be edited in such a way that a client with numerous showreels to review won't have a lull in which to shut off the tape and pop in another. Even though you are a guerrilla and may be working out of a studio that looks like an underground bunker, the reel should look clean and professional. If you want to give it some personality and sardonic twist, by all means do so, but don't be sloppy about it. The client wants to know that even though you may be a renegade media maven, their project is in good hands.

➤ **Work Ethic:** When you think about it, life during our parents' time was more like, "Gee, what church do you belong to? What university did you get your degree from?" and "Are you married?" These were real determining factors as to whether you got a job or not. But then after that, all you had to do is wear a tie and show up 9 to 5, you could put your kid through college. You were judged on different criteria. So hey, now we get to wear T-shirts, we get to work long hours and it's like, "Hey as soon as you can't cut it, there's five people waiting out in the lobby that would love to sit down at your station." That's really the way it should be. I mean, I'd rather be a bullet-ridden corpse than go out on a heart lung machine after a prolonged illness. (Doug Barnard)

Lastly, if you are doing a high volume of diverse work, you may want to create separate subcategories of showreels (e.g., one for bumpers and promos, one for movie titles, one for sports graphics). Usually this isn't necessary but clients who are narrowly focused will appreciate a reel aimed precisely at their needs. In certain circumstances, you may want to build a custom reel for a particular prospective client who is looking for something very specific. Use your discretion when asessing how decisive a custom reel would be and how much extra effort it will require.

Digital Video: Now More than Ever

We came like bedouins or goldseekers to a place with unimaginably great possibilities, only a small section of which has even now been developed.
—*Sergei Eisenstein,* Film Form

In the early stages of the video revolution, it was enough to just know how the machine or software worked. It was a revolution of old school creatives riding the backs of technical operators. The diguerrilla has changed this scenario because the tools are now directly in the hands of the creatives. Though it is continually evolving, today's production software is easier to use; it is more tactile, more WYSIWYG, and most of the cryptic programming math is buried out of the user's view.

The rise of the digital guerrilla is in some ways a reactionary revolution; it is a return to the ascendancy of well-executed ideas over the worship of the machine.

> ➤ **Cinephiles:** Because Slingshot™ exists we now have a multitude of options and most people didn't know that and so, a large part of our effort is just getting the word out, because once people find out about it, it's a perfect fit for the independent filmmaker. The guy out on the street, he's got a 16mm film camera, is able to finagle some transfer time from the telecine house and he's got $10,000 worth of computer equipment. He can make a film very easily. Edit, shoot, relatively inexpensively as well. So, to me that whole idea is exciting to me. We came up with the motto "Film Editing for the Masses." Because it really makes it accessible, those same kind of film options you would get on an expensive machine you can now get on a much cheaper machine because it works with Media 100, it works with Premiere, it works with pretty much any editing system that will produce an EDL. (Barry Silver)

The era of the diguerrilla is a more even playing field for video artists and entrepreneurs. It is no longer a case of the haves and have-nots in professional video. Almost anyone who wants to can now produce digital moving images. The real divide is no longer the brand of equipment but what you squeeze out of it. The diguerrilla, by nature, is prepared to squeeze like hell.

As was noted in chapter 8, the market for video is expanding dramatically from its traditional broadcast roots toward a server-

➤ **Rubber Meeting Road:** For starters, you need to get a little bit of gear and go down to your basement, just crank on your stuff. Just like if you were a musician, you can go to school and you can learn as much music theory as you want, but, what's really gonna make you a good musician is how many hours you spend practicing. And digital artists need to practice; they just need to keep making stuff. Once you've gained that skill and that mastery and you have the workload to really justify it, then getting the good gear is a smart move. (Doug Barnard)

⇨ ⇨ ⇨ **REALTIME VS. DOWNTIME**

The big thing about 3D rendering is that you've got all the machines running full speed ahead and then what do you do? I like that concept of going to the beach while the machines are working. If I can set up something to make the production process more efficient, great. I got back into animation because of computers. I was turned off by the fact that I didn't have that much patience to in-between the key frames. I wasn't the greatest artist, but the computer really brought me right back in because now it's all key frames and the in-betweening is automatic. I guess that appeals to my lazy nature. (Cody Harrington) managed pipeline streaming "video on tap" whenever and wherever you want it. From community-based news reporting to corporate intranets to K–12 education to new media entertainment—the video market continues to mushroom. Never before have the tools, talent, and transmission technology converged in such an abundant mix. Never before has there been such an enormous demand for video that is fast, cheap, and good. Though hardly a cushy ride, it is a good time to be a digital guerrilla.

> ➤ **Heaven Helps Those Who Help Themselves:** I just bid a project on doing a 3D architectural flythrough for this huge church project. These people five years ago wouldn't have thought about paying someone big dollars to do a computer visualization of the church. Well, granted it's sort of one of those evangelical places, it's more like a 3,500-seat auditorium rather than a chapel, but for them it makes a lot of sense, because what they're trying to do is squeeze more cash out of their parishioners. If they can get everyone excited with Hollywood special effects and it gets their church built, hey, more power to them. (Doug Barnard)

No Fear on the Frontier

In an unstable world, with unstable operating systems, the only certainty is uncertainty. That bodes well for the fortune-tellers' union but what of the diguerrilla's ultimate fate? Will he or she brave the struggle over time? It is always calming, even in your darkest hour, to be reasonably sure that you will live to fight yet another day. Long-term survival is a different kind of preparation. Just as the stewardess wants you to note the emergency exits in advance of a crash landing, you should be thinking about alternative scenarios for your project from the outset so you aren't the last one left screaming down the aisle groping to find a flotation device.

The best way to be prepared for changes in equipment or software is to archive your project thoroughly (see chapter 3) with as much metadata in as many formats as possible. We looked at media resource strategy in chapter 3, and I touched on the concept of MetaData, but here I can elaborate and describe how skillful use of metadata is actually your best hedge against being buried by advancing technology.

In chapter 3, I described the four basic categories of media data: source data (the tape or original digital file), encoded data (the converted, digitized, or copied media), synthesized data (rendered media such as effects and transitions), and metadata (descriptions of how the media is used). While you are by now, hopefully, aware that you must archive this data or risk irreparable technical catastrophes, it is not as clear what proactive benefits are available from the use of this so-called metadata. In fact, the era of metadata management is still in its infancy.

The Metaphysics of Metadata

Metadata, as it applies to media, in its simplest iteration, metadata file is like a Pagemaker or Quark file that describes where the text will flow, what font will display, where the pictures will appear, and what size. It doesn't have to contain all the source data; it merely needs to point to it and describe its use.

While a project file is an important element of metadata, it's only as good as its master application. That is, if you make modifications, you are limited to using that specific application/post-production system if you want full access to all your decisions, tracks, filters, plug-ins, mixes, and titles. But what if your system has certain limitations, or if you don't have access to it a year later, or if a post house in Spain using a completely different digital editing environment sends you a project to prep for the U.S. market.

Metadata: Next Gen

What if files could come wrapped with sticky notes about how they are intended to be used? And what if they could be read by nearly any application? And what if all the history of the project could be deconstructed so that various versions and additions could easily be extracted? If this were possible, you might be able to work with video almost as effortlessly as you work with images floating around in your head.

Methods for encoding metadata have been proposed by several product manufacturers and professional video industry task forces assigned to design standards for data interchange. As yet, the fulfillment of this mission is pending, but the implications are clear: This is the future of digital video production and a huge leap for digital guerrillas.

Living in a metadata world, it would be possible to view how a sound mix was put together or how an animation super is constructed without having to commit to one specific platform or software environment. Ideally, there would be notation channels that the originating parties could indicate production questions or special instructions to the next contributor. Missing pieces of media would generate their own placeholders, and with a mouse click, the user could request a copy of the original element from whatever server it was stored on in any location.

A true "app-nostic" protocol would give diguerrillas tremendous freedom to work virtually with one another in remote locations without having to have identical workstation setups or even all the corresponding media layers. The dream of working with diguerrillas across the globe quickly and cheaply has the potential to shift the economics of digital video even further into the hands of the proletariat.

Today, even with the rise of digital guerrilla video, there is still a command-and-control approach to creating media. It is still heard through the various stages of production I have outlined in this book. It still often resembles a bird building her nest one twig at a time (though the twigs are now much easier to rearrange).

Imagine something like an electronically connected beehive of activity with many people working on small pieces of the whole simultaneously so that the final product, when viewed from a distance, seems to be assembling itself. This kind of distributed swarming, similar to the concept of "parallel processing," when orchestrated with a bit of foresight and intelligent software, can dramatically expand the capacity of an individual or small band of guerrillas.

⇨ ⇨ ⇨ **TOWARD SOME 3D METADATA STANDARDS**

MGLA (Motion Graphics Los Angeles) was originally formed as the merger of the After Effects, Electric Image, and Hollywood 3D users groups. The feeling was that the 2D and 3D worlds were starting to merge—2D artists were being asked to include more 3D elements and perspective in their work; 3D artists were realizing a 2D program was the best place to composite and finish their animations. The most interesting results come when you blend the two.

A file format called RLA, originally developed by Alias/Wavefront and significantly extended by Kinetix, is one such link that makes blending the two easier. When a 3D program renders a scene to a file, in addition to the normal RGB color and alpha channels, it can also save in an RLA file up to 8 additional channels of information per pixel of the rendered image:

1. Z buffer (distance from camera; 32-bit floating point precision)
2. material ID (which master material was used; up to 256)
3. object ID (which object group or parent it belongs to; up to 65,536)
4. object coverage (percentage of pixel covered by object in front; 8-bit precision)
5. background (color of object behind frontmost object; 24-bit color)
6. normals (direction a surface points; 10-bit precision per axis)
7. UV coordinates (helps with texture mapping)
8. nonclamped RGB

Although this is a lot of extra information, it is packed in a format similar to a loss-less PICT file, and supposedly only doubles a normal file size on average. Note too that not all programs that support the RLA format necessarily write (or read) all of these channels.

In plain English, this means that after a scene has been rendered, you can know how far an object was from the camera, what material was used to texture map it, what group of objects it belonged to, and what direction to bounce light off it—on a pixel-by-pixel basis.

The simplest use of this information is for selecting specific objects easily. Previously, if you wanted to posttreat a particular object differently than the rest of the scene (e.g., color correct it, apply a filter to it, composite an object behind it, etc.), you either had to render it as a separate pass, or spend a lot of time carefully masking it. Instead, a 2D program that can read and use the information in an RLA file can create an automatic selection or mask based on its group ID. The additional object ID and object coverage information allow cleaner antialiasing for the selection, including some simple transparency calculation.

The material ID information can greatly help the labor-intensive process of trying to get colors right while working inside a 3D application. Now, after the render has finished, with RLA-savvy applications you can make masks and selections based on what material was used, and then perform color corrections, blurring or sharpening, etc., without affecting the rest of the scene. How many times have you been in a situation where, after a long render, a client says the equivalent of "Can those tiles be less red?" or "Did we say the logo should be blue or purple?" If the 3D application you used writes the material ID information to an RLA file, and the 2D application you use can read and use that information to create selections, these sort of corrections are suddenly much easier.

Beyond intelligent selections is the ability to use Z buffer—the distance from the camera—for processing and compositing. The simplest case would be using Z depth to create depth of field effects, using the distance to decide how much to blur each pixel, akin to an intelligent "compound blur" filter. A more advanced version would blur objects both closer and further away from the designated focal distance. Other atmospheric effects such as fog obscuration are also possible.

More interesting is the way more 2D compositing applications are adding a sense of Z depth. These programs should be able to take advantage of the Z information in an RLA file to automatically mask 2D objects into an already-rendered 3D scene, properly sorting which object is supposed to be in front of which.

Beyond that, the more a 2D program can think in 3D space, the more it can take advantage of the information to cast proper lights, shadows, reflections, and other 3D effects, after the main 3D scene has already been rendered.

RLA is not perfect—for example, it does not tell you how far behind an object is if the foreground object is partially transparent—but it is here now and is capable of being extended. It does indeed take additional software coding to support it, but its advantages are both strong and obvious. More information on the RLA format is available on Discreet Logic's website (http://www.discreet.com; look for the White Papers section) as well as http://www.ipahome.com/gff/textonly/summary/waverla.htm).

The metadata conundrum in tandem with remote networking represent the last major hurdle for diguerrillas to break out from the media niches that are currently economic strongholds into even more ambitious areas of media production. The distributed production model, with lower overhead and quicker revision/reaction time, has begun to creep into the production mainstream. It has already begun in the visual FX business and will trickle into other areas.

> ➤ **Revolution.Net:** We're all on the Web and you can see problems that come up and then people will instantly try to help them and figure it out. So yeah, I think the Web has really opened up the community. Anything can be done in someone's imagination and you can bet that someone is gonna ask you to do something that's never been done before. I'm finding people wanting to share that knowledge instead of holding on to it, at least in the animation community; I know in the software business the secrets are closely guarded. But in animation, people try to help one another if they share the tool, they're more than willing to share the information. I like it because I need it. It's so daunting that you've got to have help—some kind of a way to peel away the layers and get it done. Otherwise it's too difficult to do it for one person, one guerrilla guy out here in the woods. (Cody Harrington)

It will be digital guerrillas who will be the harbingers of this shift. They are inventing it with every user group gathering, list-server, subcontract, swap of services, electronic file transfer, and desperate phone call. They were the people, a few years ago, who asked their personal computers to do more than they should have. They are the people that ask themselves to do more than just jockey a software application. They are the people whose clients, per capita (or is that *per capital?*) are the most demanding. They are the ones who must constantly innovate or go offline.

Everyone has a mind full of wonderful moving images. The diguerrilla is just bold enough to click-and-drag them out of his mind into a digital, distributable form. This boldness, this willing-ness to ride the rough rails of a technology train in third class delivering first-class product, continues to change not only the face of the entire video industry, but also the world that watches.

Have more than thou showest, Speak less than thou knowest. —William Shakespeare

.... and then go kick *some* ass.

Appendix A

Ten Basic Principles of Traditional Cel Animation

These guidelines are useful for digital guerrillas doing any kind of keyframe work from animation to compositing to effects.

Paraphrased from *The Illusion Of Life* by Frank Thomas and Ollie Johnston (pp.47–69). Look these up in the original version and read them for a complete understanding.

1. Squash and stretch
2. Anticipation
3. Staging
4. Straight Ahead Action and Pose to Pose
5. Follow Through and Overlapping Action
6. Slow In and Slow Out
7. Arcs
8. Secondary Action
9. Timing
10. Exaggeration

1. Squash and Stretch

This action gives the illusion of weight and volume to a character as it moves. Also squash and stretch is useful in animating dialogue and doing facial expressions. How extreme the use of squash and stretch is, depends on what is required in animating the scene. Usually it is broader in a short style of picture and subtler in a feature. It is used in all forms of character animation and can be adapted to objects and geometrics. This is the most important element you will be required to master and will be used often.

2. Anticipation

This movement prepares the audience for a major action the object or character is about to perform, such as starting to run, jump or change expression. A dancer does not just leap off the floor. A backwards motion occurs before the forward action is executed. The backward motion is the anticipation. A comic effect can be done by not using anticipation after a series of gags that used anticipation. Almost all real action has major or minor anticipation such as a pitcher's wind-up or a golfer's back swing. Helps develop tension and personality.

3. Staging

A pose or action should clearly communicate to the audience the attitude, mood, reaction or idea of the object or character as it relates to the action and continuity. The effective use of long, medium or close up shots, as well as camera angles, also helps in telling the story. There is a limited amount of time in a film, so each sequence, scene and frame of film must relate to the overall story. Do not confuse the audience with too many actions at once. Use one action clearly stated to get the idea across, unless you are animating a scene that is to depict clutter and confusion. Staging directs the audience's attention to the story or idea being told. Care must be taken in designing foreground and background layers so it isn't obscuring the animation or competing with it due to excess detail behind the animation. Layers should work together as a pictorial unit.

4. Straight Ahead and Pose-to-Pose (Keyframe) Anticipation

Straight ahead animation (equivalent to just dropping keyframes as you go) starts at the first drawing and works drawing to drawing to the end of a scene. You can lose size, volume and proportions with this method, but it does have spontaneity and freshness. Fast, wild action scenes are done this way. Pose-to-Pose (work both ends towards the middle) is more planned out and charted with key drawings done at intervals throughout the scene. Size, volumes and proportions are controlled better this way, as is the action. The lead animator will turn charting and keys over to his assistant. An assistant can be better used with this method so that the animator doesn't have to draw every drawing in a scene. An animator can do more scenes this way and concentrate on the planning of the animation. Use straight ahead animation for uniqueness, and pose-to-pose for more mathematical animation like motion control and camera moves.

5. Follow Through and Overlapping Action

When the main body of the character stops, all other parts (or linked polygons) continue to catch up to the main mass of the character or object following the path of action. Nothing stops all at once. Timing becomes critical to the effectiveness of drag and the overlapping action.

6. Ease-Out and Ease-In

As action starts, we have more keyframes or acceleration curve near the starting pose, one or two in the middle, and more keyframes or acceleration curve near the next pose. Fewer drawings make the action faster and more drawings make the action slower. Slow-ins and slow-outs soften the action, making it more life-like. For a gag action, we may omit some slow-out or slow-ins for shock appeal or the surprise element. This will give more snap to the scene.

7. Arcs

All actions, with few exceptions (such as the animation of a mechanical device), follow an arc or slightly circular path. This is especially true of the human figure and the action of animals. Arcs give animation a more natural action and better flow. Think of natural movements in the terms of a pendulum swinging. All arm movement, head turns and even eye movements are executed on an arcs.

8. Secondary Action

This action adds to and enriches the main action and adds more dimension to the character animation, supplementing and/or re-enforcing the main action. Example: A character is angrily walking toward another character. The walk is forceful, aggressive and forward leaning. The leg action is just short of a stomping walk. The secondary action is a few strong gestures of the arms working with the walk. Also, the possibility of dialogue being delivered at the same time with tilts and turns of the head to accentuate the walk and dialogue, but not so much as to distract from the walking action. All of these actions should work together in support of one another. Think of the walk as the primary action and arm swings, head bounce and all other actions of the body as secondary or supporting action.

9. Timing

Expertise in timing comes best with experience and personal experimentation, using the trial and error method in refining technique. The basics are more subtle changes between poses slow and smooth the action. Rapid changes (few keyframes) make the action faster and crisper. A variety of slow and fast timing within a scene adds texture and interest to the movement. Also, there is timing in the acting of a character to establish mood, emotion and reaction to another character or to a situation. Studying movement of actors and performers on stage and in films is useful when creating characters or anthropomorphic objects. This frame by frame examination of film footage will aid you in understanding timing for animation.

10. Exaggeration

Exaggeration is not necessarily extreme distortion of a drawing or extremely broad, violent action. It's like a caricature of features, expressions, poses, attitudes and actions. Exaggeration in a walk or an eye movement or even a head turn will give your film more appeal. Be careful, a little goes a long way.

Appendix B

CD-ROM Contents

Artbeats

Film clips from the Artbeats Digital Film Library, copyright 1996-99 Artbeats Software Inc. All rights reserved. Artbeats is pleased to include these clips from various Artbeats Digital Film Library titles for your use and enjoyment. This is only a small sampling of the large volume of imagery available. Please visit the Artbeats website to see a broader view of what they have to offer: http://www.artbeats.com. For more information about Artbeats contact:

Artbeats Software, Inc.

1405 North Myrtle, Suite 5

Myrtle Creek, OR 97457

(541)863-4429,

Fax: (541) 863-4547.

E-mail: info@artbeats.com.

Artbeats—creator of the Artbeats Digital Film Library and many collections of still imagery—is a leading source of royalty-free content designed for use with digital editing and compositing, desktop video, multimedia internet content creation and 3D animation and rendering. To provide the highest possible quality, most footage is sourced from 35mm film. The clips are then processed by Artbeats for color correction, dust and scratch removal and—where applicable—looping, tiling and alpha channel creation.

Subjects include pyrotechnic effects, water, backgrounds, clouds, archival footage, suface maps and much more. Frame sizes range from D1 NTSC or PAL resolutions through 2K (2048x1536) film resolution. All products available on CD-ROM for multiple platforms.

Avid Xpress Glossary

Avid Technology created this glossary of the ever-growing array of technical terms used in the digital video industry. You will find terms used in this book as well as many others, from A/B roll to zero duration dissolve.

BetaCapsule

The folks at BetaCapsule created this mock webmentary about digital video production that contains some amusing and fun graphics, images, film clips and sounds.

Britishaudio

Britishaudio.com provides great production music to enhance the audio dimension of your digital video. They offer both traditional CD and digital downloads. A sample of some of their music is provided for your listening pleasure.

Masks

Try these rip, burn or melt masks of grayscale image sequences with various organic actions. These images can be used individually or together for masking and animation purposes to create some dynamic effects.

Oddball Film + Video Clips

Oddball Fim + Video offers a collection of rare, entertaining, unique and eye-opening stock footage. Take a look at the samples provided and see why Oddball Film + Video Oddball is the definitive source for eclectic images in all media.

Pixelan Software

Pixelan Software offers some free video spiceracks to be used as studio-quality transitions and dynamic mattes for desktop video editing. These spice-racks create beautiful visual effects that can spice up your video production.

Quick Movie 1.0.1

QuickMovie allows you to create QuickTime movies out of a series of images on your home computer. Chaotic Software Ltd. developed Quick-Movie as an easy way to create and edit your own digital movie. Sample films clips are provided as well as instructions on paying for the use of the application.

Sounddogs

Sound Dogs provides a comprehensive on-line library of sound effects and production music that have been used by Hollywood studios and directors and software developers. You can sample Sound Dog's eclectic collection of sounds from cars to crickets, water dripping to whistling.

1,001 Digital Video Weblinks

Well, there's not really 1,001 weblinks, but there are plenty and you shouldn't surf the web too much anyway. Believe me, I had to look at a lot more than a thousand websites just to skim the cream off the top of the rancid glut of non-information out there. If you've ever used a search engine, you know what I mean. While I can't promise every link will rock your world (nor even be active by the time you read this), there is some nugget of gold for every reader in this list—of this I am certain.

In an industry that changes as fast as digital video technology, the web is the only way to stay au currant with what's what. So in lieu of any long glossaries or tables or appendixes, I give you something that will remain relevant for a good while. For some of you, this may even be the most useful portion of the book.

www.books.mfi.com/dv/dgv/

Even more links and files are posted on the URL above. Check it for updates and additional information about this book, digital video and Avi Hoffer.

Index

Also available from Miller Freeman Books

Producing Great Sound for Digital Video
By Jay Rose
This practical guide is for any digital video producer who has asked, "My video is fine, but my audio isn't as clear as I'd like it to be. What am I doing wrong?" Covering the entire process of creating compelling audio for digital video, this book offers guidance in the four key areas of desktop soundtrack production: technical principles, pre-production, acquisition—both in-studio and on location, and post-production.
Paperback with audio CD, 352pp, ISBN 0-87930-597-5, $39.95

The Reel World
Scoring for Pictures
By Jeff Rona
Written by a leading Hollywood composer, this book addresses the art, technology, and business of composing music for film and television. The author explores three key areas of film and television scoring: technology and technique, musical aesthetics, and business savvy. Packed with on-the-job stories and practical examples, *The Reel World* will help any composer succeed in film or television.
Paperback, 240pp, ISBN 0-87930-591-6, $24.95

The Finale Primer
Mastering the Art of Music Notation with Finale—Second Edition
By Bill Purse
Fully updated to include Finale 2000 for both the Mac and Windows, this step-by-step guide unravels the intricacies of music preparation on the desktop using Finale software. This book covers Finale's sophisticated real-time MIDI implementation with notational graphic options. Includes helpful exercise drills and projects for composers, orchestrators, and arrangers.
Paperback, 245pp, ISBN 0-87930-602-5, $24.95

Digital Home Recording
Tips, Techniques, and Tools for Home Studio Production
Edited by Carolyn Keating; Craig Anderton, Technical Editor
This all-in-one guide helps musicians and audio engineers create a cost-effective digital studio for recording CDs at home. Tips and techniques show how to choose and use the right equipment, and set up and maintain the studio.
Paperback, 180pp, illustrated, ISBN 0-87930-380-8, $19.95

Available at book and music stores everywhere. Or contact:
Miller Freeman Books • 6600 Silacci Way, Gilroy, CA 95020 USA
Phone: (800) 848-5594 • Fax: (408) 848-5784
E-mail: mfi@rushorder.com • Web: www.books.mfi.com